Praise for Roger Lowenstein's *While America Aged*

"*While America Aged* is about more than just pensions. It's really an excellent case study of a bigger and more general problem in the modern economy."

—James Surowiecki, *Columbia Journalism Review*

"[Lowenstein] has a gift for explaining complex topics in disarmingly simple prose. . . . If I had my way, every American voter would read this book and recommend it to corporate executives, labor leaders, and lawmakers." —James Pressley, Bloomberg News

"Lowenstein depicts the pension crisis like entertaining historical fiction with lessons in history, business, and human nature."

—Ellen Marsden, *BookPage*

"A chilling anatomy of one bad decision followed by another—and another." —*Kirkus Reviews*

PENGUIN BOOKS

WHILE AMERICA AGED

Roger Lowenstein, author of three bestselling books, reported for *The Wall Street Journal* for more than a decade and wrote the *Journal's* stock market column "Heard on the Street" and also its "Intrinsic Value" column. He is now a regular contributor to *The New York Times Magazine, Smart Money,* and *Portfolio,* among other publications. He divides his time between Newton, Massachusetts, and Westfield, New Jersey.

WHILE AMERICA AGED

How Pension Debts Ruined General Motors, Stopped the NYC Subways, Bankrupted San Diego, and Loom as the Next Financial Crisis

ROGER LOWENSTEIN

PENGUIN BOOKS

PENGUIN BOOKS
Published by the Penguin Group
Penguin Group (USA) Inc., 375 Hudson Street, New York, New York 10014, U.S.A.
Penguin Group (Canada), 90 Eglinton Avenue East, Suite 700, Toronto,
Ontario, Canada M4P 2Y3 (a division of Pearson Penguin Canada Inc.)
Penguin Books Ltd, 80 Strand, London WC2R 0RL, England
Penguin Ireland, 25 St Stephen's Green, Dublin 2, Ireland (a division of Penguin Books Ltd)
Penguin Group (Australia), 250 Camberwell Road, Camberwell,
Victoria 3124, Australia (a division of Pearson Australia Group Pty Ltd)
Penguin Books India Pvt Ltd, 11 Community Centre, Panchsheel Park, New Delhi – 110 017, India
Penguin Group (NZ), 67 Apollo Drive, Rosedale, North Shore 0632,
New Zealan (a division of Pearson New Zealand Ltd)
Penguin Books (South Africa) (Pty) Ltd, 24 Sturdee Avenue,
Rosebank, Johannesburg 2196, South Africa

Penguin Books Ltd, Registered Offices:
80 Strand, London WC2R 0RL, England

First published in in the United States of America by The Penguin Press,
a member of Penguin Group (USA) Inc. 2008
Published in Penguin Books 2009

1 3 5 7 9 10 8 6 4 2

THE LIBRARY OF CONGRESS HAS CATALOGED THE HARDCOVER EDITION AS FOLLOWS:
Lowenstein, Roger.
While America Aged : how pension debts ruined General Motors, stopped the NYC subways,
bankrupted San Diego, and loom as the next financial crisis / Roger Lowenstein.
p. cm.
Includes bibliographical references and index.
ISBN 978-1-59420-167-7 (hc.)
ISBN 978-0-14-311538-0 (pbk.)
1. Pensions—United States—Finance. 2. Defined benefit pension plans—United States.
3. Retirement income—United States. I. Title
HD7125.L68 2008 2007042508
331.25'240973—dc22

Printed in the United States of America
DESIGNED BY MEIGHAN CAVANAUGH

To my father

CONTENTS

Introduction *1*

PART ONE: WHO OWNS GENERAL MOTORS? *7*

1. Walter Reuther and the Treaty of Detroit *9*
2. The Anti-Reuther *39*

PART TWO: THE PUBLIC FREIGHT *81*

3. An Entitled Class *83*
4. On Strike! *117*

PART THREE: DEBACLE IN SAN DIEGO *153*

5. Finest City *155*
6. Pension Plot *175*
7. The Bill Comes Due *195*

Conclusion: The Way Out *221*

Acknowledgments *233*

Notes *235*

Index *267*

WHILE AMERICA AGED

INTRODUCTION

In the late 1960s, six of every ten Americans were covered by a pension plan, and it was possible to envision that soon the entire workforce would have its retirement security guaranteed. That dream has gone terribly sour. Pension sponsors from airlines to textile manufacturers to steel mills have gone belly up, and hundreds of others are now deeply in the red. More alarmingly, government employers such as cities and states have fallen behind—far behind—on funding the promises they made to their retired workers.

America now faces a crisis of epidemic proportions. The fabric of the nation's pension system is collapsing—at the very moment when the population is rapidly aging. Today, America has approximately 38 million senior citizens; in a generation, the number will virtually double, to 72 million. Indeed, by 2030 one in five Americans will be over sixty-five.[1]

Who will be there to provide for them? More than 60 million Americans either are receiving or have been promised pensions; however, their numbers are shrinking rapidly. In the private sector, the proportion of jobs with pensions has plummeted to just under 20 percent.[2] Perhaps even scarier, a third of the workforce does not have any retirement savings—pension, 401(k), or private account—at all.[3]

For workers still with pensions, plan assets are grossly inadequate. In the private sector, employers' pension funds are, cumulatively, an astounding $350 billion in deficit.[4] Many employers—from Sears to IBM to Verizon—are freezing their plans to keep their obligations from growing further. Others did not act quickly enough and were forced to file for bankruptcy. The auto industry, burdened with legions of retired factory workers, is teetering on the brink. So many pension plans have gone bust already that the federal agency that *insures* pensions is itself in trouble. This agency, the Pension Benefit Guaranty Corporation, is responsible for the pensions of 1.3 million people whose plans have failed. Thanks to a spate of recent costly failures (ninety-four sponsors collapsed in 2006 alone), the PBGC is now $19 billion in the red, and could eventually require a taxpayer bailout.[5]

Even worse, the states and localities, which have promised pensions to millions of present and future retired policemen, teachers, clerical workers and others, are *hundreds of billions* of dollars behind on their payments to state pension funds.[6] This is money owed by the taxpayers—and under the state constitutions, the debts *must* be paid; pensions can never be defaulted upon. Thus, the deficits will require a combination of layoffs, service cuts, and higher taxes in a majority of the states for decades to come. In the case of some of the worst offenders, such as New Jersey, West Virginia, and Illinois, the cuts will likely be draconian. Thanks to their grossly underfunded pensions, these states are essentially insolvent.

THIS BOOK examines how the pension system went so badly off course. All financial debacles have a human element—greed or self-delusion or perhaps sheer dishonesty. In this one, retirement systems fell prey to a basic part of our nature—the urge to delay that which we find unpleasant now.

Such behavior comes naturally to any child with a homework assignment ("after dinner" . . . "when the game is over"), and so it did to pension sponsors who deferred the required contributions.

Pensions are a perfect vehicle for procrastination; in the financial world, they are the most long-enduring promises that exist. The only rival is the federal Social Security system—but there, surprisingly, the commitment is not so airtight. Congress, if it chose, could reduce or cancel Social Security benefits tomorrow. Pensions are forever.

The young men who went to work for General Motors after World War II, when GM ruled the roost of American business, were promised pension and health care benefits that remained in force for half a century. One GM retiree, who died at 111 in 2006, had been collecting pension and retiree health benefits for forty-eight years. When he first went to work, in 1926, GM's managers could not have had the faintest conception of what the company could or would be paying in benefits eighty years later.

The very remoteness of the pension guarantee seduced many employers into overpromising (after all, when the benefits came due, they would be somebody else's problem). This tendency to overpromise was especially acute in the public sector, where employee unions had the power to vote politicians who weren't sufficiently generous out of a job.

The story of pensions is, in fact, largely the story of the slow accretion of power by the labor unions. The first third of this book concerns the United Automobile Workers, who in a decade went from a ragtag bunch whose members were being beaten by paid union-busters to a formidable trade union that wrested pension and health care benefits from Detroit. (Retiree health care entails the same sort of long-term commitments, the same crushing obligations, and may be thought of as a companion to the pension problem.) Ultimately, the UAW drained out the value from once colossal companies, General Motors in particular. For impoverished GM shareholders, the sad irony is that Walter Reuther, the UAW's inspirational early leader, pointed the way toward a solution in the very beginning—and GM's encrusted management did not want to hear it.

In 2007, with the UAW and GM fighting a pitched battle over benefits, the union struck and shut the company down. Reuther's vision, which was carried to a dubious extreme, fueled the present crisis, but it also pointed to a way out.

The second part shifts the scene to the remarkable story of the then communist-run Transport Workers Union—which in the midst of the Great Depression organized the New York City subways. The TWU and its fiery leader, Mike Quill, played much the same role in the public sector as Reuther and the UAW did in private. Previous to the TWU, subway employees had to work until age seventy to qualify for a pension (and a meager one at that). Through a combination of strikes, threats, and not-so-subtle politicking, unions such as the TWU became a power in the legislature. Thanks to their efforts, New York's public servants now stand a fair chance of collecting a pension for longer than they worked, and in many cases they earn *more* in retirement (including Social Security) than they did on the job.[7] Thus "retirement" has expanded from a modest sinecure at the sunset of life to a long and lucrative second career.

This is a topsy-turvy state of affairs, contrary to economic logic as well as common sense. Subway riders are paying higher fares so that the system's middle-class employees can retire at fifty-five and spend, like as not, three decades in a comfortable retirement. The Metropolitan Transportation Authority finally demanded reforms, and over Christmas 2005 New Yorkers got a frightening glimpse of the future—when a pension strike shut down their fabled transit system.

The drama in the subways pitted the people who operated the trains against the people who rode them: the public servants against the public. This is suggestive of the crisis in public pensions everywhere. In New York, at least, the battle was waged openly and on the issues. But many other pension sponsors have not been so forthright. For institutions under stress, pensions have been a tool for escaping the tough decisions. A sort of devil's bargain is struck, whereby the unions (which know that pensions are constitutionally guaranteed) push for benefits that are beyond the ability of governments to properly fund. The unions get their promises; the politicians get to satisfy a powerful constituency. And by shortchanging their pension funds, they can run their budgets on borrowed time and put off the necessity to tax until a later generation.

The final section of this book concerns the City of San Diego, where just such a devil's pact led to a sensational scandal that toppled the mayor, cost the local government its credit rating, and brought the city to the edge of bankruptcy. The scandal had its origins in the fertile soil of San Diego's laissez-faire political culture. The pressure on politicians to keep taxes low was unrelenting, and public servants brazenly conspired with union officials to raise benefits in the future in return for permission to underfund the pension now. This relaxed the immediate pressure on the budget, though it weakened the city's future finances for years and possibly decades. Many officials behaved less like councilmen and pension trustees than like the artful dodgers at Enron. But the essential abuse—appealing to the electorate by shifting liabilities into the future—is altogether common. And the investigations and indictments that have riddled this still beleaguered city could happen anywhere. San Diego is a wake-up call to every community.

MANY COMMENTATORS have taken comfort in the notion that pensions are not the U.S.'s only retirement vehicle; they are part of a triad of options along with private savings and Social Security. But the fact is, outside of the rich, very few people have adequate savings. If pensions cannot be put right, preserving (and strengthening) the third leg—Social Security—will be the only option left. Social Security itself is under fierce attack by the right wing of the Republican Party. Many younger Americans do not believe that it will be there when they retire. What, then, is to be done?

It is too late to resurrect the companies already destroyed by runaway pensions and health care benefits. Nor can the huge obligations run up by the states be unraveled, except painfully and over the very long term. But for those not yet burned, those with the hope of digging out, and for the country at large, the sagas of General Motors, the New York City subways, and San Diego need not be a portent. Disaster can be averted if only their essential lesson is heeded: those who mortgage the future come to rue the day.

PART I

WHO OWNS GENERAL MOTORS?

ONE

WALTER REUTHER AND THE TREATY OF DETROIT

The weight of history on our results has been significant.

—Rick Wagoner, *chairman and chief executive officer, General Motors*

Once upon a time, General Motors was a symbol of success. After World War II, the automaker routinely captured more than 40 percent of the American automobile market, and in 1955, when an entry-level Chevrolet cost $1,450, GM's market share climbed to 51 percent. The company's brass was moved to complain (or so went the joke) "We're still losing five out of every ten sales."[1] In an age when GM was criticized for pursuing its own selfish aims rather than those of the country, Charlie Wilson, its outgoing president, testified, rather memorably, before the Senate Armed Services Committee, "What was good for the country *was* good for General Motors, and vice versa."[2] Wilson's remark didn't fool anybody; GM, of course, was in business for its stockholders. To ensure that its profit targets were met, it methodically raised the prices of its cars, and year after year it had the highest sales, the highest profits of any company in America. The shareholders made out like bandits. From the end of the war until 1965, a span of two decades, the stock registered a stupendous, eightfold gain.

But as an institution, General Motors was already beginning to age. Shareholders did not at first notice the great transformation that was occurring in their status—their great *disenfranchisement.* But in a manner of speaking, they lost their claim; General Motors was sold out from under them. Oh, it wasn't literally sold. But the gushing stream that was GM's cash flow, which previously and properly had flowed to the stockholders, was quietly but most assuredly diverted. Over the next four decades, GM's stock lost 60 percent of its value. The company continued to pay dividends, but the owners of America's biggest industrial enterprise would have done better holding T-bills. Even though, over those many years, GM sold as many cars or more as in Wilson's day, the putative owners—the stockholders—for all practical purposes had lost their title.

So who owned General Motors? Gradually, a revolution had taken place. A vanguard force—GM's retired workers and its future retirees—had attached an opposing title; they had become *en*titled. Modestly at first, but in time overwhelmingly, Wilson's car company became beholden to the huge pension benefits, as well as the lavish standard of health care, that it had pledged to its retired workers and their dependents. "What is good for General Motors is good for its *retirees*" was the new mantra.

By the dawn of the twenty-first century, Wilson would not have recognized his former employer. Over a fifteen-year stretch ending in 2006, GM poured $55 *billion* into its workers' pension plan, compared to only $13 billion that it paid out in dividends. In other words, the company paid its pensioners four times as much—not including the money it spent on their generous health care benefits—as it did to its ostensible owners!

Walter Reuther was both the person most responsible for this crisis and one of the first to propose a solution. A passionate and scrupulous labor leader, Reuther came of age during the Great Depression, and the experience of seeing thousands of autoworkers (and millions of Americans) lose their jobs instilled in him a lifelong desire for basic security—what he was to call "social insurance." Because Reuther was born in the first decade of the twentieth century, and because he grew up just as workers were organizing and demanding security, his life story would chart the evolution of social insurance in the United States—everything from pensions and health care to unemployment compensation. These benefits already existed in Europe, and much of Reuther's philosophy was imported via his German-born father and grandfather, both of whom were ardent Social Democrats.

But in the United States, until very late in the nineteenth century, pensions were almost unheard of. Union Army veterans got pensions, but they had begun as compensation for war injuries, and only later had been extended to older veterans generally. Private employers simply did not offer pensions. "Retirement" as we know it—that is, a distinct phase of life devoted to family and to leisure after one's working years—did not exist. Nor did the concept of unemployment.

Most people worked on farms or in small shops or mills. As they got older they didn't stop working, they simply worked a little less. If old age did catch up with them, they turned to their families for food and shelter. The "problem" of old age was in any case not widespread. In 1900, only 4 percent of the population was over sixty-five. Retirement was less one of life's standard passages, like adolescence or middle age, than it was an infrequent and brief preamble to the grave.

However, by the early twentieth century, notions of retirement were beginning to evolve. If you want to fix a date, 1907, the year Reuther was born, is as good as any. One reason was that people were living longer. Some of this was because of medical advances, and a good deal was due to the installation of sanitary plumbing and the eradication of unhygienic dwellings (and slums) where people were more likely to spread contagions.

A second factor was industrialization. The man who tended a farm could gracefully age on the job; the factory worker couldn't. Shop stewards and department managers wanted their graybeards out, to make room for younger blood. The desire to manage its labor force motivated a newly formed rail freight business, American Express, to institute the first corporate pension, in 1875.[3] The railroads gradually followed suit. Railroad pensions were similar in spirit to army pensions; the work was exceedingly dangerous, and benefits were largely a reward for risking injury and death.

As the "workplace" shifted to the city, companies figured that employees, white-collar workers in particular, would be easier to recruit if they were promised a pension. Also, since employees generally had to serve thirty years to be eligible, they would be more likely to *stay* on the job. As an executive of the Pennsylvania Railroad reckoned, "We feel sure that the pension system tends to keep our best men."[4] The rails were followed by banks, insurers, utilities—the sorts of companies interested in nurturing a stable and skilled workforce. Also, the tax code was amended so that money put into pension plans was deductible. For all these reasons, by the end of the 1920s a sizable minority of businesses offered plans.

This progress, however, accomplished very little for most blue-collar workers. Pensions were created by companies that reckoned it to be in the *corporate* interest. They were a tool for managing labor, not an entitlement due to labor. Even if some executives chose to award benefits for humanitarian reasons, the decision was theirs. The workers did not have a *right* to a pension, much less to a broader social security program. But this was Reuther's ideal.

The young Reuther had been schooled on the rights of the workingman, including, especially, the right to a dignified retirement, the way other American boys were schooled in baseball. His father, Valentine, had emigrated to the United States in 1892.[5] By then, Germany had already established a state insurance program. Valentine strongly believed in benefits for the masses in America as well. He settled in West Virginia, got a job driving a brewery wagon, and became a labor leader and devotee of the socialist Eugene Debs. Walter and his four siblings grew up in a strict home in which two religions held sway: Lutheranism and trade unionism.

Walter quit school, as was the custom, at fifteen to apprentice in a tool shop. When a mammoth die slipped, he lost a big toe. There is no record that his employer paid the bill, and for the young apprentice to have demanded "insurance" for the accident would have been laughable. In any case, hearing that a craftsman in Detroit could earn a dollar an hour, then a reasonable starting wage, in 1927 he left for the Motor City.

Reuther was hired at Ford's (such was it known, for the company was identified with its proprietor). It had a huge plant, River Rouge, that functioned as a small city—machine shops, steel and glass mills, metal stamping. An intense, hardworking redhead, Reuther did not go in for drinking or after-hours carousing. Even while holding down a job, he attended high school in his spare time and then enrolled in a local college. Joined by his brother Victor, he also began to frequent left-wing political meetings in Detroit, where the talk centered on unionizing the auto industry. Auto companies paid decent wages by prevailing standards, but job security was woefully lacking. When Ford discontinued the Model T (just as Reuther arrived in Detroit) 100,000 workers were sent packing until its plant could be retooled. The Great Depression saw layoffs on a far larger scale. Jobless men would arrive at the plants at dawn and build bonfires at the gate while desperately waiting for a call to work.[6]

Reuther was especially aroused by the lack of job security. He campaigned in 1932 for Norman Thomas, the Socialist candidate for president, took photographs of local shantytowns (dubbed "Hoovervilles" after the White House incumbent), and agitated for better working conditions. Then, according to Reuther's later account, Ford's fired him for being an activist. Nelson Lichtenstein, Reuther's best biographer, says he may have simply resigned. In any case, in 1932, he and Ford's parted.[7]

There was no future for an organizer (or for much of anyone) in Detroit just then. Most of the unemployed went on relief. A smaller number, emblematic of the era, hopped freight cars and lived as hobos. Reuther and his brother conceived a far more novel—indeed, remarkable—plan. They resolved to travel the world. This was to be no grand tour of museums and opera houses, but a proletarian journey, via bicycle, of factories and mills. The Reuthers aimed to sample working conditions around the globe, so that they might import the best ideas to America. Crossing the Atlantic by ship, they disembarked in Hamburg early in 1933, just as the Nazi revolution was engulfing their ancestral homeland. The brothers had an idea of linking up with the opposition, and they did make contact with left-wing students as well as with some of their relatives. However, as Hitler's control was becoming absolute, remaining in Germany seemed futile and they left for Austria and the Netherlands. There they waited until visas arrived for the Soviet Union. By late 1933, Walter and Vic were employed at the giant Gorky auto factory, a Stalinist imitation of the Ford plant at River Rouge.

Conditions were spartan, even though Walter and Vic were housed in the more favorable dorms reserved for foreigners. In terms of efficiency, the plant was light-years behind River Rouge. However, the brothers were infected with Gorky's pioneering spirit. Walter, who learned passable Russian, published a critique of the plant in a Moscow English-language paper, and judging from their letters home, both Reuthers were smitten with the Soviet experiment. The Russian workers, though poorly paid, had at least minimal job protection and health care. That Stalin was already employing forced labor on a mass scale seems to have escaped their notice. Victor wrote, "We are watching daily socialism being taken down from the books and shelves and put into actual application."[8]

After Gorky, they boarded a train for the Far East, where they saw appalling poverty in China and an ominous militarism on the rise in Japan. They returned home, in 1935, after thirty-two months. Irving Howe, the socialist writer who was the first to profile Reuther, said, "History had been thrust into their faces."[9] But their effect on history was only beginning.

In Detroit, the newly formed United Automobile Workers was attempting to organize the auto industry. Reuther threw himself into union work, and quickly became president of the big UAW local on Detroit's West Side. It was rough going; the auto companies (especially Ford) were adamantly opposed to unions. They hired spies and thugs to intimidate members, and as the Depression still raged workers were naturally afraid to enlist and risk their jobs. Many of the union's shock troops were communists—who at the time, it should be said, were not quite the pariahs in American life they later became. Reuther was close to the communists and may have briefly been a member.[10] However, he resisted the party's attempt to enforce an ideological line, and as his power in the union rose, he distanced himself.

In 1937, the UAW shut down a critical GM plant in Flint. Alfred Sloan, the president of GM, viewed the action as illegal and refused to negotiate. Sloan was a managerial genius who had rescued GM from failure in the 1920s and propelled it into the number one spot, ahead of Ford. He was also very much opposed to organized labor activity. Like most corporate executives of that time, Sloan was ardently opposed to Franklin D. Roosevelt's New Deal, and especially to FDR's welfare programs. Unlike most, he had worked behind the scenes to finance the anti-Roosevelt American Liberty League, a racist and anti-Semitic fringe group.[11]

If Sloan did not want a government welfare state, he certainly did not want a private one imposed on GM by employees. During the Depression, General Motors had continued to pay dividends to its stockholders even while twice cutting its meager wages and laying off half its workforce.[12] Sloan saw no reason to apologize. He ran the company for the benefit of the stockholders; he assuredly did not run a welfare agency.

Sloan beseeched the federal government to send in troops to break up the strike. Frances Perkins, the secretary of labor, refused. A passionate New Dealer and a proponent of welfare, Perkins leaned on GM to compromise. Sloan read the tea leaves and agreed to start talking. Henry Ford did not. In the spring of 1937, during a demonstration at River Rouge, he unleashed his goons, who caught up with Reuther on an overpass above the plant and severely beat him. However, the union agitation continued. In 1941, the UAW managed to shut down River Rouge. With the plant surrounded by thousands of striking picketers, Ford capitulated and agreed to government-supervised elections. Thus, by the time of Pearl Harbor, the UAW had been duly elected as the bargaining agent for most American autoworkers.

By now, Reuther, a member of the UAW's executive board, was very much focused on pensions. The Depression had exposed the plight of the number of elderly poor, and America was visited by all manner of political extremists, who stepped up the pressure for various forms of welfare benefits. The oddest of these was an elderly, out-of-work physician and onetime mining speculator in Long Beach, California, a Dr. Francis Townsend. Dr. Townsend wrote to the local newspaper suggesting a fantastic retirement scheme: that the government distribute $200 a month to each American over sixty and pay for it with a sales tax. When recycled through the economy, he argued, these lavish pensions would "abolish unemployment" forever. His proposal was fiscally unworkable, but in rural America it had the lure of an elixir. Millions of Americans joined "Townsend Clubs" and dozens of congressmen lined up in support.[13]

Social Security was enacted, in 1935, partly as a response. Roosevelt told Perkins, his labor secretary, "The Congress can't stand the pressure of the Townsend Plan unless we have a real old-age insurance system, nor can I face the country without one." But the new program hardly defused the pressure for pensions and other benefits. For one thing, Social Security fell badly short of its planners' goals—which had been to provide universal, cradle-to-grave protection. New Dealers reluctantly omitted health insurance, which they feared was politically unsalable. Moreover, millions of workers were excluded from the retirement plan. Out of deference to the southern bloc in Congress, agricultural workers, many of whom were black, were deemed ineligible, as were local government workers. Even for those who did participate, benefits were too low to provide true "security."

Also, from the day that Social Security was passed, conservatives agitated to repeal it. Reuther's old boss, Henry Ford, fulminated that it would regiment society and diminish Americans' freedom. Alf Landon, the Republican candidate for president in 1936, labeled it "a cruel hoax."[14]

The opposition focused on whether the money would really be there to fund such a large entitlement, and the early experience with private pension plans was not exactly encouraging. Actuarial science was in its early days, and many corporate sponsors of pensions did not bother to fund their plans, or did so only on a halfhearted basis. (They simply paid benefits from general funds.) As business conditions worsened during the

1930s, sponsors came under stress, the railroads in particular. For instance, the Pennsylvania Railroad's pension expense, only $235,000 in 1900, had swelled to an enormous $8 million in 1931.[15] The burden of funding the railroads' pensions was aggravated by the industry's decline. Competition from trucking had sapped the railroads' growth and led to an aging of their labor force. And the rails discovered, to their horror, that unlike wages, pension expenses could not be trimmed with the business cycle. Ultimately, railroad pensions had to be bailed out by Congress.[16] This early pension fiasco was one that executives in other industries—autos, steel, and airlines, for example—should have committed to memory.

But no graying was visible in automobiles then. It was a young industry, poised for growth. Reuther spent the war years building a power base in Detroit and struggling with the UAW's communist faction for control. He also forged ties to Washington. During the war, he made a splashy proposal to convert Detroit into a vast airplane factory; though his plan was impractical, it raised his public profile and established him as a political figure to be reckoned with. The union earned more points by pledging not to strike, and by putting up with wartime wage controls.

By the time Reuther gained unchallenged authority over the UAW, in 1947, the war was over and he had a pent-up list of demands. He also was envisioning a broader social role for the UAW, as an agent for achieving the welfare state that the New Deal had left unfinished. And he wanted it not just for autoworkers but for everyone. As early as 1949, the writer Irving Howe could see that the UAW could become a revolutionary catalyst: "a force molding American life."[17]

Pensions and job security were first on Reuther's agenda, with health care a close second. Sloan recorded his view of these demands in his memoir: "extravagant beyond reason."[18] However, the world was changing. By the war's end, more than 7 percent of Americans were over sixty-five, nearly double the ratio of 1900. And experts in the new field of demography were forecasting (correctly) that the ratio would virtually double again, to 12 percent, by 1980.[19] Retirees as a sociopolitical force were coming of age.

In a curious way, Americans' first decade of experience with Social

Security heightened, rather than alleviated, their concern for the aged. The level of the government benefit was unchanged since the Depression, and its value had been decimated by inflation. The program's very inadequacy focused attention on the need for private pensions.

Government policy further stimulated the pension bandwagon. The United States levied an excess profits tax on corporations during the war, which sent companies scurrying for the tax shelter offered by retirement plans. Also, the government froze wages while still allowing firms to grant (or increase) noncash benefits. Thus pensions became a way to give *something* to strapped employees. The result was a pension stampede, tripling the number of Americans with coverage to six and a half million, or a sixth of the workforce.[20] However, many of these plans—including the one at General Motors—included only salaried (not hourly, or unionized) workers. This seemed patently unfair; what's more, the government's tax policy had changed the terms of the debate. If the United States was going to subsidize pensions, Washington was entitled to some say in how they were used. Pensions were now viewed as a benefit to labor; as the pension historian Steven Sass put it, Congress expected a "social return for its tax favors."[21]

Congress had laid the groundwork during the New Deal with legislation establishing the right of workers to form unions and to bargain collectively. The key legislation was the National Labor Relations Act, or Wagner Act, in 1935. Though its effect was muted during the Depression, after the war union membership surged. Starved for wage hikes and squeezed by wartime inflation, the unions erupted after V-J Day with a series of crippling strikes against steel mills, packing plants, shippers, refineries—and General Motors. Unions might have derailed the entire economy, but President Truman intervened and seized the coal mines and the railroads.

The eruption turned out to be brief. As the cold war escalated, public sentiment turned rightward and less sympathetic to labor. Inflation ebbed, making wage hikes harder to justify. Big Business, as it was known, was dominated by a handful of cartels, and in the late 1940s it took a tough line. Some firms insisted on an outright pay freeze. However, pensions were seen as less inflationary. Reuther and other union leaders were nothing if not opportunistic, and increasingly demanded welfare-type benefits, or what they referred to as social insurance.

Ford Motor was at least mildly receptive. Now led by the founder's grandson, Henry II, it was eager to soften the hard-edged image of the original Henry. In 1947 the company offered a small pension. But there was a large catch: workers would have to contribute to the plan, and it was packaged with a smaller wage hike (seven cents an hour instead of fifteen cents) than if the UAW opted for a contract with no pension. Reuther, uncharacteristically, was thrown off his game. He asked the members, most of whom did not have high school diplomas, to vote. Perhaps not surprisingly, they opted for the cash-only contract by a big margin—an embarrassment to their leader.[22]

Reuther suffered a different sort of wound the next year, when gunmen fired through the kitchen window of his Northwest Detroit bungalow, nearly killing him (one bullet struck his chest) and permanently damaging his right arm. The assassination attempt boosted his moral stature just as the pension issue was coming to a head.*

Ford's new contract expired in 1949, and this time Reuther demanded a pension that was noncontributory for the workers. Warming the rhetorical flames, he insisted that the UAW would no longer tolerate a "double standard"—pensions for executives but not for men on the line.

Ford responded that if the employees didn't fund their pension, the company would have to pay for it by raising car prices, which it was unwilling to do. John Bugas, a Ford vice president, sent Reuther a condescending rejection, which he also released to the press. "Old-age security is a highly desirable goal, but it must be paid for," Bugas said dismissively.

---

*The assailants were never apprehended. Suspicion pointed to union underworld gangs threatened by Reuther's rise, probably linked to Jimmy Hoffa's Teamsters local in Detroit.

"There is no 'kitty' from which Ford can draw." Reuther cheekily retorted that Ford could fund its workers' pensions "from the same source that is used to finance security for high paid executives."[23]

At the UAW convention in Milwaukee that summer, he demanded a $100 a month pension and a hospitalization plan equivalent to 5 percent of payroll. At a time when Social Security provided retirees with on average only $28 a month, this was bold in the extreme. But it was only the beginning of Reuther's demands. What the union required, he declared to twenty-five hundred cheering delegates, was nothing short of "a full social welfare program"—health care, a pension, death benefits, disability: the works.[24] Noting that Ford, as well as Chrysler, had already said no, Reuther sarcastically observed, "Security in your old age . . . is reserved to only the blue bloods. They can have security, but if you live on the wrong side of the railroad tracks you are not entitled to it." As for GM, its president, Charlie Wilson, stood to get a pension of $25,000 a year (the equivalent of about $250,000 today). Contrasting this with the rank and file, Reuther thundered, "If you make $1.65 an hour they say, 'You don't need it [a pension], you are not entitled to it, and we are not going to give it to you.' We are going to change that in America, and we are going to start in the next couple of weeks."[25]

And now Reuther had the political wind at his back. The recent labor laws had significantly enhanced the unions' power. John L. Lewis's coal miners successfully struck for pensions after the war. Moreover, government policy, which was looking for a way to reward workers without stoking inflation, increasingly tilted toward pensions. The National Labor Relations Board, a federal agency created during the Depression to, among other things, investigate unfair labor practices, was watching pension negotiations closely. In 1948, in a case involving Inland Steel, the board ruled that companies had to at least *bargain* on pensions. That was a critical breakthrough. The next year saw dozens of strikes against steelmakers. Trying to avert an economic collapse, President Truman formed a special panel that recommended pensions (but not inflationary wage hikes) for steelworkers. The steel industry rapidly capitulated.[26]

Perhaps more relevant to the UAW's impasse with Ford, the auto market was booming. Families migrating to the suburbs were buying their very first cars. Once chosen, their preferred brand could be hard to shake—or so argued Reuther, who had an instinct for the companies' most tender spot. If Ford was struck, GM would be handed a golden opportunity to win the loyalty of first-time consumers. Record sales had weakened Ford's appetite for a strike, and the Wagner Act weakened it further. Management now had to play by rules; the days when it could send in goons to crush a few skulls were over. *Fortune* predicted, "The industry probably cannot stand off for long the auto worker's drive for security in the form of a pension scheme."[27] Two months after Reuther's appearance in Milwaukee, Ford agreed to provide the workers with a monthly pension of $100, *less* whatever a worker stood to receive from Social Security.

Reuther actually liked this convoluted structure, theorizing that it would give Ford an incentive "to go down to Washington and fight with us."[28] (The higher the federal benefit, the less that Ford had to chip in.) The unions had been waiting, with growing impatience, for Congress to raise Social Security, and also to pass national health insurance, which Truman had proposed in 1947. For a brief interlude after the war, a federal pension was considered not just probable but "a political certainty." Even Senator Robert A. Taft, a conservative who had famously opposed New Deal welfare programs, argued that the government had a duty to redress the disadvantage suffered by nonunion labor. "If a steelworker and a miner are to receive [a pension]," the senator reasoned, "why not a molder or a waiter?"[29]

Though he bargained for private benefits, Reuther strongly preferred public ones. He had a European notion of labor and industry as economic partners (a notion wholly foreign to Sloan and Wilson at GM). Within the UAW, the benefits section was known as the "social security department," signaling Reuther's credo that, ultimately, welfare benefits were the responsibility of government. Corporate pensions were a stopgap.

Proof of Reuther's socialistic attitude was his frequent demand for higher wages and benefits *without* any increase in car prices. The latter ran counter to his members' economic interests (since higher prices would mean more dollars available for autoworkers). But Reuther fancifully included the general public, and especially the workingman, in the UAW's constituency; he did not want the car-buying public to pay the price for union gains. He frequently argued that labor, management, and the public each had a worthy and defensible stake in corporate institutions—notably in GM—an argument that infuriated Wilson. For one thing, Reuther did not represent car buyers per se. For another, prices were none of the UAW's business.

GM had been forced to put up with government quotas, price controls, and meddling by the Labor Board during the war and its aftermath; now the company was anxious to return to normalcy, which the executives defined as operating its business with a free hand. Sloan, who had retired from day-to-day management but was still presiding as chairman, feared that expanding the federal welfare state would further, and perhaps irretrievably, entangle his company in the maws of government.

Looking across the Atlantic, welfare states were already emerging in Europe. Between the end of the war and 1948, the British government took over the country's coal mines, railroads, and gas and electric companies, all with rather little ado. The French leader General Charles de Gaulle nationalized Renault, France's leading automaker. In speeches and interviews, Wilson, an engineer like Sloan but fifteen years younger and less parochial in his worldview, argued that American industry and labor should work through their issues rather than submit to takeovers by the state—what Wilson termed "the philosophy of class conflict from Europe." The fear of creeping statism was very real. As *Business Week* warned, "British socialism seems a closer threat than Russian communism."[30]

Strangely, Big Business, which led the attack against expanded government benefits, seemed not to notice that *it* was the only alternative provider. As Harry Becker, who headed the UAW social security department, wrote, either Congress would deliver on social insurance or it would be "sought from employers across the collective bargaining table."[31] Business was determining who would carry the burden of benefits several generations hence—and it was choosing itself rather than Washington!

The UAW pressed the issue by dabbling with collective, union-run health plans and pensions. In an intriguing case, in the city of Toledo, Ohio, where auto-industry workers labored in hundreds of smaller shops, the UAW local proposed an area-wide "social security plan," including a pension for every worker. It would be jointly administered—that is, all of the local businesses' pension contributions would be pooled. At a stroke, this would resolve two major issues. Unlike in a single-company plan, workers could change jobs and keep their pension rights intact. And the risk of pension default was obviously much less when the assets were pooled.

Business liked it no better than it liked Social Security. Red-baiting was becoming a popular sport (Senator Joseph McCarthy was on the brink of celebrity) and any approach with a whiff of collectivism raised the fear of socialism. Toledo executives, led by the publisher of the *Toledo Blade*, mobilized to stop the pension pool with an all-out newspaper and radio campaign. As the historian Jennifer Klein has written, the attack became vitriolic, culminating in a front-page *Blade* editorial decrying the "blight" that the pension proposal "casts on this industrial community."[32] Not surprisingly, the plan withered.

However, to marginalize the Toledo plan, companies were forced to grant single-employer pensions, committing them to provide a "defined benefit" (that is, a stipulated monthly sum to retirees for the duration of their lives) regardless of the eventual obligation to the company. While Wilson was pondering this doleful precedent, Reuther played his final card.

Both GM and Chrysler had contracts expiring in 1950, but as it happened, Chrysler's expired first. Intuitively sensing the potential to divide and conquer, Reuther demanded from the company not just a pension but a contractual promise to *fund* the pension. Chrysler insisted that the union could rely on its overall corporate good health (an assurance that would seem laughable a generation later). Reuther wisely refused to take Chrysler's word for it, and the UAW struck. Chrysler still delegated labor relations to an outside law firm, as though negotiating with the UAW were just a detail.[33] Perhaps the company doubted that the UAW could enforce a strike over such a technical issue as actuarial soundness. "That was a new expression," Douglas Fraser, a unionist who had joined the industry as a metal finisher in 1936, admitted.[34] The UAW hired actuaries to explain it to the rank and file. The workers stayed out for a hundred days, after which Chrysler surrendered. The crushing loss of business dashed all hopes that Chrysler might overtake Ford as the number two producer.

GM met with the union while Chrysler was suffering through its agony. Further lessening GM's appetite for confrontation was the fact that it had earned record profits in 1949 and had just declared a stockholder dividend of $190 million—the largest payout ever by an American corporation. GM's main problem was a lack of enough cars to meet the insatiable appetite for its product, a deficit GM was promising to remedy with "plenty of new cars." It surely did not want a strike.

The UAW submitted a thirty-seven-page bargaining proposal, illustrated with a drawing of a well-groomed autoworker, in suspenders and necktie, who looked altogether respectable (not the sort who might walk off the job or seize your plant). The brief made a point of noting that its average worker had only seven years' experience, and only a fifth were over fifty—so few would be drawing pensions anytime soon. As regards health security, the union trenchantly remarked, "Although we in America are foremost in our efforts to analyze and cure disease, we have lagged far behind in organizing ourselves to meet the economic and social costs of medical care."[35]

Left unstated was the fact that those young GM workers *eventually* would age. GM knew that, of course. But they would not age overnight. And Reuther put an enticing carrot on the table—a willingness to sign a five-year deal, thus a respite from labor strife until 1955. To Charlie Wilson, the GM executive, that was too much to resist. Talks proceeded swiftly. Two weeks after the end of the Chrysler strike, GM agreed to a landmark deal: a pension of $125 a month (minus the Social Security benefit) funded by the company, a wage hike with a cost-of-living formula, and hospital and medical insurance at half the cost.

Fortune billed it "The Treaty of Detroit." The union had won the basic welfare protections (the pension was equivalent to $1,040 a month in today's money) that Reuther had craved. What is notable is that American business was so starved for labor peace that it also greeted the "treaty" with enthusiasm. *Fortune* crowed, "It has been so long since any big U.S. manufacturer could plan with complete confidence in its labor relations that industry has almost forgotten what it felt like." Sloan emphasized this aspect in his memoir, writing that the accord "represented an effort to introduce an element of reason, and of predictability" into GM's labor relations.[36]

But a few voices recognized the danger. Noting the long-term, nearly incalculable nature of pension obligations, the *Nation* checked its liberal instincts and wondered, "Who knows whether the steel, coal, or any other companies will be able for a long and uninterrupted period of years to continue to pay the agreed amounts into the funds now set up?"[37]

Peter Drucker, a young management consultant, struck a similarly foreboding note in an article titled "The Mirage of Pensions."[38] He doubted whether any company—even GM—could gauge the strength of its capital structure four decades hence. Drucker was more prescient about GM than were its own executives. The consultant also observed that *new* pension plans presented a particularly knotty financial problem. In theory, from the day an employee was vested, his employer would make annual contributions to finance his retirement. But a new plan typically endowed all the existing employees—for whom no money had been set aside—with full credit. Therefore, firms faced a catch-up obligation, particularly for employees who were nearing retirement. At Ford Motor, still a privately owned firm, the estimated liability was a staggering $200 million.

AFTER THE BREAKTHROUGH in automobiles, numerous other unions won pensions, many of which were similarly linked to Social Security. As Reuther had hoped, in the early 1950s Social Security was repeatedly raised. But with the federal benefit rising, the link became a chain that dragged the company pensions lower—something the unions hadn't really intended. Thus the UAW demanded an end to the link. Reuther now felt free to seek higher company benefits *in addition* to whatever was awarded in Washington.

Reuther found clever ways to extract more in every round, both higher levels and new types of benefits. Companies watched their cash wages closely; they found it easier to say yes on items such as pensions, disability, and health care. The UAW exploited this by negotiating wages first; then, as Fraser recalled, "we fit in the programs, pensions, health care." The seemingly routine process of "fitting in" higher benefits began to build daunting future obligations. But to the companies, pensions seemed painless. The near-term cash expense was small, the day of reckoning distant. The accounting was primitive; a pension sweetener didn't necessarily "cost" the company in terms of reported profits.

Also, there were sizable tax advantages to the employee as well as to the employer. A worker was taxed on each dollar of wages; he wasn't taxed on his pension until many years later, and if he instead received a dollar in the form of medical benefits, he wasn't taxed at all. The system thus conspired to push both management and unions into the margins of the contract; the battle increasingly was over fringe benefits.

For Reuther, no form of security was truly a "fringe." In 1955, he began to agitate for protection against layoffs, the bane of autoworkers since the Depression. The auto industry was still quite cyclical, and in each downturn thousands of workers were sent home. What Reuther wanted was a "guaranteed" wage (regardless of whether the employee was actually working). Ford Motor released a statement loaded with self-serving truth:

> The only security—the only guarantee—worth anything to Ford employees is that their company will be healthy, competitive and progressive enough to be able to employ them at a high rate of wages and benefits. When any proposed security scheme impairs this healthy condition—no matter how attractive may seem the arguments in its favor—such scheme will impair the real security of the worker.[39]

Reuther made it plain the union would strike, a point he was careful to repeat with regularity. During a negotiating session, Ford offered what it felt was a reasonable compromise. As Bugas, the Ford executive, read the details aloud, Reuther recognized it as similar to a GM proposal he had already rejected and blurted out, "How the hell do you get a Chevy on a Ford assembly line?" Then he led his team out of the room.[40]

The automakers' real problem, in the sense that it weakened their negotiating hand, was that they were rolling in money. In 1955, GM earned more than $1 billion—a first for an American corporation. Most of its profits were paid out in dividends; in the postwar era, companies felt a keener responsibility to provide stockholders with income. Dividend yields ranged in the high single digits, and increases in GM's dividend were big news. The *New York Times* would report that the directors had gathered around the oval table in the boardroom, following a meal of "roast turkey and cranberry sauce with fresh peas and mashed turnips," and hoisted the dividend like Santa delivering goodies to his children.[41] To refuse a union demand, no matter how much it might have been in the corporate interest, ran a risk in the short run of a strike that would turn off the golden spigot to shareholders.

Bargaining in such a balmy climate, the UAW did even better in 1955 than it had in 1950. Pensions were boosted 50 percent. Including Social Security, workers could expect to retire on $175 a month—a heady 75 percent increase in five years.

Disabled workers got a double pension.[42] Paid vacations were stretched to three weeks, plus seven holidays. And idled workers would now get a "supplemental" benefit in addition to state unemployment compensation. The "supplemental" stipend was small, but Reuther knew it was just an opener. After three subsequent contract rounds, laid-off workers would be guaranteed an astonishing 95 percent of regular pay for at least six months while they were on furlough.

Sloan was especially stung by the supplemental benefit. He wrote in his memoir that GM had disagreed with several aspects of the plan but, "Ultimately, the entire industry conceded the point," as if even he were unsure how it had happened.[43] However, the UAW was already planning for an even costlier benefit—health care for *retirees.* Once the employers' essential responsibility for social insurance was established, the Big Three found it impossible to resist—partly because there *were* only three manufacturers, or only three that counted. GM, Ford, and Chrysler routinely carved up 90 percent of the market, with GM alone claiming roughly half of that share. As oligopolists, they could build benefit costs into the price of cars and not suffer a competitive loss. GM knew when it announced a price hike that Ford and Chrysler would follow suit. For all their talk of open markets, Big Auto (like Big Steel) lived in a cloistered universe in which true competition was lacking. Therefore, almost any cost seemed tolerable. The automakers failed to grasp that pensions were different. Pensions created *long*-term obligations that could outlast even their prosperity.

By 1960, 40 percent of American workers (including most of those who belonged to unions) had won or been granted pensions.[44] Only a decade after the Treaty of Detroit, pensions had become an American institution, one that was radically reshaping people's lives. Fewer men were working after sixty-five, and as the UAW social security department, which kept close track of national trends, reported to Reuther with some astonishment, "an increasing number of older men in good health are choosing to retire rather than go on working." The trend was stark; in 1920 among U.S. males, six of ten senior citizens were in the labor force; in 1960, only three of ten.[45] Older Americans, their pensions safely in hand, were looking forward to a few years of fun, not just a rocking chair.

With its usual impeccable timing, the UAW set its sights on a new entitlement—*early* retirement with full pensions. This would liberate autoworkers from the factory while still in vigorous middle age, and serve the union's purpose of moving workers through the system faster, so that more younger members could be recruited.

However, a hint of the danger embedded in its pension strategy unexpectedly emerged right under the UAW's nose. The union had always had trouble getting the automakers to inject the cash to *fund* their pension plans. GM's plan was frequently 30 percent or more below full funding; Chrysler's occasionally dipped 50 percent under.[46] Such proportions reflected the amount that employees stood to lose if a plan was terminated—in a bankruptcy, for instance.* This was not a worry for the Big Three, but as the auto industry consolidated in the 1950s, the "independent" producers—Nash, Hudson, Studebaker, and Packard—increasingly struggled.

In 1954, Packard failed, and the employees lost a hefty chunk of their pensions. The remaining independents, American Motors (formed by a merger of Hudson and Nash) and Studebaker, were obliged to keep raising pension benefits, in line with the industry leaders. However, they did not have the cash to fully fund. As a UAW actuary, quoted in James Wooten's chronicle of pension legislation, recounted, "we soon woke up to the sad fact that 'fully funded pension plans' are among the rarest animals."[47]

Pensions *without* funding were merely expressions of intent that, if things went well, the workers would get paid. Put differently, they were an attempt to fob off on a future generation the burden accrued by the present one. (In pension plans, this is an ever-present danger.) In truth, unfunded pensions did not provide security; as Drucker warned, they were more a "mirage" than real. But in 1959 Studebaker agreed, as it were, to burnish the mirage—to increase the pension, its third such hike in six years.

This was a reckless step, and the union was partially complicit. The UAW permitted companies that were behind in their contributions to amortize their catch-up payments over thirty years, much like a family with a mortgage. With each liberalization of benefits, payments were restructured over a new thirty years, as if a new mortgage had been issued. This deferred the ultimate due date, fostering an illusion of solvency. Putting off the pension funding date was a way of stretching the math, and enabled (or so it seemed) a firm to pay greater benefits.[48]

---

*Literally, full funding was defined as having assets equal to the *present value* of future pension obligations. This required actuaries to estimate when workers would retire, how long they would live, and also the rate at which assets in the pension fund would grow.

In Studebaker's case, both union and management found something to celebrate (at least in the short term). The union could revel in a pension increase while Studebaker could hang on to more of its scarce cash. In effect, they jointly signed on to the fiction that Studebaker could afford a pension plan that was clearly beyond its means. It was a cynical arrangement, one that illustrated the strong temptation to award gains in the present at the expense of a later generation.

Studebaker enjoyed a revival when it introduced the Lark, a boxy compact intended to compete with Volkswagen's popular, hump-shaped Beetle. As if besotted with its momentary prosperity, Studebaker approved a *fourth*, if modest, pension increase in 1961. Then the Lark fizzled, and in 1963 Studebaker went belly up. Reuther implored the company to do what it could for pensioners. Studebaker's reply signaled that there was nothing *to* be done.[49] Thousands of employees, including some who had worked forty years on the line, lost the bulk of their pensions. The failure was truly a watershed. The workers lost a devastating $15 million in benefits.[50]

Even before the collapse, the UAW's social security department was thinking about the need for federal insurance of pensions, much like deposit insurance in banks. The Studebaker bust put pension solvency on the front page. A pension committee formed by President Kennedy was tasked to explore reforms, and the UAW began a protracted push for legislation.

Reuther by now was a force in American politics, and in particular in the Democratic Party. The UAW was a formidable vote-getting machine, and Reuther had the ear of senators and presidents. He frequently testified on issues such as retirement, health care, jobs, and poverty. He also underwrote civil rights demonstrations, including the epochal March on Washington.* Nor did he let up on socialized insurance. As he reminded a

---

*Though he was overshadowed by Martin Luther King Jr.'s "I have a dream" speech, it was Reuther that day who most forcefully criticized President Kennedy for his slowness to act on civil rights. Alluding to Kennedy's preoccupation with defending the West against communism, Reuther told the marchers, "We cannot *defend* freedom in Berlin so long as we *deny* freedom in Birmingham."

business audience, "The drive for collective bargaining programs did not mean a relaxation of Labor's interest in governmental programs."[51] He was ahead of his time on a range of issues, such as the need for pension portability for workers who changed jobs, the lack of health care for the uninsured, and the already alarming increase in medical costs.

However, Reuther had less success in Washington than he did in Detroit. Although Medicare was introduced in the mid-1960s, America refused to adopt the velvety universal protections of European welfare states. Welfare gains came mostly at the bargaining table, which meant that unionized labor such as factory workers made out much better than those nonunion "molders and waiters." And the future obligations of unionized industry—autos, steel, rubber, and so forth—grew apace.

IF THE UAW was energized by the Studebaker collapse, the automakers blithely ignored it. In the short run, the disappearance of a competitor merely strengthened their oligopoly. As one-car families became two-car families, assembly lines were humming. GM had an aura of invincibility: in the early 1960s its Chevrolet division alone sold more passenger cars than all of Ford.[52] At the corporate level, its sales and also its profits ranked first among all U.S. companies for ten years running—an awesome streak.

With GM's prosperity seemingly limitless, the expedient course in any one year was to give the union what, or nearly what, it wanted. Sloan, who published his memoir in 1963, the year he retired, claimed credit for preventing the union from seizing control of "basic management prerogatives" such as production schedules; he was silent on the costs of benefits, perhaps because they would become clear only over time. Looking back over his decades of bitter dispute with the UAW, Sloan concluded, "The issue of unionism at General Motors is long since settled," with "workable relations" having been achieved.[53] This was a wishful appraisal.

Negotiations had become a ritual, almost Shakespearean struggle, certain to go down to the last moment when a strike would either begin or, mercifully, be avoided. The talks in 1961 took place in the massive GM headquarters, then located four miles from downtown Detroit, in a room with a long mahogany table, two dozen blue upholstered chairs, microphones, and golden drapes. A reporter described how "Mr. Reuther" would emerge from the endless sessions, smile at the waiting cameras, and, in response to shouted questions, combatively stake his ground before he and his "entourage" were whisked into a union-owned Oldsmobile.[54]

Generally, contracts lasted three years, so the pressure on the companies was nearly relentless. In 1961, Reuther led 255,000 GM workers on strike and scored a deceptively costly settlement. Though wages rose by only 2½ percent, pensions were boosted by much more—12 percent—and Reuther also won *full* health insurance for employees and half the cost of hospital, medical, and surgical insurance for retirees. There were myriad small improvements in benefits, too.[55] From the standpoint of the corporate books, such promises were "free" (they did not appear on GM's balance sheet). But in economic terms, they were practically suicidal.

The longer-term pattern was that pensions and other benefits were leaping well ahead of inflation, wages, or other costs. The growing complexity of the benefit structure fueled the union's ability to navigate the system and, inevitably, to boost its take. Perusing the union archives, one has the feeling of wandering through the files of a vast institution of the state—a cabinet-level bureaucracy, maybe, or a government insurance agency. There is voluminous information on, and correspondence with, pension and health plans around the country, a veritable trove of data on the expanding social safety network.

As its expertise grew, the union began to sound faintly presumptuous, almost arrogant. A statement from the UAW to General Motors on proposed improvements to the benefit for laid-off workers, in preparation for the 1964 round, runs to fifteen pages. It asserts that the previous supplemental benefit "fell far short of meeting management's full responsibility to laid-off workers."[56] It is no longer a matter for GM to negotiate; it is GM's *responsibility*.

But the union, of course, was entitled to craft its agenda. It was management's job to hold the line. By granting ever richer benefits that would encumber GM into the hereafter, the executives were banking on GM's continued strength into the distant twenty-first century. At the time, GM's execs felt they had every reason for confidence. In 1963, the company's profit margins were at a peak.[57] What's more, it employed some 405,000 active workers, a solid base from which to support its pensioners, of whom there were just 31,000. Its contributions into the pension fund (plus the fund's income) totaled $95 million, compared with only $25 million that it paid in benefits, so the plan was operating at a tidy surplus.[58] GM did not consider that it might repeat the experience of the railroads, which had become saddled with an aging workforce just as their growth waned. On reflection, it was the executives in Detroit who were truly presumptuous.

THE 1964 BARGAINING was the last to occur before, in the well-greased General Motors engine, one could detect the first faint sounds of a cough. GM continued to sell one out of every two cars in America, and the contract that emerged from the 1964 talks was a monument to its, and the overall industry's, prosperity. GM had just reported the highest net income by any U.S. company ever, and the contract raised pensions by an astounding 50 percent. In 1950, the GM benefit had been equivalent to a $45 a month pension for a thirty-year veteran, or $125 a month including Social Security. In only fourteen years the pension had tripled; a single worker could now retire on $315 a month.

Retirees got a further and very significant boost from 50 percent to 100 percent of health care costs. In a pen stroke, the company thus committed to pay for procedures and drugs whose range would be limited in the future only by the (unforeseeable) powers of medical science. Even in that year, the list of covered treatments ran to nine pages, from X-ray and radiation therapy to in-hospital treatment for "nervous or mental conditions" to obstetric and pre- and postnatal care. With improved technology and society's liberalizing view of health care, the cost of caring for an army of hundreds of thousands of people and their families was rising exponentially.[59] This posed a grave future risk, even if it barely dented the companies at the time.

WITH SUCH IMPRESSIVE GAINS, Reuther feared that the union was becoming vulnerable. If the automakers ran into hard times, UAW benefits would surely become a target. Thus, in the mid- and late 1960s, Reuther increasingly focused on how to make secure what the union had won. In 1966, he testified in favor of government pension insurance. Private pensions were now a leviathan industry with $85 billion in assets. (The UAW alone had a thousand different plans with employers in autos, aerospace, and related industries.) It was not hard to imagine that another Studebaker was out there somewhere. The next year, Reuther returned to Congress to speak on Social Security. Though the union was still pushing for a full federal pension, Reuther was more concerned with the system's solvency. Sounding like a latter-day Republican, he warned that Social Security's reserves, which were held in trust funds, would only be as sound "as the willingness of the American people to support them."[60]

He was back on the Hill again to recommend an experimental program of incentives (again, a pretty Republican idea) for hospitals "to encourage methods of holding down unit costs [and] ascertain optimal utilization patterns."[61] At first glance, this was strange: Reuther's members had their health care paid for, no matter what the price or how frequent the service. But with costs rising so speedily, Reuther sensed that sooner or later the golden protections he had won might come under attack. A brief prepared by an aide, "Salient Facts Relative to Health Care in the U.S.," laid out the galloping rate of health care inflation (double that of the economy at large). What was worse, 60 percent of Americans had no insurance for prescription drugs; 34 percent had none for hospitalization.[62] Someone in the UAW underlined in magic marker the subheading "Failure of Private Health Insurance." A full generation before Hillary Clinton, as First Lady, would attempt to pass a national health care bill, the UAW had glimpsed the essential inability of the private sector to deal with health care.

IN THE MID-1960S, as Reuther had feared, auto profits did slow down. In 1966 GM cut the dividend. By the following year, the stock was off by a third. The trouble first appeared in a mild, seemingly remediable form. GM was having to placate the government's new safety director and address mechanical defects in its vehicles brought to the public's attention by a pesky Harvard law school graduate, Ralph Nader.[63] (Nader's 1965 best seller, *Unsafe at Any Speed*, specifically targeted the GM Corvair.) But GM's troubles went deeper. In 1967, the Japanese Datsun made its debut in American showrooms; it was an instant hit. Late that year, an analysis in the *New York Times* of the problems facing James Roche, GM's new chief executive, highlighted the efforts of a U.S. senator to break up the company as a would-be monopolist. Way down in the article, the *Times* mentioned a more ominous problem—"the rapid rise of foreign car sales in the home market."[64] The problem, which "could not be ignored much longer," according to the article, did not dissuade GM's new management team from adhering to the usual pattern with labor. One month later, they agreed to yet another lofty raise in the pension (about 24 percent), plus an escalator with built-in raises in subsequent contract years.[65]

Would it ever stop? By now, no one in the upper echelons of the auto companies had as long an institutional memory as Reuther. They scarcely realized how their companies had aged, but Reuther, marking the twentieth anniversary of the first automobile pension, compiled some figures that should have awakened the executives at long last. Since 1949, Ford had paid pensions to 49,000 employees, for a total of $387 million. And as those formerly young workers aged the expense was rising sharply. By the end of the 1960s the annual payout was $60 million, and in the future it would be much more.[66] An independent analysis of pensions in rubber, autos, and steel concluded that pensions had been rising at nearly triple the rate of wages.[67]

And the pressure was on for more, as inflation was eroding the value of pension checks. Inflation terrified Reuther—it was a scourge that neither the companies nor the union could check, and it reaffirmed his view that only society at large, rather than collective bargaining, could provide his members with the ultimate security he hungered for. In the late '60s, the political and the economic were frequently intertwined: union bosses commonly spoke out on the Vietnam War (which, in turn, spurred economic troubles) or on the nascent environmental movement. Such issues now aroused Reuther nearly as much as wages and production schedules.

In keeping with his broader agenda, Reuther was building a conference center for the UAW, on remote Black Lake in lower Michigan, where he envisioned that the union might explore such themes. This took him back to his days as a blue-collar traveler offering prescriptions for Soviet industry. At heart, he was a social engineer as much as a labor leader—a trait that inevitably irked the executives. Black Lake was his indulgence. Reuther frequently visited the construction site, and in May 1970 he set off in a small Lear airplane with his wife, his architect, and his nephew for a final inspection before the center opened. They were late taking off, and a light rain was falling. Just short of the airport, the plane crashed in the woods. Reuther and everyone else on board was killed. Thirty thousand autoworkers stayed home to mark Reuther's funeral, and even the automakers paid tribute to their longtime foe, halting their assembly lines for a precious three minutes.[68]

REUTHER'S SUCCESSORS were bent on showing that the UAW would improve on his gains, starting with the contract round that year. Their demands, which included larger pensions and full benefits for early retirees, genuinely alarmed the bosses at GM. One out of seven American car buyers was defecting to imports—whose labor costs were dramatically lower—

and the combination of slowing sales and rising costs was putting a squeeze on GM's profits. Perhaps GM felt it was necessary to take a strike to demonstrate that the game had changed. In any event, the union did strike. The company bore it for nine weeks—the most costly work stoppage in industry history.[69] Then it could bear no more. Acknowledging defeat, GM dropped its demand that workers pay a share of the future increase in medical costs—in fact, medical benefits were *improved.* What's more, GM raised the pension more than 40 percent above the previous contract, to five times as high as in the famous 1950 treaty.[70] Reuther was dead, but the welfare state was alive and well. It would be the burden of American industry in the future—and of the auto industry in particular—to pay for it.

TWO

THE ANTI-REUTHER

Companies would deal with the burden of pensions in different ways. Airlines and steelmakers, sagging under impossible pension loads, would be forced to file for bankruptcy. Firms in healthier industries—IBM, for instance, or Hewlett-Packard—would survive by paying off their older workers and jettisoning pensions for the next generation. The newest companies, such as those in Silicon Valley, wouldn't offer pensions at all, though even they would have to grapple with the mounting cost of health care. In the 1990s, Wal-Mart was besieged by liberal activists who complained about its paltry level of insurance—though why some companies and not others should be made to provide such benefits was never quite clear. (This is why Reuther had always pushed for *public* health care.) Even Starbucks would announce in 2005 that it was spending more on health care than it was on coffee beans, proof that social benefits were *not* an issue restricted to old-line manufacturers such as GM.

But the burdens fell hardest on the older, unionized firms. It was their experience—their slow unraveling over the 1970s, '80s, and '90s—that sounded the general alarm. A pair of auto executives, in particular, were cast in the role of unwinding the benefits that Reuther and the UAW had championed. For these two executives, saving their companies would depend on it.

IN THE FALL OF 1973, Rick Wagoner was twenty years old, an economics major at Duke University. He had his sights set on Harvard Business School, but he had no particular interest in General Motors, the company he would one day lead. He was not paying attention to the labor negotiations in Detroit that year, not even when the UAW struck the Chrysler Corp.—once again, over pensions. People in the industry did not recognize it as a milestone either. Steve Miller, a young executive at Ford, would not have guessed that the settlement agreed to by Chrysler, and quickly adopted by the others, would come to haunt him three decades later. In the minds of its executives at least, the auto industry was characterized by stability, not change. Miller, a whiz kid with a Harvard Law degree and a Stanford MBA, was working his way though Ford's overseas operations, in exotic posts such as Melbourne and Mexico City. He figured he would spend the rest of his career at Ford (though in fact he would work with a dozen companies, many on the brink—or in the midst—of bankruptcy). It did not occur to Miller that, thanks to the untenable burden of pension and health care benefits for the workers, comfortable careers in the auto industry would become as outmoded as the Edsel, and that the 1973 labor settlement in particular would be a franchise-wrecker and the subject of his own last act in business.

But pensions have long lead times. In 1973, the UAW won full pensions for early retirees, a plum known to the rank and file as "thirty-and-out." This was an extraordinary expansion of private welfare, the crippling burden of which would become clear only as Wagoner and Miller rose through the ranks. As it was, any employee with thirty years under his belt was immediately eligible for a pension. A young man (and most UAW workers *were* men) who started at the factory out of high school could retire with full benefits before the age of fifty.

Actually, the benefits were more than "full." At fifty, that worker would be twelve years shy of collecting Social Security. A pension alone wouldn't suffice. So . . . the companies agreed to pay an *enhanced* pension—very greatly enhanced—until their retirees reached age sixty-two. This way, younger retirees would have as much total income as if they *were* receiving Social Security. Why wait for that condo in St. Pete until you were sixty-five and gray? Why not travel the world at *fifty-five*? Why not indeed! GM would pay for it.

The UAW had tried to win a federal pension; having failed, it persuaded the automakers to, in effect, subsidize Social Security. This was a breathtaking step. Autoworkers were now endowed with—and contractually entitled to—a full pension while still in the prime of their adulthood and, as far as the rest of the world was concerned, their working lives. This dramatically increased the burden on their employers.

Suppose, for example, that in 1945 GM had hired a fresh-faced twenty-five-year-old worker, likely just returned from the war. In 1974, when the new contract took effect, that worker would be fifty-four. He probably had a family, maybe a son of his own had served in Vietnam. He was eager to retire, but would stay on the job until he got his pension. He might have worked another eight or ten years—that is, to his early sixties or perhaps until sixty-five—stamping metal, fitting fenders, or otherwise contributing productive labor.

With "thirty-and-out," he could retire at fifty-five with an enhanced pension of, incredibly, $550 a month—more than double the pension of workers who retired at the traditional age.[1] What was worse (from the employer's standpoint), suppose our worker lived to, say, seventy-five: under the old system he would have retired in his early sixties and lived off his pension for a decade or so. Now he might retire at fifty-five, and thus be a ward of the company for twice as long. Actually, since life spans were increasing, the change was even more pronounced. Pensioners would be retiring earlier and they, as well as their spouses, would be living longer, taxing the employer at each end of the spectrum. Once a tool for promoting loyalty, pensions had been contorted through collective bargaining into a scheme for encouraging early and expensive departures.

As GM's actuaries toted up the costs of thirty-and-out, even they were shocked. In 1972, the pension obligation at GM was equivalent to forty-three cents an hour in labor costs; by 1975 it had jumped to eighty-three cents. "Pension costs have substantially exceeded estimates," the head of the UAW benefits department confided in a memo to Leonard Woodcock, Reuther's successor.[2] From the start, more workers retired early than either the union or the companies expected. And why not? Early retirement was a good deal. Looking forward, there was a risk of GM's becoming a dangerously bloated enterprise, one with more retirees than active workers.

Thirty-and-out posed a more immediate peril. Since it increased funding requirements, it tended to increase the extent to which pension plans became *under*funded. This reignited the issue of pension insurance.*

Legislation to create government insurance had been brewing since the Studebaker bust in the early 1960s, but business had been cool to it. After much delay, the Johnson administration was finally about to propose a bill. But at the last minute, Henry Ford II told President Johnson that pension insurance would cost the Democrats the business community's support in the 1968 election. With that, the proposal withered.[3]

Aside from its usual hostility to federal involvement, corporate America feared that insurance, by making pension failures less painful, would encourage companies as well as unions to take more risk, perhaps by pushing benefits to unrealistic levels. Just as welfare (in the neoconservative view at least) encouraged people to be lazy, pension insurance would create a moral hazard by "rewarding" workers for corporate failure, endangering the very system it was meant to preserve.[4]

---

*The legal status of pension benefits had already been resolved, in favor of the employee—that is, companies were not allowed to walk away from their obligations. The point of insurance, of course, was that the "right" to a pension was only as good as the funding behind it.

Surprisingly, organized labor was also wary of reform. Any legislation that committed the government to insuring pensions would also toughen funding requirements. Unions recognized that if corporations were required to fund—and not just promise—pensions, they would be slower to increase benefits. Therefore, many of the big labor unions lobbied *against* the emerging legislation. Labor leaders, who were acutely sensitive to their own political interests, preferred to bargain for lavish benefits, even if unsound, over benefits that were more modest but secure.[5] This explained a curious irony of the pension world. At nonunion sponsors, such as Kodak and IBM, pension funds were typically better funded than they were at unionized industries, such as steel, where organized labor was supposedly watching out for the workers' interests.[6]

The UAW was an exception: following Reuther's lead, it consistently pushed for insurance *and* for adequate funding, though it had trouble achieving the latter. Reuther had argued that pensions should not be a "lottery" to be enjoyed only by those who were lucky enough to work for a fiscally healthy employer.[7] Old-age security was simply too important.

The UAW argued that the "gross inadequacy" of Social Security made pension insurance all the more necessary.[8] By the 1970s, the goal of a full federal pension was more or less dead, and experts were coming to terms with the fact that America did not really have a retirement "system." What it had was a patchwork with plenty of rents in the quilt.

At the most basic level was Social Security. The federal program now included most of the workforce. However, it could be expected to replace only about 35 percent of a typical worker's income (considered the bare minimum to retire on). The wealthy, of course, supplemented Social Security with private savings. But most people did not have savings. In between the rich and poor were a vast group of workers—some 30 million Americans and their families—who were counting on supplementing Social Security with a private pension. Insuring them was hardly a trivial matter.[9]

A handful of congressmen kept the issue alive, with hearings that dramatized the plight of workers who had lost their pensions. In 1972, Representative Elwood H. Hillis, a first-term congressman from Indiana, made an emotional plea, citing the letters he received "every week . . . from persons who, after a lifetime of work, have discovered they cannot qualify for the pension which they have planned on over the years." Representative Hillis cited the example of a blacksmith who had worked thirty-four years at the Drop Forging Co. and was due to receive a modest pension, $119 a month, when he turned sixty-five. Four months before his birthday, the company folded. The blacksmith got only a lump sum of $1,400 (less than a year of his promised pension) as well as, Hillis added with evident sarcasm, "a pat on the back. . . . Is it right to leave this type of thing to chance like this?"[10]

Congress's answer for years had been yes. However, the early 1970s were hard times for blue-collar America, and lawmakers felt under pressure to do *something*. The Arab oil embargo had sent shudders through manufacturing, and waves of layoffs began to ripple through the Rust Belt.

Autoworkers, long the standard for blue-collar families aspiring to the middle class, feared that their dream of making it was slipping away. A malaise spread through the ranks, and a smattering of members turned to drugs (workers on the Cadillac, then a nineteen-foot gas guzzler, would listen to Jimi Hendrix during lunch breaks while they drank beer and smoked marijuana). One UAW local backed the conservative former Alabama governor and onetime segregationist, George Wallace, for president in 1972. This backlash against the union's traditional liberalism reflected the members' growing insecurity. Reuther had championed the interests of the larger society, but in the early '70s the UAW began to lobby for import quotas, which would punish American consumers.[11]

In 1974, the U.S. economy slumped and 100,000 autoworkers were put on furlough.[12] Pension insurance reemerged as a handy bone to throw to the workers. The most innovative proposal was advanced by Ralph Nader, who suggested that corporate pensions be transferred to personal (and portable) accounts that the government, rather than private employers, would supervise.[13] That proved a shade too radical. In August, after the Watergate scandal toppled President Nixon, a Congress eager to demonstrate that the federal government could still do something positive enacted the Employee Retirement Income Security Act.

ERISA launched a new era for pensions. It established a federal agency, the Pension Benefit Guaranty Corporation, to insure pension benefits up to a reasonable limit. The PBGC operated like an insurance company; it would collect premiums from corporations and pay out claims to retirees whose plans failed. ERISA also established funding rules to, in theory, lessen the likelihood of a future Studebaker.* However, the rules were notoriously lax, and, in a sop to industry, premium levels were set too low. The PBGC was thus an insurer that minimized the risks and undercharged the customer—a dubious proposition.

THE LAW did nothing to stop the UAW benefits steamroller. In 1976, the UAW got vision care, hearing aids, and a comprehensive substance abuse program added to the menu, which already included dental care including 100 percent of the cost of preventive treatment. Then, in 1979, hours before a strike deadline, GM agreed to raise pensions to $555 a month, and to a whopping $925 for early retirees. This was nine times the original Reuther pension, and 30 percent higher than in the previous year. GM rationalized that the lavish pension settlement bought it relief on wages, and that much was true.[14] "Bargainers held the line on wages for current workers to win significant gains for retirees," the *New York Times* observed. It did not comment on what such an arrangement would mean for GM's finances in the future.[15] But with the number of retirees mushrooming, it was not hard to guess. To top it off, the barnburner 1979 pact doubled time off to fifteen paid holidays in addition to nine paid personal

---

*ERISA also set up rules governing pension investments, requiring adequate diversification and setting limits on portfolio risk. It also established rules to prevent a recurrence of Teamster-type pension fraud.

days, *plus* several weeks of vacation, competitive with the cushiest welfare states in Europe. Douglas Fraser, then the UAW president, admitted later that the 1979 accord was "a hell of a settlement."[16]

The pension increases, perhaps understandable in a more benign economic era, were now completely out of sync with the verities of the auto industry. Largely thanks to cheaper labor, Japanese carmakers could manufacture a car and ship it to the United States for $1,650 less than the Big Three could produce one here.[17] And it was only a matter of time before the Japanese expanded from small cars (a market they controlled) to mid-sized vehicles, Detroit's bread and butter. Even the chief economist at Ford believed that labor contracts were putting the industry at serious risk. One sign that reality had not sunk in was that Ford dispensed bonuses of $630,000 each to its president and executive vice president.[18] Fat bonuses at the top made it impossible to win sacrifices from the union.

Whether the executives were in denial or uninformed (probably it was a combination of the two), prospects for the industry had profoundly waned. As opposed to 1950, when the United States had had only four cars per every ten Americans, by the mid-'70s there were ten for ten.[19] The family driveway was essentially saturated, and growth in car sales was certain to taper off.* Detroit faced a double whammy: a slower-growing pie, and more carmakers angling for a slice. For the first time in decades, the Big Three had to hold the line on prices or risk losing market share.

The larger truth was that pensions in Detroit were ultimately "paid" for not by the companies, but by car buyers. And consumers now had a choice. In effect, they could buy cars with pensions from GM, Ford, and Chrysler—or cars without them from Toyota. In Japan, as in Germany, worker pensions were paid by the state.

This should have persuaded the auto negotiators to restrain pension and health benefits, which would burden their finances for decades to

---

*And it did. From 1947 to 1977, auto sales grew from 4 million vehicles to 15 million, a brisk, 4.5 percent annual growth rate. In the three subsequent decades, growth slowed to a crawl: well under 1 percent a year.

come. However, their response was nearly the opposite. Retiree benefits were a *future* cost. Forced to choose, executives inevitably found more slack in future budgets (if they bothered to calculate them at all) than in present ones. Thus they repeatedly offered richer pensions later in exchange for modest increases in wages now. "Pensions got better every year," noted Dan Luria, a UAW economist. "There was little resistance."[20]

It is doubtful that the executives truly understood the long-term impact of the pension. Even the nomenclature was misleading. Unions bargained for pensions in terms of dollars and cents per year of service; what mattered to a company actuary was the total benefit as a percentage of the worker's final salary or, alternately, the yearly expense as a percentage of total labor costs. Both of these figures were skyrocketing.

IN 1981, an independent actuary named Robert C. Kryvicky finally delved into the thirty-year history of collectively bargained pensions.[21] His report was seen by almost no one outside his field (it was published by the Society of Actuaries), but it should have been required reading in Detroit. Kryvicky concluded that an "upward bias" in the bargaining dynamics had lifted benefits ever higher. And the effects of concessions such as early retirement, though underappreciated, were devastating. In autos (Kryvicky specifically examined Ford), while wages had risen five times since 1950, pensions had vaulted ten times. As a result, benefits had soared from an average of 14 percent of workers' final salaries to 32 percent. Kryvicky found a similar pattern in rubber and steel. This spiraling of benefits had left many plans less than half-funded.

To appreciate how alarming this was, keep in mind that if employers had been making the requisite contributions to their plans, funding deficits should have been zero. But, as Kryvicky showed, the "ratcheting up" of benefits led insidiously to underfunding. Recall that for each covered worker, an employer was supposed to make an annual contribution, the size of which depended on the future benefit. When a union negotiated a higher benefit, not only did the employer have to raise its *future* contributions, it had to make up for the shortfall in *previous* years as well. You can think of a pension as a deferred wage, which the employer was (hopefully) paying on the installment plan. Benefit hikes rendered all of the past installments deficient.

The problem was especially acute in the case of workers who had already retired. In theory, their pensions were both fixed and fully financed, thus no further payments were due. In fact, unions regularly bargained for increases for *current* retirees as well as for their active members. At the UAW, such increases were especially large. (Not coincidentally, the UAW permitted retirees to vote in its elections.) An autoworker who had retired from GM in 1950 at a pension of $45 a month was, by 1980, collecting $435 a month. Even after adjusting for inflation, his pension had tripled. The point is not that auto retirees were rich (they were not), but that the burden on their employers was becoming intolerable.

The lopsided demography of the auto industry posed another risk (similar to the problems experienced by Social Security). The companies lumped the cost of their retirees in with the expense of active workers. Thus it was no big deal for companies with many active workers and only a few retirees, as had once been the case at GM. But as Kryvicky had noticed, during the 1970s, "each recession had taken a toll" on employment. GM's domestic workforce, which hit a peak in the late '70s of 468,000 unionized workers, was already in decline.[22] What would happen if the decline, there or elsewhere, became severe? Kryvicky foresaw that an imbalanced retirees-to-actives ratio would spell "very considerable problems."

As if on cue, Chrysler, the weakest of the Big Three, began to run seriously short of cash. The company hired Lee Iacocca, a charismatic former Ford executive, to stave off a bankruptcy. His plan centered on obtaining a loan guarantee from the federal government, so that private banks would extend it credit. Iacocca recruited a Ford executive, Gerald Greenwald, as chief financial officer, and Greenwald brought along Miller, the onetime whiz kid. Miller got off the plane from Caracas, where he had been stationed with Ford, and was given the job of lobbying Congress to rescue his new company. The lawmakers agreed—on one condition. All the other parties involved with Chrysler—including the UAW—had to share some of the pain.

While pensions were not at the heart of Chrysler's problem, the crisis opened its eyes to the need to rein in benefits and other labor costs. It also got Miller, an ambitious and impressionable executive, thinking more deeply about the future of unions. That Chrysler—or any of the automakers—could withstand another decade of benefit hikes was unthinkable.

To win the loan guarantee, the UAW agreed to forgo wage hikes and some holidays. For political reasons, Chrysler pretended that the givebacks were a major coup. "It was all about winning the government supports," according to Luria, the UAW economist. "We all [Chrysler and the union] agreed to exaggerate what the concessions were worth."[23] Fraser, the UAW president, joined Chrysler's board, and enthusiastically supported the deal. Even so, the UAW had a hard time persuading its members to vote in favor. Miller concluded that union members were simply unwilling to face reality.[24]

Once the immediate crisis was past, Chrysler began to examine its cost structure. At a board meeting, Greenwald asked the directors to identify the company's biggest supplier. Some said U.S. Steel; others Goodyear Tire & Rubber or Dana, the automotive parts supplier. "Nope; you're all wrong," Greenwald said with the air of a man revealing a well-kept secret. "It's Blue Cross."[25]

Such exercises were to become a staple in American boardrooms, but in the early 1980s the idea that an auto manufacturer could spend more on a fringe benefit such as health care than on steel was shocking. As Greenwald went through his presentation, elaborating on the rise in health care costs, Iacocca had an epiphany. He turned to two of his board members, Fraser, the union man, and Joseph A. Califano Jr., a former secretary of health, education, and welfare, and declared, "The three of us—we're the ones who created this problem." This was a clever, if oblique, reference to labor, government, and business—the unhappy trinity of health care policy.[26]

Greenwald's pitch led Chrysler to undertake an in-depth study of health care costs. Management and the UAW, working together, concluded that under the union's cushy plan, workers were essentially indifferent to the level of medical spending, which was fostering random and unnecessarily costly treatment patterns. Rates of certain elective surgeries, or of cesarian deliveries, were dramatically higher in some regions, implying excessive rates of spending. Iacocca became especially irked by the bills for podiatrists, who were operating on members a toe at a time. He told Fraser, "We must have the healthiest feet in the country."[27]

The Chrysler project briefly slowed, but did not derail, the freight train of increasing health care costs. In the late 1980s, the company fell into trouble again. Looking for another rescue, it entered merger discussions with Fiat. However, as the talks progressed, Gianni Agnelli, Fiat's chairman, became worried about Chrysler's now truly soaring benefit obligations. Agnelli was no stranger to social welfare; he had just broken the grip of Italy's powerful trade unions. But in a meeting with Iacocca and Miller in New York, he confessed that he had serious misgivings with regard to Chrysler's contracts with the UAW. "I am fearful of the social liability," he told them. That signaled that the deal was dead.[28]

Greenwald made one other attempt to corral Chrysler's ruinous labor costs. The UAW tactic of designating one of the Big Three to bargain with in each round inevitably weakened all of them, because each company lived in dread of a strike. Greenwald's fantasy, which he duly proposed, was that the Big Three negotiate as a unit. But he could never get GM and Ford to go along; they did not seem to think they had much in common with Chrysler.[29] Like blind men, they kept strolling toward the cliff.

The Motown brass had generally spent their formative years in the industry when it was insulated from competition. Roger Smith, GM's new CEO, had been hired, as an accounting clerk, in 1949—the last executive from the pre-pension era. Having operated in a cartel for so long, he failed to grasp how serious the situation was, or to realize that the old arrangements wouldn't work. His first instinct was to push for so-called voluntary restraints on Japanese imports, duly agreed to by the Reagan administration. This merely insulated the companies for a little longer.

Smith jauntily defended his protectionist policy. "The Japanese are a trading nation," he told a reporter. "They have to trade to live, and in my opinion, they must be terribly worried about what their trading-partner status has gotten to be," he added, as though the Japanese were mere merchants who would soon come begging to Detroit for higher quotas.[30] Instead, Japanese exporters accelerated plans to build on GM's turf. Honda retooled its new motorcycle plant in the tiny hamlet of Marysville, Ohio, and by 1982, American-made Accords were rolling off the conveyor.

Since Marysville was nonunion, and more such transplant factories were in the works, the union was terrified. Even scarier to the UAW, manufacturers were making progress in automation. For instance, the side of a car body, formerly welded from as many as fifteen jigsaw pieces, now was being stamped from a single roll of steel. The welders were no longer needed. By 1984, productivity improvements, as well as declining market share, had sliced 100,000 union jobs from GM and 300,000 from the industry.[31]

Job losses and demands for cuts to pensions and heath care each provoked similar anxieties. They threatened the union's hard-earned security blanket and revived deep-seated fears that harkened back to the Depression. Owen Bieber, who had just become the UAW president, had a searing memory from his childhood, in Grand Rapids, of his dad's trudging off to a UAW job at McInerney Spring & Wire for a seventy-hour week, during which he would be paid *only* for the time when the factory had sufficient work as well as materials on hand—maybe sixty hours, maybe forty—just so long as the company had labor when it needed it, as if Bieber's dad were responsible for management's well-being. With productivity improvements looming as a new job-killer, Bieber wanted to turn the tables, so that, as he put it, the company could not "throw people on the scrap heap."[32] But who would pay for such security?

The UAW's approach was to push for job *guarantees.* Rather than recognize that old-style contractual protections might not work in a global economy, in which consumers would be free to buy elsewhere, the union sought more protections. Its conscious aim was to make labor a *fixed* cost.[33] Pensions were the ultimate fixed cost (by law, an accrued benefit could not be undone), but the union wanted more. Guaranteed health care, a job, retirement. That way, if sales deteriorated, GM would have scant incentive to curtail production, since it would be paying for the labor anyway. As much as GM loathed the union's strategy, the company's approach was not so different. The trade quotas GM advocated were simply another tactic for interfering with supply and demand. Neither party was willing to trust the market.

But GM's market share was falling anyway. In the early 1980s, it began to consume more cash than it was taking in. Smith was spending billions to modernize plants (in part for ambitious robot gadgetry that would miserably backfire, with the robots spray-painting each other instead of the cars on the line) while also straining to maintain the dividend and still feed the relentless pension genie.[34] It could not raise prices, as that would lead to a further decline in sales. Thus, GM entered the 1984 labor round determined to win concessions.

Though GM could not fiddle with accrued pension benefits—that is, those already earned—companies *were* free, at least in theory, to negotiate lower benefits going forward. However, as GM knew, the UAW viewed pensions as "sacrosanct."[35]

The company had higher hopes for restraining health care, which now accounted for $430 on every car.[36] The expense put GM at a severe disadvantage, since foreign carmakers had virtually no such costs. In Japan, as in Western Europe, workers got insurance from the government (what Reuther had advocated for America). Even in Marysville, since Honda had no older workers and, of course, no retirees, its expenses were trivial.

But rather than roll back the Reuther-era protections, GM, fearing a strike that would idle its plants, agreed to broaden them again. Pension rates were raised, health benefits maintained. What's more, GM gave Bieber what he really wanted—a "jobs bank," or protection program. In theory, laid-off workers were to be assigned to a reserve pool or "bank" while waiting for a transfer to another GM job or company retraining. In practice, redundant employees would report to "work," shuffle through employment papers, watch television, play Ping-Pong, all at regular pay for the duration of the contract. Effectively, it was a *lifetime* guarantee because, as Bieber reflected, "once you put something like that in a contract it is very hard to change."*[37] The jobs bank could have been the creation of an ultraliberal government planner—and in a sense it was. It was the ultimate embodiment of the welfare state inside General Motors.

Though wage increases under the new contract were modest—only 1 percent in the first year—this reflected the tacit bargain struck by the UAW and the company, under which the latter committed to an ever-widening raft of welfare protections. This kept the factories humming but mortgaged GM's future. In truth, GM was being managed for the benefit of the *institution* of GM, rather than for its owners. A pair of auto-industry writers observed that GM was operating more like a "nation" than a business—responsible for the welfare of tens of thousands of workers as well as a vast archipelago of dealers and suppliers.[38] But nations have the power to tax; companies (and their shareholders) need profits. By 1990, GM's stockholders had endured no less than a twenty-five-year run without a single dollar of increase in the stock price.

Alfred Sloan, GM's most influential steward, had run plants at 80 percent of capacity, when necessary, in the interest of profitability, but his successors could not afford to let factories sit idle. The fixed costs were simply too great. Therefore, they developed the ruinous habit of producing more vehicles than consumers wanted.[39] GM unloaded its surplus (on the cheap) on rental agencies, but that soon glutted the used-car market, with devastating effects on resale value. As consumers discovered that Chevys did not retain their value like Camrys or Accords, the GM brand suffered irreparable harm. Not all of this was due to the pension and benefit structure, but the legacy overhang greatly limited GM's flexibility. The execu-

---

*Under the 1984 contract, the jobs bank was available only up to a specified dollar amount, and only to workers laid off under certain conditions. The restrictions were gradually eliminated.

tives felt roped in, like a man whose family had grown too large. The publicity-conscious Roger Smith obsessed over propping up his falling market share when a more nimble operator would have simply—and quickly—shrunk to profitable size.[40]

Smith was rarely challenged inside GM, as internal dissension was inimical to the culture.* The decentralized management structure created by Sloan had slowly ossified. The organization had come to resemble a field of silos, rigorously separated according to responsibility and overseen only at the very top by executives with a lateral view. It was not a place that nurtured rebels. However, the younger generation was less wedded to GM traditions. Executives recruited in the 1970s had never known the luxury of operating as a quasi-monopolist. When Wagoner was hired, as a financial manager, in 1977, GM's market share was 45 percent. By 1987, the end of his first decade, it had plummeted to 35 percent. Wagoner observed much of this dismal slippage from afar, in GM outposts in Brazil, Canada, and Europe, where he at least gained a broader perspective than that of the managers in Detroit.

Wagoner could see that the auto model of labor relations was self-destructive. Outside of steel, airlines, and autos, it also was increasingly archaic. In the new era of deregulation and global competition, plush benefits were out of step. Corporations were oriented toward profit and stock price, not stability and security. Thus, in the 1980s, the pension in corporate America began a protracted decline. The proportion of private sector workers who had coverage, once as high as 45 percent, steadily shrank.

The most frequently cited reason for the decline was the boom in 401(k)s. This was wholly unplanned. In 1980, Congress had added a paragraph—letter "k"—to section 401 of the Internal Revenue Code. This allowed

---

*The career of John DeLorean illustrated GM's inability to cope with rebels. After designing the hot-rod Pontiac GTO, he quickly rose through the ranks but ruffled too many feathers along the way. In 1973, he resigned. He later published a biting memoir, *On a Clear Day You Can See General Motors.*

employees to defer taxes on money put into profit-sharing plans, as long as the plans were open to all workers and not just the executives. This seemingly minor administrative adjustment blossomed into a new savings vehicle for millions of Americans. For corporate treasurers, the 401(k) had obvious appeal. Unlike with a pension, the company was *not* responsible for its employees' retirement. Companies generally made a yearly contribution, but it was not a fixed cost in the sense of a pension (such plans could be amended or even terminated by the sponsor at will). And the sponsor's future liability was zero. Undeniably, 401(k)s also appealed to workers. Employees could manage their own retirement portfolios, and since, by happy accident, the stock market was rising in the 1980s and 1990s, novices concluded that investing was hardly more challenging than picking a college or planning a vacation.

However, there is no question that 401(k) holders were worse off than traditional pensioners. Their benefits were both lower and less secure. Even after many years, most workers had accumulated only trivial sums. Indeed, by the first decade of the twenty-first century—that is, a full generation into the 401(k) era—half of those with plans had accumulated less than $31,000.[41]

This begs a question: why did younger workers not insist on pensions, as had Reuther's generation in the 1940s and '50s? The answer, quite simply, is that workers no longer had the muscle. Labor's bargaining power suffered a rapid decline from the 1970s onward, as evidenced by the dramatic fall in union membership.[42] For nonunionized workers, 401(k)s eased the pain, but they were less the *reason* for the decline of pensions than the excuse. Fewer companies had to submit to union demands for a pension, and therefore fewer companies offered one.

Could Detroit survive as the exception? In 1990, trying to buy peace with the UAW yet again, GM hiked the thirty-and-out pension to $1,600 a month. Since 1950, the pension was up fifteen times; the sticker price of a new Chevrolet was up only eight times. GM also added new coverage for mental health and substance abuse, and committed to spending *$4 billion* on idled workers, meaning, mostly, those in the jobs bank.[43] Five months later, GM cut the dividend, from seventy-five cents to forty cents—vivid proof that employee entitlements were being paid from the pockets of shareholders. In the early '90s, the company suffered huge losses. Even when business revived, since the old workers were remote from the plants with work, GM would be in the humbling position of paying existing workers to be idle while hiring new ones.[44] Such trends could not continue, and, as the late economist Herbert Stein remarked, if something cannot go on then it will stop. But no one—including Stein—could predict *when* it would stop.

The countercurrents began to swirl far from Detroit, in Norwalk, Connecticut, a quaint suburb overlooking the Long Island Sound that is the domicile of an obscure entity known as the Financial Accounting Standards Board. It is doubtful that even one pensioner in a thousand had ever heard of FASB. Yet the board, which sets the accounting rules for U.S. corporations (not just the auto companies but all of them), was to play a vital role in determining the effect of pension and health benefits on American companies' profits. And this was to greatly affect their willingness to provide them.

In the mid-'80s, FASB decided that the rules for pension accounting suffered from a gaping hole. Corporations were required to disclose on their balance sheets the money they borrowed from banks, bondholders, or anyone else—but not the pension benefits that they would owe to their retirees. FAS 87, as the new rule was known, required them to come clean: to disclose their pension liabilities. It did not have an immediate impact, as pension funds at the moment were relatively flush. By the early 1990s, however, they were anything but.

Pension accounting follows its own particular rules—impenetrable to the outsider but to an actuary altogether logical. The basic idea is that the size of the obligation moves in the opposite direction as interest rates. If interest rates go up, the obligation becomes smaller; if rates go down, bigger.

How such a backwards rule was developed, or rather, why, is really simple. Pensions are a future expense, like saving for your children's college. You know, approximately, how big the college (or the pension) expense will be when it comes due. The question is, how much does one have to put aside *now* to meet that expense? The answer is known as the *net present value* of the future obligation. If money is compounding at a high rate, your nest egg will grow faster, thus the present obligation—what you need to save now—is smaller.

In the 1980s and early '90s, interest rates fell and fell and continued to fall. The stock market attracted more attention, but the truly unprecedented move was in interest rates. From mid-1981 to mid-1993—almost exactly the period of Smith's chairmanship at GM—the rate on the ten-year government bond fell, with little interruption, from a sky-high 16 percent to 6 percent.

To consumers, lower rates were wonderful news (cheaper mortgages, less expensive credit card debt). To actuaries they were like a noose, tugging pension obligations ever higher. Smith tried to paper it over. GM, which under Sloan and Wilson had been a model of accurate reporting, began to monkey around with the numbers. Accounting is fun that way—if no one is paying attention it lets you do almost anything. For instance, GM's number crunchers decided to adjust the expected life of their plants, thus magically reducing depreciation charges and boosting earnings.[45] It was so much easier than selling cars.

In pensions, GM made two potent assumptions. One was that its pension fund would earn 11 percent a year—a very aggressive mark. The other was that its retirees would die two years earlier (to a pension actuary, this was good news!) than had previously been assumed.[46] Both of these assumptions lowered GM's *apparent* pension obligation, which thanks to FAS 87 had become a matter of grave importance to management, though in the real world nothing changed. Retirees were not going to roll over and die just because Smith told his actuary he thought it was a good idea. Smith's own pension, incidentally, was more than $1 million a year.[47]

Smith's elastic approach to bookkeeping, when it came out, hurt GM's image almost as much as his bland car styling and low vehicle ratings. Strong companies do not need to cheat. Consumers sense this. And the suspect accounting was anyway overwhelmed by reality. By the early '90s, pension funds around the country were suffering due to falling interest rates. GM was in the worst shape of all. Its pension was underfunded by $23 billion—an eye-popping, potentially bankrupting sum.[48]

At this moment, FASB chose to adopt a *second*, quite similar rule—to become effective in 1993—requiring companies to recognize the future cost of their retirees' health care. The new standard, FAS 106, did not, of course, mean that health care was now more expensive or that retirees would suddenly get sicker—only that companies who had promised to pay their bills would have to own up to it, thus erasing billions of dollars of their equity. This sent financial officers into a tizzy. Paying for retirees was one thing; admitting to your shareholders you were doing it was something else. In short order, scores of companies cut back on health care, their workers never quite realizing what hit them. "It was a consequence FASB never thought of," according to Rob Moroni, a health care consultant. "They thought they would help investors. What they did, they killed retirees."[49]

At the time, Moroni worked at GM. Once FAS 106 was adopted, GM got very interested in health care. Hillary Clinton, the incoming First Lady, was formulating a proposal tilted toward national health care, and GM tasked Moroni to model its effect on the company. Business in general favored reform, for the same reasons as GM. Health costs were chewing up their profits. As President Clinton took office, the Chamber of Commerce (the principal business lobby) actually favored universal health care.[50]

However, under heavy pressure from Republican Party ideologues, business turned sharply against the plan. And GM executives, who were wary of upsetting their corporate brethren, as well as their customary political allies, toed the line. In other words, GM did *not* go to Congress and say, "We have a problem, we need government health care in the United States or we won't be able to compete with Toyota." Nor did other companies. And when Mrs. Clinton's plan hit a roadblock, business let the proposal die.

Still, its days of passively writing checks were over. GM had a new CEO, Jack Smith (unrelated to Roger Smith, who had retired). He proposed to the UAW that new workers be hired on a different, and lower, benefit scale. He got nowhere. Smith had more license with salaried (nonunion) workers—and to them he unveiled a shocker. From 1993 on, people who took salaried jobs at GM would not get a traditional pension plan, nor would they get retiree health care. The counterrevolution had begun: for the first time since the Reuther era, GM was eschewing a full slate of benefits.

With respect to union employees (where most of the expenses lay), Smith tried several approaches. He created a health care staff, of which Moroni became the director, and made a study of costs, much as Chrysler had done earlier. With the UAW's cooperation, it educated workers on the value of preventive care. Autoworkers tended to be heavy smokers and disproportionately overweight, and GM, which was already footing the bill to treat their lung cancers and diabetes, now got into the business of dispensing, free of charge, expert advice on keeping fit, living healthy, and eating green vegetables. Well and good, but pharmaceutical companies kept developing new drugs, and autoworkers (both retired and active) were filling fifteen prescriptions on average a year, and so Moroni's efforts barely made a dent in GM's rapidly escalating bill.[51] Though its future obligation for health care now was starkly disclosed in black and white, the company was not required to set aside funds for the purpose, and so for the most part GM simply let the obligation build.

ERISA forbade that approach on pensions, and GM was forced to resort to Herculean measures to pay off its pension underfunding. It was able to do this because, first, it sold a pair of valuable subsidiaries, and, second, it had a very hot product line: the minivan and sport utility vehicle.* In effect, a huge chunk of its wealth was transferred from the

*The subsidiaries were Hughes Electronics and Electronic Data Systems.

corporation to the pension fund, where it would be walled off from shareholders forever. Funding the pension also drained immense resources from what GM could invest in product design, which set back its efforts to build better cars. "They were absolutely related," one executive confirmed. "Quality is expensive."[52] Pouring its funds into pensions, GM was late to invest in hybrid vehicles—one of its many forgone opportunities. In fact, GM invested so much in its pension fund in the mid-1990s that, with the same money, it could have acquired half of Toyota Motor Corp.

Wagoner was, at last, brought to Detroit to try to fix the North American Operations. He struck a hard line on labor, pushing the UAW for productivity improvements and also the right to outsource. The union was infuriated. Over a span of a few years, with Wagoner calling the shots, GM endured thirteen work stoppages.[53] Perhaps that was a measure of Wagoner's success. In 1998, he suffered a very costly strike in Flint. Then both sides moderated. Wagoner, while still seeking concessions, concluded he needed the UAW as a partner. The union accepted the need for enhanced productivity—that is, building cars with fewer workers. But it did not give ground on legacy issues, as pensions, health care, and such were coming to be known. Indeed, legacy became more costly as the ratio of retirees to active workers grew.

By the late '90s, GM was facing the demographic nightmare forecast by Kryvicky. It was down to 180,000 hourly employees, compared with a dizzying 400,000 retirees. That offset the positive impact of anything the company did right. GM did not truly reap the gains from productivity savings, or from its heady SUV sales—or at least the shareholders didn't reap them. The company had to use those savings to repay the debt incurred by the past.

When GM's market share fell below 30 percent, it faced the possibility of a death spiral: fewer sales, thus a worsening employee ratio leading to lessened cash flow and, conceivably, lower sales. Something had to be done. One gnawing disadvantage was that GM's parts were made in-house, meaning by GM employees with full union benefits. Japanese carmakers bought parts from outside suppliers, who did not have pension plans.

SMITH OPTED FOR A radical break. In 1998, GM decided to spin out its auto parts subsidiary into a separate corporation. The spin-out company, to be christened Delphi, was itself huge. Delphi would employ 60,000 workers, or a third of the old GM—producing everything from dashboard electronics to airbag systems to wheel bearings—in 160 plants in the United States and overseas. At least superficially, spinning off Delphi was clever. The pensions of those 60,000 workers would not be GM's burden anymore. At a stroke, the weight of its past would be diminished. In addition, GM would be free to buy its parts from independents, who used cheaper labor, as well as from Delphi. But the plan had to pass muster with the UAW.

Richard Shoemaker, the official in charge of the GM department at the UAW, was a slight, silver-haired man with wire-rimmed glasses and a clipped mustache. His demeanor was soft-spoken and gentlemanly; he could have passed for a college professor rather than a labor leader who had gotten his union card in 1957, right after high school, when he had gone to work for Deere & Co. in his hometown of East Moline.

Shoemaker had serious doubts about the Delphi deal. People who had worked at GM their entire careers, and had depended on GM's guarantees, would be forced to rely on a new corporation, which he believed was undercapitalized and whose future would be uncertain.

Contractually, the UAW had the power to stop the spin-off—a power that Shoemaker demurely referred to as "the leverage."[54] But Shoemaker was also a realist who recognized that the union's power was declining. Therefore, he didn't try to block the spin-off; he merely made it conditional on certain protections. GM would have to agree to pay Delphi's pension and health care expenses if Delphi ever became unable to do so. GM also promised that it would hire back surplus workers that Delphi didn't need. And GM would have to keep buying Delphi parts. So, thanks to these conditions, GM wouldn't really be off the hook. The Delphi legacy would not be so easy to shake.

Shoemaker also had conditions for Delphi. When the UAW's contract expired, it would have to renew on the same terms as GM—not once, but twice—so that wages and benefits at Delphi would continue to mirror those at GM for almost a decade after it had supposedly become independent. Delphi wouldn't be born with a clean slate; GM's tired blood would be running through its veins. The prospectus for Delphi's new stock made a point of warning investors, "A substantial portion of our cash flow will be dedicated to meet our pension funding obligations."

At the beginning of 1999, the spin-off became official. Superficially, GM seemed like a different company, one with only 120,000 hourly workers and a smaller legacy obligation. The next year, Wagoner became chief executive—at forty-seven, GM's youngest ever. He inherited a General Motors that was one-fourth the size of the company he had joined. Wagoner was optimistic. He predicted that GM would earn $10 a share by mid-decade. In 2000 and early 2001 the stock traded well above its old highs. However, an analyst at Goldman Sachs, Gary Lapidus, injected a note of skepticism. Lapidus did an analysis similar to Kryvicky's—only with twenty years' more history. He said GM had a lot of value, but 90 percent of it would never reach the shareholders; it would go to retirees.[55] As Lapidus's report began to circulate, Wall Street began to think about GM in a different light. It was a pension firm on wheels, so went the joke—an HMO with a showroom.

Wall Street was far more enamored of the newer, faster-growing firms in what it was beginning to call the "new economy." Many of these were in high tech, such as Microsoft and Amazon. New-age retailers such as Starbucks and Wal-Mart were also prize examples. Though in different industries, such companies had one thing in common: they had structured their operations to *minimize* their future commitments. For instance, Wal-Mart kept merchandise on the shelves for far less time than a traditional retailer (and Amazon did not have shelves at all). Nowhere was this quality more evident than in employee benefits. These companies did not—and would not—offer pensions. Microsoft would never have to worry about its aging software designers—they would be someone else's problem.

For such reasons, the proportion of Americans with pensions (in the private sector, at least) continued to decline, and they were more and more constrained to the so-called old economy. They were in unionized industries such as autos, airlines, and mining that had grown up with pensioned (and protected) workforces, and these industries were suffering dearly as a result.

It was steel, whose history most closely resembled that of automobiles, that woke Detroit to the realization that pensions could literally tip companies into bankruptcy. In the steel industry, employment in traditional mills had withered due to improved industrial processes, and also as a result of competition from newer, nonunion mills. Bethlehem Steel, a once great institution that built more than a thousand ships in World War II and whose product still sparkled from the Golden Gate Bridge in San Francisco to the Chrysler Building in New York City, bore a striking resemblance to the lions of Detroit. By 2001, Bethlehem had shrunk to a pitiably small labor force of 12,000—one worker for every eight retirees. This ratio was a kind of mathematical madness, as if a roomful of nurses had been summoned to care for thousands of elderly. Two weeks after the attack on the Twin Towers, Bethlehem hit a wall. It needed a new CEO, and the executive it found was Steve Miller, the onetime rescue artist at Chrysler.

After leaving the automaker in 1992, Miller had pursued an improbable second career as a corporate Mr. Fix-It. He joined a banking firm and worked on the restructuring of Olympia & York, a high-flying real estate developer that filed for bankruptcy. Then he retired to Oregon, his home, but in 1995 he got a call from the general counsel of Morrison-Knudsen, a construction firm whose CEO had been forced out after it came to light that he had misused corporate assets. "Our CEO was fired or quit, the shareholders are suing us, and we are running out of cash to meet the payroll. How would you like to be our chairman?" he said. Miller took the company through bankruptcy and restructured it. The assignment lasted more than a year. Then he got another call, this time from Federal Mogul, a distressed auto parts supplier.[56]

By then, the pattern was set. The bankruptcy fraternity is close-knit, and when a company got into trouble, they often called Miller. Bethlehem was his eighth repair job in a decade. His experience as a cost-cutter, as well as his privileged upbringing (his family had owned a successful lumber business), had turned him into an apostle against rigid labor contracts, especially pensions. At Bethlehem, he decided that legacy benefits had to go. On his first weekend on the job, he flew to New York and met with Leo Gerard, president of the United Steelworkers. Miller said, "If we don't do something about this labor contract we're going in the tank."[57]

The union resented the way Miller, an outsider to the steel industry, was quick to assign the blame. Aging steelworkers were hardly living high. But although Miller *was* simplistic, on pensions he was right. Bethlehem's pension fund was $3.7 billion in the hole. Nobody was going to invest in Bethlehem again—ever—if it meant having to restore the workers' pensions.

Miller put Bethlehem into bankruptcy, and its pension fund was terminated. Retirees got their benefits from the PBGC (the government insurance agency), though the amount that a retiree could collect was capped. Benefits above the cap, as well as health care, were out. With the legacy burden out of the way, the union found a new investor, the financier Wilbur Ross, to buy the steel mills. Ross turned Bethlehem into a profitable, low-cost company—one that was totally unburdened by the past. Rules restricting productivity were scotched. It employed fewer workers, but individually they earned more. The pension was replaced by a multiemployer plan, managed by the union, which relieved the new owner of the burden. Miller, who retired once the company was sold, thought he had seen the future. The problem wasn't steel, or autos, or any of these old industries: it was the labor contracts and especially pensions that had squashed them. Miller became an evangelist for shedding legacy benefits: an *anti*-Reuther. He told a group of newspaper reporters, "No company should be making open-ended promises to its workers for events 50 years down the road."[58]

As pension problems spread, Miller began to seem prescient. After the attacks on September 11, 2001, the stock market shook off the final vestiges of high-tech euphoria; the bottom fell out of the Nasdaq and the

Standard & Poor's 500, too. Pension funds, like other investors, suffered devastating losses. But for pension funds, the problem was worse, because *interest rates* also crashed. By 2003, long-term bond rates had fallen to forty-year lows and pension plans everywhere were underwater.

The PBGC was forced to bail out more plans, including those of a wave of airlines. With so many claims coming due, the PBGC itself developed a serious deficit. As predicted, companies had taken advantage of lax funding rules and allowed their pension plans to become deeply underfunded before going bankrupt. (Unions, knowing that benefits were insured, had played along.) United Airlines did not make any contributions to its employee plans for three straight years. Rather shockingly, even after two of its jets had been turned into weapons by the September 11 terrorists, and when the airline industry was pleading for emergency relief from Congress, United granted a 40 percent *increase* in pension benefits for 23,000 ground workers. Then it filed for bankruptcy and dropped its pension fund—whose liabilities surpassed its assets by $10 billion—into the lap of the PBGC.[59]

In the aftermath of September 11, the PBGC's financial position quickly deteriorated, raising the specter that it might need a federal bailout just as had, earlier, the agency that insured savings and loans when the S&L industry collapsed.[60] Claims from failed pension sponsors ran into the billions of dollars a year; in fact, in the first five years of the new century the PBGC's losses were four times as high as the total in the previous twenty-five years.[61]

The agency's nightmare was that the auto industry, where pension insurance had gotten its inspiration, would follow steel and airlines and stick it with the most costly claims of all. In the recession that followed September 11, auto parts firms in the Midwest started to fail. Delphi was suddenly wobbly. GM, its sales collapsing, cut vehicle prices and offered consumers zero percent financing. Trying not to seem desperate, the company billed this as a patriotic effort to revive the American economy. But after a brief spurt, its market share continued to slide. And its pension fund suffered terrible losses in the stock market. By 2002, it was $20 billion underfunded—potentially another Studebaker, only orders of magnitude larger.

Worrisomely to the brass, GM was being talked about in the press not for its cars but for its soaring pensions and benefit expense. "Every article on General Motors was about the pension hole," a spokesperson recalled. It was grating, demoralizing. Wagoner called in John Devine, the chief financial officer, and the pair decided they had to go on the attack—specifically against legacy costs. It had to be the highest priority.[62]

Wagoner did two things. First, in 2003, GM sold a staggering $13.5 billion in bonds—the biggest corporate bond sale in U.S. history. It plowed the money (and more) into its pension fund. The bond offering was shrewdly timed, when interest rates were low. Still, it merely transferred the pension obligation from the fund to General Motors's own balance sheet. It did not, of course, erase the obligation.

Second, Wagoner began to speak out about GM's intolerable health care burden. He pounded away at the idea that America's health care system needed reform, that it was both too expensive and failing to deliver quality results, and that it left out millions (the uninsured). It was difficult to tell who his intended audience was—the UAW or the U.S. government. The Bush administration had shown zero interest in health care reform, and Wagoner carefully avoided sounding as if he were soliciting, Chrysler-style, for federal help. When a GM lobbyist, Annette Gaurisco, made a closed-door pitch to lawmakers for a "level playing field," Senator Tom Daschle, the senior Democrat in the room, pounced on the obvious implication and queried, "A level playing field? It sounds like GM is for public health care financing." Guarisco went silent. GM was always tongue-tied on the subject of government relief. Aside from that notable omission, Wagoner's health care sermons were becoming indistinguishable from Walter Reuther's.

Internally, Wagoner was convening a monthly meeting on health care issues—an improbable diversion for the head of the world's largest car company. He started offering detailed suggestions (why couldn't GM force employees who smoked to pay more for coverage, for instance?) as if he *were* running an HMO. GM had previously downplayed the issue, but now it made sure that the reporters writing about the auto industry were well aware that in every GM car, $1,525 of cost represented health care. Not coincidentally, Toyota's profit margin per vehicle was greater than GM's by roughly the same amount.[63] The UAW did not quite get that such a gap was unsustainable. In the view of union leaders, GM's management, by demanding cuts, was merely kowtowing to Wall Street.[64] But Wall Street represented the rightful owners.

In the 2003 negotiating round, the union and GM battled to a draw. The pension level was—once again—raised. Early retirees were hiked to just over $3,000 a month.[65] A worker who retired in his early fifties was thus assured of $36,000 a year—a reasonable middle-class stipend. However, the union agreed to give back a little on health care. Previously, members had paid five dollars per prescription, whether generic or otherwise; now they would pay ten dollars for branded drugs (still only a tiny fraction of the cost). In total, UAW workers would still pay only 7 percent of their health care expenses—compared with a national average of 32 percent.[66] Wagoner made it clear he would be back for more concessions.

But the legacy issue reemerged sooner than Wagoner expected—not at GM but at its offspring, Delphi. For various reasons, Delphi was even less prepared to handle the legacy burden than General Motors. Its pension plan, $1.7 billion in the red at the time of the spin-off, had been falling deeper in the hole ever since.[67] Delphi was a strange creation—a newborn conceived with the hardened arteries of an old man. As a UAW shop, its costs were in the stratosphere. Wages for Delphi production workers were roughly $26 an hour—double those of comparable workers elsewhere.[68] This doomed the company's ability to price competitively. For instance, it cost Delphi $2.05 to make a spark plug that could be purchased in China for $1.05. Due to its agreement with its former parent, Delphi sold the plugs to GM for $1.70, so each party suffered a loss.[69] But wherever the contract permitted, GM was diversifying away from Delphi to lower-cost suppliers.

As business with GM slumped, Delphi had no choice but to try to coax thousands of its workers into retirement. Its population of retirees—initially zero—began to mushroom. By 2004, it was spending a third as much on health care as it was on wages—as if every third factory hand were accompanied by a full-time medic.[70] Aside from hospital care and prescription drugs, Delphi workers got dental, vision, a pension, life insurance, sickness, disability, and accident coverage, as well as approximately five weeks' vacation a year and free legal services when they purchased a home, filed for divorce, or got a speeding ticket. When averaged over its declining number of employees, these benefits alone padded its labor costs by $29 an hour (compared to $7.50 at a typical nonunion firm)—an astronomical and, again, unsustainable expense.[71]

Hemorrhaging cash, Delphi went begging to the union. Shoemaker, the official in charge of the GM department at the UAW, and Richard Gettelfinger, the union president, agreed to a major concession: Delphi could hire a "second tier" of employees who would work under a less generous contract. This second tier could work at lower wages and with a more meager, *non*traditional form of pension.[72] For the union, this was a bitter pill—it spelled the beginning of the end of Reuther's pension plan. But the concession did little good: Delphi did not have enough orders to hire new workers on any terms. In 2004, it lost a staggering $4.8 billion. Absent a recovery at GM, its biggest customer by far, Delphi would not survive.

But GM was obsessed with its own survival. Delphi's premium prices were costing GM $2 billion a year, and GM was demanding cuts. In the winter of 2005, the situation turned critical. Oil prices soared above $55 a barrel, a by-product of the endless war in Iraq. Demand for SUVs, Detroit's lifeblood for the past decade, began to weaken. GM's market share fell, sickeningly, to 25 percent—half its peak level. Incredibly, it was selling fewer cars in the United States than in 1964, when Rick Wagoner was eleven years old.

Wall Street began to agitate for change. The problem, many believed, was neither GM's lack of market appeal nor its legacy burden but the two in concert. Toyota was spending roughly twice as much as GM to develop the next generation of cars—all but ensuring its continued supremacy.[73] Where were GM's resources? The obvious answer was: in its pension funds, which were disbursing a staggering $7 billion in benefits a year.[74]

And GM's health care tab still was rising at double-digit rates. By 2005, the company was spending at a rate of $5.3 billion a year.[75] It was filling a prescription every two seconds—not just in every state in the nation but in nearly every *zip code*.[76] Including retirees as well as their dependents, GM was paying for the care of 1.1 million souls, of whom only 140,000 (white-collar as well as blue-collar) were still on the job.[77] Reuther's creation was imploding; it was devouring itself.

In March 2005, Wagoner glumly announced that GM expected to lose nearly a billion dollars in the first quarter. On that very day its stock plummeted 14 percent. GM was now trading at $29 a share, back to its level of the early 1970s. Events now moved quickly. Standard & Poor's lowered its rating on GM's bonds to speculative, or junk bond, level—raising the cost of GM financings (a critical item for its car loan subsidiary). Then GM admitted that sales were worsening and pulled all forecasts for the rest of the year. Kirk Kerkorian, a Las Vegas mogul-cum-raider, bought a chunk of GM stock, and hinted he might try to shake up the company's management. Wall Street began to speak, first in a whisper and then quite openly, of the possibility of GM's filing for bankruptcy. *Fortune* wrote in April, in surprisingly strong language, ". . . the evidence points, with increasing certitude, to bankruptcy."[78]

Wagoner spent the spring and early summer jawing with Gettelfinger, the union president, and with Shoemaker, demanding that the UAW reopen its contract and make concessions on health care. Wagoner was under enormous strain. GM was losing money. Its directors were pressuring him to reduce costs. He had to deliver *some* concession from the union. Meanwhile, the press (egged on by Kerkorian) was lambasting Wagoner for supposedly not having a sufficient sense of urgency. There were constant rumors his days were numbered.

Gettelfinger did not want to see Wagoner removed (his successor might well be worse) or provoked to take desperate action. The union chief promised to take a look at health care and see what he could do. But Gettelfinger was in a jam too. When he visited retired autoworkers in Florida, they were up in arms. Wages, they reminded him, were always negotiable, but benefits were why they had *become* autoworkers.[79] Two storied American institutions—GM and the UAW—hung in the balance.

While Gettelfinger dithered, Wagoner did his best to rebut the bankruptcy talk and calm markets, while still making clear (for the union's benefit) that GM was fighting for its life. A broad-shouldered former basketball player at Duke, Wagoner seemed suddenly drawn and withered. Though incisive in small groups, he was not a charismatic leader like Iacocca. Methodical and determined, he came across in public as wooden, almost hapless. But contrary to what his critics said, he and his team were well aware that the situation was critical. When Devine, the CFO, was asked whether a bankruptcy was possible, he said no but added, startlingly, that "a liquidation was."[80]

Devine was worried about a new, potentially catastrophic problem. He was worried about Delphi.[81] The parts firm was on the edge—a goblin from GM's past it couldn't be rid of. Following an admission of accounting problems, Delphi was looking for a new CEO. It placed a call to the one former auto executive who had extensive experience with legacy benefits: Steve Miller. Though having sworn to stay retired this time, the sixty-three-year-old Miller was intrigued. Delphi could be a laboratory for his post-industrial vision. He confided in a colleague who told him, "You could have an impact on the world; it's your *duty* to take it."[82] This appealed to Miller's vanity. He went to work in July of 2005, a $3 million bonus in hand.

Miller immediately met with Gettelfinger and Shoemaker and pressed them for concessions. His demands were harsh. He wanted wages rolled back to $10–$12 an hour (competitive with local Burger King outlets) and an end to defined pension benefits. What's more, he wanted to abolish the jobs bank and health care for retirees and to brutally downsize health care for active employees, and to cut insurance, tuition assistance, and other benefits. This would undo virtually everything the UAW had fought for in its seventy-year history.[83] Unlike Wagoner, who preferred quiet, incremental solutions, the blustery Miller was inclined toward drama. He saw Delphi as a pivotal act in a national movement against legacy benefits, with himself playing the part of the "messenger"—a term he used often and one that infuriated the rank and file.

Miller's message was that the era in which a factory job could deliver a middle-class life with a secure retirement was over. This, in truth, was hard to deny. Miller acknowledged that this was a tragedy for employees, but it was a tragedy, he seemed to say, that was unavoidable—even healthy for American industry.[84] At a press conference, he asserted, "Paying $65 an hour for someone mowing the lawn at one of our plants is just not going to cut it in industrial America." When he visited a Delphi factory in upstate New York, he was met by workers clad in green T-shirts reading, "Miller's Lawn-Care Service: Mowing Down Wages."[85]

Gettelfinger despised Miller. A former Ford chassis repairman, who spoke in the earthy language of his native Indiana, where he'd been raised on a farm, he told a colleague, "I would rather pick shit with chickens and eat every other beakful than negotiate with this guy." Miller made a conciliatory gesture of refusing his salary, but it rang hollow because he kept his seven-figure bonus and boasted of his sacrifice nonetheless.[86] When he visited the UAW, Shoemaker and Gettelfinger told him "you can count on a strike" if the cuts he was proposing went through. After he left, Gettelfinger was so enraged he told an aide to remove the chair where Miller had been sitting.[87]

While pushing the union, Miller was simultaneously seeking help from GM. However, Wagoner was preoccupied with his own troubles. Miller had the feeling that Wagoner did not quite get that GM's and Delphi's fates were intertwined. If Delphi, GM's principal supplier, were to shut down, GM's plants would grind to a halt within the month. Its neat little spin-off had backfired. Instead of shedding legacy obligations by transferring them to Delphi, it had made them more combustible. Delphi epitomized all that was wrong with Detroit, and it was threatening to drag down General Motors with it.

In the fall, three months after coming to work, Miller took the step he had surely envisioned from the start: he filed for bankruptcy. The Delphi filing was the largest ever by a U.S. manufacturer. (Delta Air Lines and Northwest Airlines, whose pension promises to workers exceeded the assets in their pension funds by $16 billion, had filed for bankruptcy the previous month.[88]) The primary cause, Miller said, was simple: it was the straitjacket of pension and related legacy obligations. In only six years, Delphi had accumulated an unfunded liability of $8 billion for retiree health care. Its pension hole was $4 billion, of which, if it ever emerged from bankruptcy, half would immediately come due. There was simply no place to get the money. "Delphi needs a pension solution," the company declared in court filings. "It cannot afford to fund the pension . . . and no business can operate successfully if it cannot respond to market forces."[89]

A court is among the worst of all venues to design, or redesign, a social contract. But that was where the parties were. Miller now had the weapon of the bankruptcy process to reverse what the UAW had won in decades of bargaining. He filed a pair of motions seeking authorization to tear up Delphi's contracts with the UAW and other unions and to renege on its post-retirement benefits. (The pension could be terminated only by the PBGC, in a separate process.) Bruce Simon, the UAW lawyer, chose to contrast Miller in open court with Charlie Wilson, GM's fabled president during its golden era of the 1950s:

> Your honor, in the early 1950s the then-CEO of General Motors famously declared that what's good for GM is good for America.* Some of us in the room are old enough to remember that. Today we have Delphi spawned

*Wilson has been misquoted so many times that this version has passed into history. The correct quotation is cited on page 9.

> by GM telling us that closing 21 plants in America, eliminating 25,000 middle-class jobs in America, slashing the wages, pensions and benefits of the 5,000 or so American workers in Delphi's seven remaining American plants is good for Delphi. . . . Delphi's plan is to substantially exit its United States operations and transfer its production to low-wage foreign facilities, to convert [its] remaining few American workers from the middle class to the financial margins.[90]

Simon was hardly exaggerating. Employees bitterly testified to the grim futures that would await if their contracts were broken. Some would lose their cars and homes, or be forced to take their kids out of college. Roger Struckman, a shop steward for fourteen years in Columbus, testified that three members in his unit would have to take second jobs to pay for the care of chronically ailing spouses, one with multiple sclerosis and two with diabetes. "We have *counted* on having good affordable health insurance throughout retirement," Struckman noted.[91] His own daughter would have to give up her dream of attending a four-year college. Chris Brown, a forty-seven-year-old who worked the night shift for Delphi assembling fuel injector parts, had taken the job (back in 1984, with GM) because his second child had been born prematurely and he needed the benefits. Now Miller wanted to take them away, and reduce his wage to $10 an hour—what Brown had earned in his first job after high school.[92]

Workers by the dozen sent scathing emails to Miller. One signed off, "Hoping You Burn In The Deepest Bowels of Hell For All Of Eternity."[93] The union's formal response was more decorous, but no less direct. It reaffirmed that it would go on strike and remain on strike.

Delphi's woes put considerable pressure on GM. A strike against Delphi would cripple GM. Already, due to Delphi's bankruptcy, GM was on the hook to make up lost benefits to Delphi employees of at least $5.5 *billion.*[94] Such miseries at the two companies spilled over, of course, to the union, whose roll of active members was steadily shrinking. All three were suffering—it was only a question of how the losses would be apportioned. As the judge overseeing the bankruptcy observed, the parties were engaged in a kind of three-dimensional chess. Each could check the other two.

Before he dealt with Delphi, Wagoner was insisting he needed a concession from the union. Legally, he believed he had the right to walk from retiree health benefits—which were not as protected as pensions—when the contract expired. He preferred a consensual solution, but he couldn't wait long. Kerkorian had upped his stake in GM to 9.9 percent, and both he and the GM directors were restless. The stock was falling, and GM's market value was down to a paltry $15 billion, compared with an absurd $195 billion that it had pledged to retirees.[95] The scale of its legacy obligations totally overwhelmed its car business. By illustration, a mere 1 percent decline in interest rates would have raised GM's retiree obligations by enough to offset *all* of the profits it had earned during Wagoner's tenure to date, that is, 2000 to 2004 inclusive.* And the crises seemed to multiply by the week: Delphi, Hurricane Katrina, a spike in oil prices.

Meeting with the union leaders, Wagoner gave them his bottom line. The unfunded portion of GM's health care obligation was roughly $60 billion. He needed $20 billion of it back.[96] And he needed it now.

Inexplicably, in the midst of the showdown, GM granted a pension increase to the Canadian Auto Workers. Steve Girsky, a GM executive recently recruited from Morgan Stanley, where he had been a longtime auto analyst, sent a note to Wagoner, the substance of which was, "How do we look Shoemaker in the eye and tell him we need cuts when we just gave 3% to the CAW?" To Girsky, GM's get-tough labor strategy was too much bark and too little bite.

Still new to GM, Girsky wanted to provoke a quick breakthrough. He suggested that *he* sit down with the UAW leadership, whom he knew from his days as an analyst. GM's labor department was cool to the idea; the UAW

---

*A percentage-point change in interest rates would raise (or lower) GM's pension and health care obligations by $8 billion each, or $16 billion in total. GM earned $13 billion from 2000 to 2004.

was their turf. But Wagoner said okay. Girsky met Shoemaker early one morning at a diner on Jefferson Avenue, near Solidarity House, the union's headquarters. Shoemaker for once behaved like a typical, and frustrated, labor leader. A quiet man, he almost shouted at Girsky: "We have no relationship with you guys. You're not talking to us." When Girsky got back to GM, he called Wagoner. "Rick," he said, "you better get engaged."

Notwithstanding Shoemaker's show of bravado, the union leaders were deeply concerned. There was a tipping point beyond which they would have to make concessions; the Delphi bankruptcy and Miller's aggressive response to it had pushed them to the brink. Shoemaker had asked Jim Millstein, an investment banker at the prestigious Lazard firm, to (at GM's expense) counsel the union. Shoemaker wanted Millstein to tell him how bad off GM was, and whether it really needed relief. Corporations always blamed the union.

Millstein pored over the numbers. He told Shoemaker that GM's condition wasn't as bad as it was saying. It was worse.

The union leaders explained to Millstein that it would be difficult for them, and for the members, to grant a concession, especially in mid-contract. They talked about the UAW's history, how it had been established during the Depression, when Americans did not have retirement benefits, guaranteed or otherwise. Millstein said the UAW had no choice.[97]

The union was working on two plans. One would impose higher expenses and copays, mostly on its retirees. It would reduce GM's health care liability by 20 percent or so. Millstein also developed another option—"Plan B."

Plan B was revolutionary. GM merely had to give the UAW a pot of money and the UAW would insure itself. GM would be out of the health care business forever.

The financial staff at GM liked Plan B. However, it was the more complicated of the two, and GM didn't have much time to work out the details.[98] Wagoner had told his board he was expecting to get an offer from the union over the summer, then in September. Now it was early October of 2005 and GM *still* did not have a formal offer. The union kept saying they were "tweaking" it. Wagoner knew that GM's third quarter would be dreadful—another billion dollars lost. He needed to show *something* positive when the company announced its results. If the union didn't act, he would cut retiree health care unilaterally. That would trigger an explosive confrontation with the union and probably a strike. GM might never recover from it.

The day before the deadline, Wagoner said, "I'm going ahead." Then the union proposed Plan A—a sizable, voluntary reduction of benefits. The night before the announcement, GM was still trying to figure out how much it would save. A bureaucrat buried in company headquarters uncovered a discrepancy of one to two billion dollars. He sent out an urgent email: "There seems to be a glitch; do we have a deal or not?" In the press release, Wagoner announced a "significant" update on health care while somehow managing to avoid disclosing the details.

No sooner did Gettelfinger cough up the health care concession, which was signed at the end of October, than Wagoner vowed to seek more-comprehensive givebacks in 2007, when the contract expired.[99] The union's only solace was a little-noticed addendum to the agreement, which took the form of a joint letter on health care. "Given the fragmented and wasteful nature of the U.S. health care system," the document said, "the parties recognize an issue-by-issue approach to reform . . . is no longer sufficient. . . . [A] lasting solution to our health care cost crisis cannot be forged at the bargaining table."

This is what Reuther had argued fifty years earlier. And there was more: "[T]he parties will develop and/or support national proposals that . . . foster cost-effective, quality health care. . . . Given the Nation's 46 million uninsured Americans, the UAW and GM will support public policies at the federal and state level that will enable all Americans to have health insurance."[100]

Reuther had invited the manufacturers to "go down to Washington and fight with us." The government, not industry, he said, should be the first line of defense on health care. A half century later, in an obscure corporate filing, GM had all but agreed. It did not quite say it *favored* national health care, perhaps because GM's board included the vice chairman of Pfizer, the big pharmaceutical concern, or perhaps because GM's culture was simply opposed. Miller, though, was under no such constraints. He admitted, "Reuther may have been right."[101]

Once Wagoner had the union concession in his pocket, he had a little room to deal with Miller. They met over Thanksgiving. Miller told Wagoner that if the UAW went on strike against Delphi it would destroy GM. And the UAW *would* strike if Miller didn't offer a compromise. The only way he could do so, he said, was if GM extended more support to Delphi. "A strike would kill you," Miller said.[102]

GM gave some ground: it agreed to continue paying higher prices on Delphi parts, and hinted that it might agree to more concessions. Now it was Miller's turn to seek an accord with the union. As a carrot, he raised wages slightly above his earlier offer. But he insisted that Gettelfinger accept the essence of his terms, including vastly stripped-down benefits.

Gettelfinger was in the least enviable spot of the three. He realized, even if he didn't say so, that the old UAW model was headed for extinction. He was fighting on behalf of the older workers, who had invested their lives in GM/Delphi and relied on its guarantees. If the model was to be ditched, at least the older workers had to be taken care of.

Similar to Reuther, Gettelfinger was scrupulous, devout, a teetotaler and enormously dedicated. He would schedule outside meetings for 6:30 in the morning and then go to work at the office *first.*[103] Also like Reuther, he saw himself as the head of a social movement, but he had lost the economic leverage to promote it. He worried about younger workers who would not have benefits, much less a living wage. Without viable auto companies, he wouldn't have union wages to offer at all.

And GM's future was by no means assured. It was still losing ground in the auto market. Oil prices ominously passed the $60-a-barrel mark. Wagoner announced in November that GM would idle twelve plants and lay off 30,000 workers, but the union was pressuring him to *rehire* thousands of employees from Delphi. And the mess at

Delphi remained unresolved; it was a tinderbox that could ignite at any moment. By Christmas 2005, GM's stock had fallen below $18, its lowest level since Wagoner's undergraduate days. General Motors, an American institution and long the country's premier manufacturer, now was valued at less than the Harley-Davidson motorcycle company. Its offspring, Delphi, was in Chapter 11. The transfer of value to pensioners was nearly complete. Other large corporations, such as Hewlett-Packard, Verizon, and IBM, as if to signal their horror at GM's predicament, were freezing their pension plans, meaning their employees would never again accrue benefits. Nationally, the retreat from pensions was gathering steam.

Early in 2006, Wagoner froze the pension of GM's salaried employees—but that was hardly enough. Most of GM's employees were union members and therefore immune, and their average compensation, including benefits, equaled an astonishing $81 an hour.[104] The only sure way to reduce that figure would be the Delphi route: bankruptcy. The White House declared that, come what may, GM could not expect a bailout à la Chrysler; it had better start making "relevant" products.[105] Wagoner seemed to have run out of options. At the next board meeting, George Fisher, the lead director, pummeled the CEO for GM's lack of progress. The verbal thrashing left Wagoner stunned.[106] Then Wagoner had to disclose the dreadful result for 2005—a staggering loss of $10.6 billion. The company could not survive another such year. In January, Girsky delivered a presentation to fifty top GM executives. He told them, "Markets think we're going out of business."

Wagoner, writing the annual letter to shareholders, was almost as blunt. "[Two thousand and five] was one of the most difficult years in General Motors' 98-year history," he said. There was a certain irony in this. In terms of cars built per man-hours, GM was a far more efficient machine than in Alfred Sloan's day. Indeed, the company's sales were its second highest ever. But in a market saturated with eleven competitors, there was too little gravy to share with the retirees and still have ample profits left for the owners. As Wagoner wrote, "It was the year in which GM's two fundamental weaknesses in the U.S. market were fully exposed: our huge legacy cost burden," and GM's inability to adjust its structural costs.[107] Despite the UAW's concession, nothing had been fixed. And given the uncertain prospects for benefit negotiations the following year, no one knew if they could be.

Part II

THE PUBLIC FREIGHT

THREE

AN ENTITLED CLASS

Unfortunately, pension plans are an easy place to defer spending to balance a government budget.

—REPRESENTATIVE ELWOOD HILLIS *(Indiana)*

The judge can drop dead in his black robes.

—MICHAEL QUILL

One person closely following GM's pension troubles was Peter S. Kalikow, the down-to-earth real estate mogul who ran the New York City subways. Kalikow was chairman of the Metropolitan Transportation Authority, a New York State agency whose purview also included the city buses and various suburban commuter lines. Ever since 2001, when he had taken the MTA job (which was a reward for his patronage to Governor George Pataki), Kalikow had worried about the MTA's pensions. At the MTA, as at public agencies across the country, pension costs were skyrocketing. As recently as 2000, the pension bill for the city subway and bus systems had been "only" $16 million. By 2005, it had soared to $165 million. And the MTA was projecting an alarming continued escalation.[1] Partly this was due to the steady ratcheting up of benefits, partly to creeping demographic trends, which had greatly stretched people's retirements. Though this had also occurred in the private sector, it was more pronounced in government, where the "right" of employees to retire early was championed by their unions. As workers were also living longer, the math had become unworkable. In the subways, for example, a typical employee in an earlier generation had worked for approximately forty years and then lived off his pension for, say, another ten years. Now employees retired after twenty-five years, after which they were likely to collect a pension for an equivalent quarter-century or even longer. It was as if two conductors were aboard each train—one of them doing the steering and the other lazing in his rocker—and both at taxpayer expense. To Kalikow, this seemed inherently unsound. He worried that the MTA was repeating the mistakes of General Motors.

A serious car buff, Kalikow had admired GM as an undergraduate and followed its fortunes ever since. He found it astonishing that a company once emblematic of success—a company, he would note, that had been profitable for decades, profitable even during the *Depression*—was now on the verge of collapse. "Had GM acted earlier, it would be a different story today," Kalikow would say. He was determined to heed this lesson at the MTA. He told an aide, "The greatest company in America is going broke over pensions. We have to do something before it catches up to us here."[2]

BY THE TIME Kalikow took office, though, the problem *had* caught up to the public sector. Virtually every government agency in New York City and State was facing a pension toll on a par with the MTA's. Nor was New York an isolated case. Other municipalities and states around the country faced a similar pension problem. In many states—California, Illinois, New Jersey, West Virginia—the problem is considerably worse.

It's no accident that the states are in worse shape than corporate America, because negotiations in the public sector are *inherently* tilted in the direction of higher benefits. This is because public unions can organize politically and influence elections—which is to say, they can vote their bosses out of office. This gives them direct clout over the people who determine their benefits. By contrast, the UAW, for all its muscle, cannot vote the CEO of General Motors out of a job.

Politicians thus face huge temptations to increase benefits. Even though this is costly in the long run, in the short run officeholders are rewarded at the ballot box. This is an example of what economists term "moral hazard," when people's incentives are tilted toward policies that are risky, harmful, or wasteful socially.

Another difference from the private sector is that public-sector pensions enjoy an enhanced legal status that makes them ultimately far more costly. As in the private sector, an employee's pension can never be revoked. But a private company at least has the option of "freezing" its plan. When that happens, the meter on benefits stops running. Employees, of course, keep the benefits already accrued, but from the time of the freeze onward they do not accrue more credits. To employers, this can be a very significant saving. (Unionized companies cannot freeze their plans without the union's permission, but legally such moves are permissible.)

In contrast, a public agency can *never* stop the meter—not even with a union's permission. As early as 1939, pension benefits had been guaranteed by the New York State Constitution—which was interpreted to mean that *any* benefit granted to an employee at any time during his employ was forever guaranteed. Other states subsequently matched this provision.

Thus, if a clerk or a teacher works a single day for a district with a pension, he or she will accrue benefits at the rate specified under the plan (or better) *for the entirety of his career.* From day one, the employer is committed for a span measured in decades. Governments do not even have the option of escaping pensions via bankruptcy. Once granted, public pensions are truly immutable.

The social calculus of public pensions is also deeply troubling, and in a way that private pensions are not. Though GM's benefit structure had been ruinous to its shareholders, it had not hurt the public at large. Whether autoworkers' pensions were higher or lower, whether GM's profits were a little more or a little less, was not *society's* problem.

Public pensions are different. Transit pensions are financed by a combination of taxes and fares; in other words, they are paid for by the public, especially the riding public. And riders and taxpayers, more than the employees, were Peter Kalikow's chief constituency—or so he maintained.

Why should the *public* pay for employee pensions? Most of the people riding the trains could not hope to retire after twenty-five years, nor did they earn as much as the average transit worker, which, including everyone from cleaners to train operators, was $58,000 a year.[3]

As it was, the public was *already* footing the bill. Squeezed by the system's rising costs, Kalikow had been forced to defer subway expansion projects; he was trimming service, eliminating bus routes, closing token booths, and reducing late-night operations. The fare had been bumped, from $1.50 to $2.00. So one way or another, his customers *were* paying. The MTA's capital needs were massive, and Kalikow was in a perpetual battle with Albany, and Washington, for subsidies. He did not want to spend them on lavish pensions.

This set the stage for a confrontation that pitted the interests of the public against those of public servants. In 2005, Kalikow demanded that the transit pension be cut. Legally he couldn't touch the pensions of employees already on the payroll. What he wanted was to reduce the benefit for *future* employees, and ease the burden on his successors. This would require the acquiescence of the state legislature, as well as the governor (and, in practice, the mayor). Most of all, he would need the agreement of Roger Toussaint, president of Local 100 of the Transport Workers Union of America.

Local 100 had a deserved reputation for being unflinching, divisive, and embittered. By comparison, it made the UAW seem a model of reasonableness. However, in other respects the two unions had much in common.

Like the UAW, Local 100 wielded fearsome power over its employer. The 35,000 hourly transit workers were as essential to the city's ordinary life, its healthy circulation, as were its police and fire services—on a daily basis probably more so. On a typical weekday, New York's subways carry four and a half million riders, making it the fifth largest transit system in the world.* The system's longest route, the A train, spans thirty-one miles,

---

*Moscow is the biggest, followed by Tokyo, Seoul, and Mexico City.

and the tracks in the entire system, if laid end to end, would reach all the way to Chicago. Operating this formidable network without the union would be unthinkable. And for reasons owing to the subways' embattled history, benefits were, for Local 100, make-or-break issues. To Toussaint, pensions were a matter not just of money but of self-respect. He had a simple response to Kalikow. If the MTA touched the union's pensions, present *or* future, the union would strike. Public strikes have been illegal in New York State since the 1940s, but the TWU had struck twice before, and devastated the city on each occasion. And so, in December 2005, New Yorkers awoke, almost surreally, to a crisis. With the holidays nearing, they were on the brink of losing their buses and trains and, for all practical purposes, their city. New York would literally grind to a halt.

Presumably, the notion that pensions could have derailed an essential public service would have struck the average New Yorker as improbable. But a showdown over pensions somewhere in the city was almost inevitable. The governor wanted it and so did the mayor, though neither would sacrifice his political capital to bring it about. Kalikow asserted that the conflagration broke out at transit, rather than at some other city agency, because no one else had "the guts"—his guts.[4] This was arguably true, but it overlooked the larger cause, which was rooted in the transit system's tortured past. The origins of the public pension problem—in New York and around the country—were bound up with the history of the subways and, indeed, that of their rebellious workers and their implacable union.

GOVERNMENT EMPLOYERS began to offer pensions somewhat before those in private industry. Predictably, the practice started in hazardous lines of work. The first modern pension was the Police Life and Health Insurance Fund, established in New York in 1857. Only cops who had been disabled (or the widows of cops who had been killed) were entitled to benefits, but in 1878 the pension was extended to all policemen who had served twenty-five years and reached the age of fifty-five.[5] Benefits were liberal, but the fund was virtually insolvent almost from the start.

Such is the nature of public pensions—benefits tied to salaries, wages steadily rising—that the obligation seems to outdistance even the most carefully wrought calculation.

The police fund offered a dramatic illustration. Initially, the city hoped to avoid incurring any of the expense. Policemen made contributions from their salaries and other revenue was supplied from the sale of pistol permits, condemned property sales and, rather quaintly, "masked ball licenses." Such sources being insufficient, the city was soon forced to make regular contributions. Nonetheless, by 1913, the fund was fully depleted. In the words of a contemporary report, it "existed as a legal fiction only."[6] The city thus had to pay benefits from its general funds. The authors of the report, trying to err on the side of prudence, estimated that during the remainder of the century—that is, for the ensuing eighty-seven years—police pension expenditures could cumulatively amount to $375 million. No doubt, this seemed an eye-popping sum at the time. Alas, New York eventually would spend three times as much on police pensions *in a single year.*[7] So much for prudent pension forecasts.

BY THE FIRST DECADE of the twentieth century, police and firefighters in more than eighty cities had pension plans.[8] Other civil servant groups followed, primarily because government employers needed stable workforces. Teachers (mostly women) would be more likely to continue working after marriage if they knew that a pension awaited them. Also, government paid less than private employers. To compensate for meager wages, civil service jobs offered "benefits." Over time, cities and workers struck an implicit bargain. Wages were low, but no one got sacked. And with a pension, a job meant security for life. In 1912, such security was a rare commodity indeed.

Government workers were generally forbidden from joining unions, which meant they were unable to bargain over terms. Police and firemen typically formed "benevolent associations," but these almost never challenged the authorities. In 1919, the Boston police tried to organize a union, but the ringleaders were fired. In retaliation, the police went on strike. With no police presence, gangs of thugs began to roam the city, robbing citizens, vandalizing property, and converting the Common, the oldest public park in America, into an open-air dice parlor. The crisis captured national attention. The governor, Calvin Coolidge, was considered a friend of labor, and sympathized with the policemen's demands (not only were their wages substandard but patrolmen were dunned for the cost of the bullets they fired while on duty). However, as the conflict turned on the policemen's right to strike, Coolidge opposed them. After dithering for days, he summoned the state guard. Samuel Gompers, head of the American Federation of Labor, sent a telegram in protest. Coolidge's reply (which was released to the press, and which would catapult him to the vice presidency the following year) was characteristically terse: "There is no right to strike against the public safety by anybody, anywhere, any time." The strike quickly collapsed.[9] Though he hardly intended so much, Coolidge's example set the template for suppressing public unions. They remained weak or nonexistent, leaving civil servants beholden to suffer whatever salary and pension their employer proffered.

The New York City subways were a prime example of the workers' lack of clout. New York's first subway was built by the Interborough Rapid Transit Co., in 1904, followed by Brooklyn Rapid Transit. Both were privately owned, with investment from Wall Street. However, as the initial development work was funded by the city, the subways were considered quasi-public entities. Fares were regulated, and capped at a nickel a ride.[10] However, the fact that the subways served a public purpose did not imply that the city took any responsibility for the employees—far from it.

In that era, the work was exceedingly dangerous. Before reliable signaling, train crashes were frequent. Even when trains were idle, workers had to crawl beneath the car couplings to attach air hoses, signal lines, and electrified cables. Track walkers trod miles of darkened and dirt-filled tunnels, prowling for broken rails and loose bolts. Though a worker might seem to be out of reach of a fast-coming train, an observer noted, "yet his coat may be open and begin to flap dangerously in the sudden rush of air."[11] That the workers were often exhausted (a function of seventy- to eighty-hour workweeks and the lack of days off) increased the risks. As late as the 1920s and early '30s, an *average* of eighteen IRT employees a year suffered fatal injuries.[12]

Recognition of the hazards moved the IRT to grant a pension in 1916. However, it was not exactly generous. Benefits were set at a meager 1 percent of wages for each year of service, and workers weren't eligible until age seventy, which relatively few were likely to reach. Disabled workers got a pension—but only if they were *totally* disabled and had twenty-five years of service under their belt. Moreover, wages, which were the basis for calculating benefits, were low even by then prevailing standards. An IRT machinist earned $2 a day; a motorman about $3 (autoworkers in Detroit were making $5). Yet, worried that the pension might prove too costly, the IRT directors imposed a further limitation: total pension benefits were capped at $50,000 a year. If too many workers qualified, individual benefits were simply reduced.[13]

Discontent among the employees—who in addition to mortal danger had to contend with restless crowds, deafening noise, extremes of temperature, and the lack of overtime or paid holidays—ran high. Workers commonly referred to themselves as "slaves."[14]

In 1916, IRT workers struck; alas, the company was prepared and quickly restored service. To undercut union activity, the lines employed scores of paid spies who reported back to their bosses on the workers' every move. Discipline was harsh. To further quell the employees, the IRT formed an in-house union, the "Brotherhood of the IRT." Involvement with outside unions brought dismissal from the job. Predictably, the Brotherhood was toothless. It repeatedly sought to have the pension plan incorporated into the workers' written employment contracts, but the IRT steadfastly refused, preferring that the pension, stingy as it was, remain revocable at the company's discretion. The lack of security left employees especially vulnerable to hard times. During the Depression, when ridership plummeted, the IRT cut back on hours and imposed a 10 percent wage cut.[15]

As the slump worsened, the costs of maintaining the system weighed heavily on the lines' deteriorating finances. The companies desperately pleaded for a fare hike, but the city refused to grant one. In 1932, the IRT declared bankruptcy and was placed under the supervision of a court-appointed receiver. As the labor historian Joshua Freeman has described, this opened a subtle window for labor organizers. Simultaneously, a pair of clandestine networks began to infiltrate the transit workers. The New York subways had disproportionately hired Irish immigrants (sought because they spoke English and would work cheap), and among the immigrants were veterans of the blood-soaked Irish insurrection. These transplanted rebels were bent on organizing the subways. They had no trouble linking up with ordinary workers, whom they knew from Irish neighborhoods, as well as from the rich stew of local Gaelic organizations and political societies.

The other network was the Communist Party. As the two groups were plying the same turf, they agreed to pool resources. A pact was made at Silver's Cafeteria on Columbus Circle. Thomas O'Shea, who had blown up police stations for the Irish Republican Army, and Michael Quill, a fellow expatriate who had been active, in a lesser role, in the rebellion, were among the Irish present. The left-wingers' delegation was led by John Santo, a Hungarian Jew who had emigrated in the 1920s, worked in the auto industry in Gary, Indiana, become a doctrinaire communist, and been dispatched by the party to New York, where he focused on organizing the transit industry. In 1934, soon after the rendezvous, the Transport Workers Union was born.[16]

It seized on the pension issue from the start. The IRT was proposing that the existing pension be scotched and replaced with a slightly more generous package (workers would be eligible at sixty-five instead of seventy). The plan would be voluntary for existing workers and compulsory for future hires. The catch was that it would be financed largely by the workers themselves, who would be required to contribute 3 percent of wages. This would be a major hardship for low-paid workers. Nonetheless, the great majority agreed to join.[17]

The TWU claimed that the workers had been coerced. The union staged a rally to demonstrate against the pension and, according to the *Daily Worker*, two thousand employees turned out.[18] For a formerly cowed workforce, this was an impressive showing. Then the union petitioned the court to declare the plan invalid. It claimed that the pension amounted to a payoff for the recent wage cut—making the TWU the first to detect the recurring trade (future benefits for wage restraint now) in American pension schemes. It is unlikely that the employees followed such particulars, but the pension remained a rallying point because the workers were contributing *twice* as much to it as was their miserly employer.[19]

For the TWU, the pension issue paved the way toward the larger goal of recruiting members. Quill was a natural organizer. Energetic and convivial, he had a gift for gab, a style at once theatrical and suffused with affinity for the ordinary worker, with whom he could lift a glass of scotch and roll a brogue. His rhetoric was impassioned but not doctrinaire, and he mixed easily in the Irish fraternal organizations and political gatherings. The second youngest of a family of eight, born to Gaelic-speaking farmers (and staunch IRA supporters) in Kilgarvan, he had emigrated and taken a job in the IRT as a gate man, at a wage of twenty-seven cents an hour, in 1926—the year before Walter Reuther arrived at Ford's. In New York, Quill lived an itinerant existence, sleeping in the union hall or rented rooms, roaming the buildings and taverns and subway barns where the workers congregated and which, to one of his later biographers, suggested the transported hills and valleys of his native land.[20] Once he got married, he lived with his wife, Mollie, in a small Bronx apartment, "like any IRT motorman."[21]

The fledgling union got a lift in 1935, when the New Deal enacted the protective Wagner Act, which restrained the IRT and the Brooklyn line, now known as the BMT, from flagrant union-busting. Also, in the case of the bankrupt IRT, the presiding judge was sympathetic to labor. Still, organizing was a battle. For money, experience, and organizational talents, the TWU was deeply dependent on Santo, the Communist Party operative, and his cohorts. Party members occupied key positions in the union, and the TWU's close association with the party was an open secret. Santo wrote in the *Daily Worker* that if the subways could be struck for even six hours, life in the city would come to a halt and "knock a few bricks off the capitalist structure."[22]

In the late 1930s, Representative Martin Dies, a Texas communist-hunter who prefigured McCarthy, held hearings on communist activity in the TWU. Quill and others were named. Quill cheekily retorted, "I'd rather be called a Red by the rats than a rat by the Reds," illustrating his talent for mockery (and for evasion). A more telling explanation emerged from a worker who testified that he wouldn't have joined the party "if the American Federation of Labor had been on the job." The truth was that the communists put more effort, money, and resources into the transit workers' cause than did mainstream labor.[23] For a mix of pragmatic and ideological motives, Quill made the party his ally and, to some extent, his master.*

The Red taint hurt the union's image in the Catholic Church, which was a chief rival for the immigrants' affections. Quill, who became the TWU's president in 1937, was undeterred. He was willing to take unpopular stands, and persistently strove to racially integrate the TWU, even at the board level. He prodded the IRT to expand opportunities for African Americans, whom the line had hired only as porters. He also was outspoken in his denunciation of anti-Semitism, of both the Nazi and the domestic variety. At a time when the radio priest Charles Coughlin was spewing vicious anti-Semitic propaganda to millions of receptive listeners, many of them Irish Catholics, this took considerable guts.[24]

Because or in spite of Quill's political unorthodoxy, the TWU rapidly gained members. In 1937 it staged a sit-down strike (modeled on the UAW demonstration then going on in Flint) to protest the firing of two pro-union engineers. By year's end, the TWU had swept employee elections at the major city transit companies (bus as well as rail), establishing it as the recognized union for 30,000 transit workers.[25]

---

*Quill was often accused of being a communist. He attended party meetings and was close to Earl Browder, head of the American Communist Party. But, as Freeman noted, Quill always denied, even under oath, that he had formally joined. He said later he had been "kind of careful where my signature went."

Now in a position to negotiate contracts, Quill consulted with John L. Lewis, the country's most powerful labor leader. "How will you take your raise—a straight increase or part in pensions?" Lewis asked. "I knew right then we were green at the game," Quill was to say.[26] Actually, pensions were already a burning issue. For retirees, the transit pension was patently inadequate. Thomas O'Brien, a seventy-two-year-old trainman who had worked twenty-seven years, was collecting a mere $38.37 a month; Henry J. Dunne, who had become disabled after twenty-four years on the job (he was now seventy), was getting only $32.69. The TWU archives are rife with such pitiable cases.[27]

The union promptly won a new pension plan in 1937, as well as a 10 percent wage hike. By 1939, the TWU had negotiated a paid vacation of one to two weeks plus sick leave and overtime—major improvements for workers who had been treated so shabbily. Also, through the efforts of Santo, who enlisted unemployed physicians to treat transit workers and their families, the TWU offered low-cost health care. The model of company health care was not yet established and the TWU saw no reason why the union, which had recreation facilities and a library, shouldn't also include a clinic.[28] For many transit workers it was the first time they saw a doctor.*

With the IRT still in receivership, New York City began to consider taking over the line and running it as a public service. This would put Quill in contact—perhaps in conflict—with the one public figure as charismatic as he was, Mayor Fiorello LaGuardia. While "the Little Flower" had campaigned as a liberal Republican and attracted labor support, as mayor he refused to give unions any meaningful role in bargaining, much less a formal contract. Elected as a "clean government" candidate opposed to patronage, the hen-shaped mayor saw union bosses as only a step above old-time ward bosses. Besides, he argued, since civil servants enjoyed the city's "full and complete protection" they had no need of a union.[29]

---

*The health plan was viable only because so many doctors were out of work and were willing to see patients at bargain rates. After the Depression it was suspended.

Early in 1940, LaGuardia decided to merge the IRT, the barely profitable BMT, and also a small city-owned line into a unified public subway. The city transit system was born in June 1940 with more than twelve hundred miles of track and five hundred stations (bus lines would come later). Quill immediately wrote the mayor and asked if the subways, under public ownership, would honor union contracts and engage in collective bargaining.

After some delay, LaGuardia replied that while the TWU would be free to *confer* with management, the city would not recognize it as an exclusive bargaining agent, nor did it accept its right to strike. To underline the point, the city mailed pamphlets to 32,000 subway workers, defiantly informing them that they were free to quit the TWU.[30]

Quill, naturally, exploded. He vowed that the union would strike, and accused the mayor of being as much an enemy of labor as Henry Ford. He thundered operatically, "Thus do you turn against labor—you who have pretended to be a staunch friend of labor."[31] Whether such outbursts were genuine or calculated was, in Quill's case, always impossible to tell.

Both parties sought help in Washington. Despite its pro-labor philosophy, the Roosevelt administration was cool to the idea of a *public* union. The secretary of labor, Frances Perkins, an old friend of unions (including the UAW), adopted a reproachful tone; she warned that if the city engaged in collective bargaining it would dilute the power of its elected officials. FDR got personally involved, opining that "the Board of Transportation in New York cannot enter into a contract with the subway workers."[32]

Quill continued to talk strike; his men "wouldn't work one hour" without a contract. But his position was weakening. Many TWU members (apparently accepting the LaGuardia position) had stopped paying dues. Public sentiment also was running against the TWU. Then, in June of 1941, Germany invaded the Soviet Union—a distant event with immediate consequences for a communist-allied union. Once the Soviet Union entered the war, the Communist Party in the United States did an about-face. Rather than try to weaken the capitalist system through strikes and disruptions, the party exhorted workers to support the war effort by keeping the economy humming. This gave Quill an excuse to back down. Six months later, the Japanese attack on Pearl Harbor brought the United States into the war, putting all strike talk on indefinite hold. During the war years, the TWU remained in an odd limbo. It was bigger by far than any other municipal union in New York, and among the biggest and best organized in the country. It also successfully expanded into other cities. And yet its flagship, Local 100, which represented New York transit workers, did not have the authority to bargain collectively or to sign contracts.

As city employees, transit workers were automatically enrolled in the New York City Employees' Retirement System. Pensions in New York were relatively generous by the standards of the day. Police and firemen who had worked twenty years immediately qualified for pensions that, in theory, would be equal to half their salary upon retirement. Other groups had to work longer, and they could not collect until they reached a specified minimum age, typically fifty-five or sixty.

However, employees contributed roughly half of the cost, in the form of salary deductions, so that their pensions were as much "earned" as they were awarded. Moreover, benefits were *not* guaranteed. If certain actuarial assumptions—how long retirees lived, for example—proved to be optimistic, employees got less than the promised "half." And many did receive less.[33]

At transit, employees had to serve thirty-five years for a pension equal to half of their final salary. And the employee contribution—6 percent of wages—was even higher than when the plan had been administered privately.[34] This enraged Santo, who made a stirring pitch to his fellows on the union board to fight for a fully paid pension:

> [They] paint us monsters from Moscow. . . . They said the only reason we are threatening trouble is because Mike Quill is looking for political power. . . . We want wage increases like the mine, steel and auto workers got, and we want shorter hours. And we want a free pension plan, because if a man worked 15 years he should be taken care of by the company for which he worked.[35]

During the 1940s, more public employers (mimicking the trend in industry) adopted pensions. The proportion of public employees with plans rose from half to two-thirds.[36] But the level of benefits scarcely budged—mostly because, in the public sector, the Walter Reuther and John L. Lewis types were scarcely able to bargain. Most state and local governments still did not recognize unions; more important, they did not think of their employees as a legitimate interest group. This was as true in New York as anywhere else. Indeed, since the city takeover of transit, Quill had seen his negotiating power seriously backslide. He reckoned that to move his agenda forward he would need an ally in City Hall.

With a new mayor, the Irish-born William O'Dwyer, who took office after the war, prospects brightened. O'Dwyer was prepared to grant the TWU more power (on the theory that it would force the union to grow up a little, and to stop resorting to work stoppages, strike threats, and so on). However, he could not be perceived as too close to a union dominated by communists.

Quill could see that the political climate was changing. Santo was being harassed by the FBI for his radicalism, and was facing probable deportation. He had already quit the union he had done so much to build, to spare it potential embarrassment.

Two simmering conflicts brought the issue of Quill's alliance with the communists to a head. One was the 1948 presidential campaign, in which Harry Truman faced an uphill battle for reelection. Labor leaders of the era played considerable roles as kingmakers, and the communists were pressuring Quill to back the third-party candidacy of Henry Wallace, a former U.S. vice president. Wallace, who was critical of Truman's tough stance against the Soviets, enjoyed considerable support on the left. Quill, however, was beginning to doubt whether the Wallace crusade, which could cost Truman the White House, was worth it.

The other issue was the nickel fare. The TWU had always been opposed to raising it, as doing so would amount to a tax on working New Yorkers. This was also the Communist Party line. However, the mayor gave Quill to know, in so many words, that without a fare hike there would be no money for increased wages or benefits. Quill, therefore, had to decide who *his* constituency was—all of the "oppressed," or transit workers alone. He was soon voicing support in radio ads for a fare hike—for which the *Daily Worker* denounced him as an opportunist. Probably Quill did not intend a total break, but in the late 1940s nothing was so impossible as to be half opposed to (or half in support of) communism. Addressing four thousand members at a TWU rally, Quill proclaimed his independence from the party in dramatic fashion. "They say I have to read the *Daily Worker* editorials to make up my mind what to do," he said derisively. Then he grabbed a copy of the newspaper, conveniently at hand, held it above his head and tore it to shreds, eliciting a cheer.[37] Promptly he went about purging the union of more than a dozen communists in leadership roles.* Meanwhile, he and O'Dwyer had arrived at a deal. The subway fare rose to a dime. And O'Dwyer gave the TWU a wage hike, a pension increase, *and* a health plan, as well as a dues check-off (which let the union collect dues directly from member paychecks). It was not quite the Treaty of Detroit, but it brought the TWU closer to full-fledged union status.

In flagrant disregard of its pact with the city, the TWU continued to stage work stoppages at a rate of four per year.[38] Every time O'Dwyer went on vacation, or so it seemed, he had to rush back to New York to avert a threatened transit strike. Though Quill generally led the insurrections, he didn't necessarily instigate them. He was continually being challenged by splinter factions and rival unions on his left (one group resorted to pelting him with eggs). To avoid losing control of his rebellious union, Quill re-

---

*Santo was arrested on immigration charges. Though TWU colleagues testified on his behalf, he chose not to fight deportation and returned to Hungary, where he rose to become the manager in charge of the national meat industry. During the 1956 anticommunist uprising he defected. In 1963, he returned to the United States. However, he and Quill were by then estranged. Looking back on his association with the party, Quill was uncommonly reflective: "We had a lot of help from the Communists. They worked for us night and day. . . . I'm sorry they didn't continue to help, but they showed allegiance to the Soviet Union and not to the American labor movement."

peatedly had to adopt more confrontational positions. L. H. Whittemore, a Quill biographer, captured the dynamic between Quill and his unruly troops when he wrote, "If they pulled a work stoppage, Mike pulled a slowdown on the whole system. If they were angry, Quill was furious."[39]

In particular, Quill kept pushing for full recognition, which meant the right to bargain collectively and to sign a contract. He had his highest hopes yet for Robert F. Wagner Jr., who was elected mayor in 1953. Wagner was the son of the U.S. senator who had authored the National Labor Relations Act that had unshackled private unions. The junior Wagner was a transitional figure in New York politics, who had been nurtured by the Tammany Hall machine and adroitly mastered the art of backroom deal-making. Like his father, he was a friend of labor.

Wagner's advisers, unsettled by the strife at transit and by more general signs of labor unrest, were urging that he rethink the city's nonrecognition policy. Perhaps it was better that worker discontent be channeled through designated unions—preferably those run by moderates? A recognized union might be controlled; disparate activists could not be. Ironically, city officials cited GM's relationship with the UAW as a role model.[40]

Quill shrewdly threw his support to Wagner early in his campaign.[41] The next year, his efforts were rewarded: the TWU was anointed the exclusive bargaining agent for transit workers and handed its first contract. In return, it pledged not to strike.[42] Thanks to its enhanced clout, the union won an improved pension, with half pay at age sixty. City employees were also admitted into Social Security, which boosted their living standard in retirement considerably.

Ominously for taxpayers, the city had little conception of what the pension would cost (it was still using actuarial assumptions from the World War I era).[43] But Quill grasped its value, at least in a human sense, when he took a vacation in Ireland. Walking a dirt road, he heard an old farmer greet him, "Good *eve*ning, Mike," as if it were the most natural thing in the world to see Quill on the old sod in County Kerry. The man was a former transit worker who had retired to his homeland on a transit pension.[44]

WITH TRANSIT as a test case, Wagner inched toward a policy of recognition for other unions. As mayor, he distanced himself from Tammany, pursued a more liberal agenda, and courted labor with renewed zeal. Whenever a union boss had a favor to ask, Wagner made it his business to listen.[45] In 1957, an election year, an aide proposed that he authorize full collective bargaining. She described it as a potential vote-getter: "You can call it the 'Little Wagner Act.' "[46]

"Executive Order 49," as it was known, was promulgated in 1958. Wagner surely thought he was containing, rather than unleashing, the labor genie. In the immediate aftermath it seemed that way. The mayor kept his thumb on the process (he set up the rules defining bargaining units, for instance), and it took a while for newly recognized unions to marshal their strength. Even when they did, out of deference to Wagner their demands were at first modest.

However, the Little Wagner Act, which had been set in motion by the transit workers, triggered a revolution. It empowered public employees in the city and, soon after, nationwide. President Kennedy (advised by the same aide as Wagner had been) authorized collective bargaining for federal employees in 1962.[47] Massachusetts enacted legislation permitting public employees to join unions in 1958, the year of Wagner's order. Soon after, the Bay State authorized the unions to bargain. Three-quarters of the states did likewise—setting in motion a process in which public employees would wrest ever bigger rewards, and especially bigger pensions.[48] Membership in public unions rose exponentially. Virtually proscribed only a decade earlier, by the mid-'60s these unions had been transformed into lobbying powerhouses with salaried staffs, hired lawyers, in-house newspapers, and (just in New York City alone) a quarter of a million dues-paying members.[49]

Unlike private-sector unions, the TWU and the Patrolmen's Benevolent Association (an organization that evolved into a union for the police force) had a secret weapon. The normal procedure was to negotiate a pension in collective bargaining, and then seek the necessary legislative approval. But unions that *failed* to get the pension terms they wanted through negotiation could also lobby Albany directly.

It is doubtful that many legislators had even the vaguest notion as to the true cost of benefits. What is worse, they didn't care. Unlike corporations, legislatures were not subject to even rudimentary controls over pension funding; thus they could grant increases without worrying about who would pay for them. This dynamic was hardly contained to New York. In Indiana, for example, the State Teachers Association had to procure a court order to force the state to contribute to its chronically deficit-ridden fund. Even then, the fund went wanting.[50]

So great was labor's clout in Albany, each state senator and assemblyman received on his desk each morning a specially tailored version of the legislative calendar—on which, beside each bill, was bluntly stamped "THIS BILL APPROVED (OR DISAPPROVED) BY THE NEW YORK STATE A.F.L.-C.I.O."[51] And from the early '60s on, the calendar was stocked with pension measures. The legislature began to dole out pension plums little by little and group by group—now to patrolmen, now to sanitation workers, now to teachers. Thus, while the size of the pension had once depended on whether actuarial forecasts came true, Albany now guaranteed it regardless. And now, too, the cash contribution of employees toward their pensions was significantly reduced—leaving the public to carry the freight. Also, the definition of hazardous work was liberalized, so that the transit police, the housing authority police, and corrections officers came to get pensions as lucrative as those of firemen and cops.[52] Albany enacted no fewer than two hundred pension bills over the course of the decade—every one of them resulting in higher costs.[53] Indeed, from the Wagner era to the early '70s, the city's payroll rose four times while retirement benefits surged nine times.[54] And of course, these benefits could not—ever—be revoked.

THE TONE of public service also changed. Teachers had once rejected the idea of belonging to a union, as they had considered it unbefitting for professionals. Hospitals had once been organized solely to serve their patients' needs, as distinct from their employees' "rights." Such genteel notions were quickly set aside. Teachers and orderlies as well as sanitation men became more strident. Public strikes, though illegal in New York and many other states, occurred with increasing frequency.[55]

In inner cities such as New York, where public employees were heavily minority, union issues became fused with the civil rights movement. This gave unions the cover of liberalism: rather than being seen as an interest group, they were often portrayed as crusaders for the underprivileged. This made for a shriller, more heated climate in the bargaining room. Employees who equated unsatisfactory working conditions with racial grievances were not inclined to compromise.

This combustible mix threatened to split apart the TWU, which by the mid-'60s was one-third African American.[56] Though Quill continued to be both active and outspoken on civil rights, particularly voting rights, he no longer resonated with younger blacks and Hispanics. They saw a leadership whose pale, lined faces still overwhelmingly reflected its Irish traditions.[57] Unhappily for Quill, upper-echelon motormen, while heavily Irish, were also dissatisfied, because Quill had focused on raising wages in transit's lower ranks. As wage scales compressed, higher-paid drivers felt neglected and threatened to break away.

Quill, therefore, was continually hustling to mollify his divided and divisive members. In 1961, the Transit Authority proposed to run a fully automated train (no motorman) along the shuttle track between Times Square and Grand Central Station. Quill spat back, "If the Transit Authority runs even one of these headless horsemen, we'll strike, no matter what."[58] And that was the end of it. Such small victories notwithstanding, the fact was that Quill had ten times sought authorization from the members to call a general strike and—always negotiating a "miracle" settlement at the eleventh hour—never once used it.[59] His members were no longer amused. One worker wrote, "Dear Mr. Quill: Nobody believe [*sic*] that you will ever call a strike in the subway. You haven't called one in thirty years."[60]

There was some truth to the charge that Quill was more pragmatic than his rabble-rousing image. His utterances were bold but his nature was cautious. Also, his heart was failing, and he now had a greater sense of life's limitations. Perhaps he also had visions of a life beyond labor conflict. Having been widowed, he had remarried his longtime secretary, Shirley Garry, in whose Yiddishisms he delighted, and with whom he shared a three-room vacation cottage in the Virgin Islands. In 1963, he dodged yet another bullet, wringing a settlement out of Wagner and forgoing yet another threatened strike.

The outlook for the next contract, which expired on New Year's Eve 1965, was less auspicious. Early that year, social service workers struck, closing most of the city's gargantuan welfare operation.[61] This marked a new phase in public employee militancy. More immediate to the TWU, transit workers remained poorly paid. Motormen earned $3.46 an hour, compared with $3.96 for those on trains run by the Port Authority, a rival agency serving commuters between New York and New Jersey.[62] But the decisive factor was a changing of the guard at City Hall. After three terms, Wagner was retiring. The mayor-elect, John V. Lindsay, was a liberal, forty-four-year-old Republican congressman who represented the wealthy Upper East Side "silk-stocking" district. Lindsay was tall, handsome, and full of ideals. Though he wasn't personally wealthy, his background could hardly have been more unlike Quill's. Educated at an elite prep school and at Yale, he campaigned against the personalized politics and backroom deals of the Wagner years, promising a more enlightened era in which labor relations would be handled by fair-minded experts and fact-finding panels.[63] Though popular with voters, he struck labor leaders as naïve.

Returning from a post-election vacation in Puerto Rico, tanned and hopeful, Lindsay discovered that transit talks were at an impasse. "I'm not an expert on labor matters," he admitted.[64]

Wagner, smelling a fiasco, distanced himself from the negotiations, which in any case went nowhere. Lindsay, not wanting to seem like a "deal-maker," also refused to take part. Quill despised the mayor-elect's do-gooder's zeal and, presumably, his Protestant rectitude.* He ridiculed him by deliberately mispronouncing his name as "Lindsley." Perhaps, had Lindsay gotten involved, as Quill was imploring him to do, they could have come to terms. It is more likely that this time, Quill had resolved to strike. The Transit Authority procured a court order enjoining the union's leaders from calling one. Quill tore it to shreds.

On the evening of Friday, December 31, just after Lindsay's swearing-in and hours before the contract expired, the new mayor joined the negotiators at the Americana Hotel. The TWU was demanding that workers get a pension after only twenty-five years on the job, as well as a four-day workweek and potloads of money. The city's offer did not come close. Lindsay airily demanded that the TWU submit to arbitration. Quill told the mayor to "grow up." Then he called Lindsay an obscenity (in Yiddish). Lindsay, who saw in Quill the antithesis of the modern, reformist, and reasonable politics he stood for, remained grimly silent.[65]

Lindsay expected a short strike—just long enough for Quill to make his point. Quill, privately, was of a similar mind. He told Joseph O'Grady, head of the Transit Authority, that he would "give the drunks time to get home [on Saturday], strike at 5 A.M. and have it settled before Monday."[66] It is not clear if Quill's lieutenants understood this crucial point. And Quill, visibly gray, had weakened physically. His suite at the Americana was stacked with medicines, and he was dizzy from popping the pain-killer Demerol.[67]

The strike commenced, as threatened, early Saturday. That night, at Lindsay's inaugural ball, Sammy Davis Jr. went to the microphone and deadpanned, "I want to congratulate the mayor for eliminating crime on the subways after only 24 hours on the job."[68] Monday morning Lindsay walked four miles to work in a show of solidarity with ordinary New Yorkers. Citizens (as well as the press) were overwhelmingly siding with the city. On Tuesday, the city moved to enforce the no-strike law. A sheriff arrived

---

*Jimmy Breslin famously declared, "When Quill looked at Lindsay he saw the Church of England."

at the Americana to arrest the leaders of the TWU. Quill snapped, "The judge can drop dead in his black robes and we would not call off the strike."[69] Shirley brought him a book on Irish history to read in his cell.

Two hours after Quill was jailed, he suffered a heart attack and was rushed to Bellevue Hospital. This sudden and ominous development seemed to endow the strike, which previously had seemed scripted and almost farcical, with the deeper character of tragedy. It hardened the strikers' resolve. More was now at stake—the life of Quill himself. Meanwhile, the forced regime of lengthy walks, missed workdays, and traffic jams was taking its toll on New Yorkers. On Thursday, according to the traffic commissioner, New York suffered the worst rush hour in its history—a tie-up that endured from approximately 4:45 a.m. to almost noon.[70]

With the city and the negotiations snarled, Lindsay resorted to the hated "back door." Robert Price, the deputy mayor, secretly visited Quill at his bedside. He offered a $500 a year pension bonus. Quill snapped it up. Then Price asked what Quill needed to settle. The ailing warrior held up four fingers—which Price understood to mean four dollars an hour for motormen—which would equate to 15 percent over just two years.[71] After thirteen days, the transit strike mercifully ended. It was an unalloyed triumph for the TWU, which received twice as large a settlement as under Wagner.[72] Flush with victory, the union hired a pension specialist and began to prepare for its next fight.

Quill was charitable to Lindsay in the aftermath. He did not really believe, or so he said, the harsh words he had spoken in battle about the mayor. But two weeks after the trains resumed operations, sixty-year-old Michael Quill died. He was buried in St. Patrick's Cathedral, his casket draped in an IRA flag.[73]

The city's wounds did not heal either quickly or well. Lindsay had squandered the tremendous optimism that had greeted his inauguration. Now he felt compelled to do his utmost to avert more strikes, putting the city in a weak negotiating position. Even when the legislature passed tougher antistrike legislation, known as the Taylor Law, unions realized they had leverage over the city and its shaken public. One exorbitant settlement followed another. As Charles Morris, a chronicler of the Lindsay era, wrote, the transit strike touched off "a wave of me-tooism."[74]

In rapid order, city employees negotiated the basic welfare protections: full health insurance, then *retiree* insurance, plus ten to twenty sick days per year, twenty-five vacation days, and eleven holidays. In addition, unions bargained for numerous work restrictions (and thus, inefficiencies). For example, the TWU secured a ban on part-time work, meaning that bus drivers would be paid for long stretches of idle time in between the morning and evening rush hour.[75] In this and myriad other ways, city employees were redefining the meaning of the term "public servant." They had become an entitled class—a group entitled to the public's largesse.

Government agencies tended to succumb because they were (not unlike the auto cartels) monopolies. New Yorkers could not shop elsewhere for subway service or police protection: the *New York* subways, and the NYPD, were all they had. No matter how much the employees earned, and no matter what their services cost, the citizens were captive customers.

AFTER THE TRANSIT STRIKE, one union after another demanded higher pensions. What is surprising is not that they succeeded, but how easily they did so. In 1966, the Patrolmen's Benevolent Association won *full* pensions (that is, equal to their full salaries) after thirty-five years.[76] A game of leapfrog ensued. The sanitation workers, arguing that they were also "uniformed," got *four* pension sweeteners over the mid-1960s, vaulting them to a half pension after twenty years and virtual parity with the firemen and cops.[77] A panicked PBA came hurrying back for more.

The TWU, which had set off the pension bandwagon, demanded that it not be left behind. Ellis Van Riper, a negotiator for Local 100 who had been jailed for nine days in 1966, met with the city's actuary and, pounding on the desk for emphasis, thundered, "Goddamn, if the garbage men get '20/50' so can we."[78] This was late 1967. With its contract nearing expiration, the union threatened a strike. This made pensions truly a citywide issue. Transit disputes always galvanized the public, and memories of the strike of '66 were still raw. Fearing a repeat, the city agreed: half of final salary—guaranteed—for workers fifty and up with twenty years' service. And there was more. Transit agreed to change the definition of the "final salary" upon which the pension was calculated. Previously, it was the average earned over an employee's final five years. Almost unbelievably, it now became the last year's salary—*including overtime.* This led to significant abuse, as retiring employees maneuvered, with the help of friendly overseers, to be assigned heroic amounts of overtime. As the TWU crowed to its members, an employee who retired after thirty years, and who had earned $9,000 in his last year, would receive an annual pension of $6,129—compared with $3,943 under the old contract.[79] In a pen stroke, the city's future commitment to transit workers had soared by more than half.

John J. Gilhooley, the head of the Transit Authority, considered it frankly excessive, but, as he admitted later, "I yielded on the pension rather than take a strike."[80] The authority made the same decision two years later, when it agreed to pay the transit pension's full cost, thus eliminating entirely the employee contribution. Transit workers—and they alone—now had the "free" pension that the fiery Santo had demanded.[81]

The transit deals opened the floodgates. Thanks to the free ride at transit, contribution rates for other unions soon fell to negligible levels. Victor Gotbaum, head of the sprawling District Council 37, which represented parks, hospital, and municipal workers, was set to sign a contract when he heard about the TWU's gold-plated pension. He barged into City Hall exclaiming, "I can't *live* with my pension deal." He negotiated a better one.

The teachers got an even richer settlement—a pension for *more* than half pay after twenty-five years (a rather short career for a white-collar professional). When Gotbaum saw he had been leapfrogged by the teachers, in 1970, he demanded yet a sweeter deal. The response of a Lindsay aide to one such pension demand was memorable: "When would we have to start paying for it?" Told that, due to the peculiarities of the pension calendar, an increase would not affect the budget until three years later, by which time Lindsay would be serving out his final year, the aide breezily approved it.[82]

Police and firemen got two quite special plums. One was the so-called heart bill. This mandated that any officer or fireman retiring with heart disease was entitled to a presumption that his sickness was job-induced, meaning he could retire with a disability benefit equal to three-quarters, instead of half, of salary—and one exempt from federal taxes.[83]

More exceptional still was the so-called variable pension supplement. Unhappy that other unions had narrowed the gap, the firefighters demanded an extra . . . something. The city said it was tapped out. The firefighters union, always intellectually creative when it came to its pension, suggested that the city, which then was investing most of its retirement funds in bonds, put a portion in stocks. Any surplus profit could be divided up among retired firemen at the end of the year.

This turned every principle of pension accounting on its head. Since the city would have to pay a full pension even in years in which its investments declined, reason dictated that it save, not distribute, the so-called surplus in good years. Nonetheless, retired firemen and also cops got the "variable supplement"—quickly dubbed a "Christmas bonus"—without shouldering any of the market risk.[84]

Although one wonders at the thinking of Arthur Goldberg, the former secretary of labor and Supreme Court justice who mediated that deal, the labor accords of the late '60s fit a pattern, and responsibility for them, at least in part, lay beyond Lindsay's (or anyone in the city's) control. All of urban America was, to one degree or another, in the midst of a broad experiment with the welfare state that had begun in the late 1950s and early '60s, largely as an effort to improve the conditions of inner-city minorities and others. Spending on social services was rising sharply, welfare rolls were soaring—ultimately accommodating nearly one in seven New Yorkers—and public-sector work rolls were expanding.[85] Interest groups gained new influence at City Hall, and unions were among the beneficiaries.

However, Lindsay's helplessness in the face of organized labor surely made it worse. In a visceral sense, the mayor spent his entire first term recovering from the debacle with Quill. Seeking to avoid work stoppages, he embraced fact-finding panels to mediate disputes—but these only played into labor's hands. Though seemingly impartial, the tendency of mediators was to "split the difference" and recommend at least a portion of union demands.[86] Transit was thus able to piggyback substantial wage gains—36 percent over four years—on top of its rich new retirement benefits.[87] The irony is that, despite Lindsay's generous treatment of labor unions, he was hit by a wave of crippling strikes anyway.

The mayor's approach—and his results—somewhat improved as he moved into a second term, in 1970. By then, however, New York had established a uniquely generous pension edifice. In effect, it bizarrely inverted the age-old wisdom that pensions should be a fraction of working income. By the end of the 1960s, and including Social Security (to which the city contributed), municipal employees earned *more* after they retired. A transit worker could retire on 120 percent of his final salary; a teacher, on 130 percent.[88]

Predictably, such rich pensions induced a wave of early retirements. In the next fifteen months, 30 percent of eligible motormen retired.[89] Within two years, *two-thirds* of the subway maintenance crew was gone.[90]

Thanks to the new, more liberal definition of "final salary," this exodus turned out to be far more costly than expected. One motorman, who had earned $13,500 in his second to last year, claimed a "final salary" (on which his pension would be based) of $29,000—an extreme example of overtime abuse. Such cases became common throughout the civil service. However, it took an actuary to fully understand their impact. For instance, the cost of employing a fireman for a day of overtime in his last year was $76 in cash wages. However, that single day could boost the fireman's lifetime pension benefits by an astonishing $1,141.[91]

Such and similar pension mathematics led to soaring obligations, which put a heavy load on the city budget. By 1970, the New York City Employees' Retirement System (an umbrella fund for transit and various other employee groups) had fallen to a funded level of only 40 percent—a dangerously low level, and down from 70 percent a decade earlier.[92]

While other municipal departments, such as police and fire, suffered similar strains, the new pension had an especially deleterious effect on transit. Strapped for funds, the authority cut back on maintenance, leading to a marked increase in the rate of breakdowns and delays.[93] The exodus of workers thinned the ranks of experienced repairmen and drivers when they were needed most. New Yorkers who were scarcely aware of the ins and outs of employee pensions *were* very much aware that trains were breaking down, employees were less attentive, stations were suddenly less clean, and incidents of crime—including violent crime—were soaring.

With the city no longer able to handle the strain, transit was absorbed into a new state agency, the MTA. However, transit employees remained a part of the city's underfunded pension plan. And the transit system continued to spiral downward. In the first half of the 1970s, the fare was hiked three times. However, the increases were partly self-defeating. In response to the higher fare, as well as to a weakening local economy and poorer service, the system lost nearly a quarter of its riders—some 300 million fares a year.[94] By the early 1970s, transit was in financial trouble.

The same was not yet being said of the city as a whole, but transit was a ripe symbol of the city's problems, fiscal and otherwise. (The subways always seemed to exert a gravitational pull on the rest of New York.) Elected officials and local business leaders were increasingly alarmed by the growth in the city's labor costs, pensions in particular. Though certainly not the city's only fiscal ill, retirement benefits had skyrocketed to $780 million in 1971—more than triple the total of a decade earlier.[95] And just as such costs were cutting into performance at transit, so they were eating into the perception of New York as a livable and affordable place to live and work.

It turned out that the city did not *quite* have a monopoly in services after all. If taxes became too high, or service too slipshod, residents might move away. It wouldn't happen overnight, but by the early '70s a migration was clearly under way. New York was hemorrhaging private-sector jobs and losing its middle-class core to the suburbs, especially out of state, where taxes were significantly lower. Just as car buyers were defecting from GM to Toyota, so "consumers" of government services were abandoning New York. In truth, the unions had overreached.

Political support for pensions now began to ebb. New Yorkers awoke to headlines like the one in the *Schenectady Union-Star*: "State Pensions: A Gravy Train." Nelson A. Rockefeller, the longtime governor, who had been the model of largesse with respect to unions, invariably supporting pension hikes and encouraging the legislature to do likewise, executed a swift about-face. This time, Rocky lobbied the legislature to say "no."[96]

Rockefeller was not so naïve as to target transit, the police, or sanitation workers. These were politically connected unions with strong ethnic identities and bases of support. (New York's cops were heavily Irish, the sanitation men Italian, the teachers Jewish.) Rockefeller focused on the pensions of the *least* powerful employees: low-ranking civil service, health and hospital workers, housing employees, security people. These lower-ranking workers were predominately Hispanic and African American.[97]

Two unions represented them: the 100,000-member-strong DC 37, and the smaller Local 237 of the Teamsters. When Barry Feinstein, who ran the Teamsters local, heard that the legislature was going after his members' pensions he went "ballistic." Local 237 had been founded by Feinstein's father, who had gotten his Teamsters charter from Jimmy Hoffa. Barry Feinstein had grown up on the Lower East Side, surrounded by a mixture of tough-talking union bosses and Democratic Party stalwarts. Unsure of a career, he attended a local college, then joined the army reserves. When his father got sick, he filled in for him at the union and fell in love with it. Meanwhile, he went to law school. The Teamsters being an institution where blood counted, by age thirty-two the younger Feinstein was running Local 237. Now, four years later, after the "no" vote on pensions, he called Victor Gotbaum, head of the other affected union. The two agreed to fight back. Both had some muscle at their disposal. Feinstein's union operated the drawbridges that spanned the city's waterways. Gotbaum's union represented heavy-equipment workers and truck drivers. They planned their response in secret.[98]

On June 7, 1971, a sweltering morning, the roads to New York were inexplicably clogged. It was the worst tie-up since the subway strike: as reported in the next day's *Times*, "hundreds of thousands of motorists were trapped in massive traffic jams on the hottest day of the year when municipal workers opened drawbridges in the city and abandoned trucks on major highways."[99] In a feat worthy of commandos, Feinstein's men had swiveled twenty-seven of the city's twenty-nine movable bridges to an open position in the early hours of the morning, then fled their posts on a Teamsters-driven skiff, taking their operating keys and much vital electrical equipment with them. They left a helpless Army Corps of Engineers to try to sort out the damage. Gotbaum's truck drivers were less effective.[100]

After two days of this patent blackmail, the city agreed to lobby the legislature to reverse itself and—in the event it failed—to compensate the workers with other benefits. Feinstein and Gotbaum called off the strike. As matters developed, the legislature didn't budge. However, the city, making good on its promise, provided *every* municipal union with a new "retiree welfare fund," including prescription drugs, dental care, and life insurance. This was considered no big deal, even by the city actuary.[101] Such benefits soon spread to public unions across the country, and of course their costs would eventually mushroom. In one bizarre stunt, Feinstein had paved the way for benefits similar to those won by the UAW over decades.*

However, the drawbridge strike left a lingering public distaste toward the unions. For the first time, legislators came under pressure to limit pensions. Rockefeller, prodded by his fiscally prudent lieutenant governor, Malcolm Wilson, now truly got on the bandwagon, and established a state commission to study New York's hodgepodge of pension systems and to recommend changes.

The commission was chaired by Otto Kinzel, a no-nonsense corporate lawyer. Kinzel concluded that the state's, and the city's, plans were overwhelmingly too generous. By his reckoning, local and state employers were spending 20 percent to 40 percent of payroll costs on pensions, making those pensions the richest in the United States by far. In the private sector, by comparison, pension expense typically was only 5 percent of payroll.[102]

---

*Feinstein was indicted for his role in planning the strike. The case never went to trial.

Since present employees were protected by law, Kinzel proposed that the state set up a new, unified plan for employees hired in the future. Benefits would be much reduced, and having a single plan, Kinzel believed, would end the game in which each union tried to leapfrog the other.[103]

The consequences of *not* adopting his plan, Kinzel implied, would be grave. "I think our system would save New York City from bankruptcy," he declared in a press conference. That was in January 1973—perhaps the first public suggestion that the city was headed for a financial crisis.[104]

Newspapers in the state enthusiastically supported Kinzel. To the editorial writers at the *Times*, the fact that public employees stood to earn more in retirement than on the job demonstrated that the city's, as well as the state's, pension system had gone badly off course.[105] Business leaders, working behind the scenes, strongly supported Kinzel as well.

Only the unions opposed him. They practically screamed bloody murder, and launched an extensive lobbying effort to stop the plan. Albert Shanker, head of the United Federation of Teachers, sent busloads of placard-wielding teachers to Albany. The TWU accused the governor of "pension plunder" and entreated its members to swamp the legislature with mail. The workers, at transit and elsewhere, responded as if their families were under attack (and perhaps they were). One assemblyman complained of receiving five hundred "anti" letters a day.[106]

The legislators now had to choose between the editorialists urging them to act with courage and the busloads of angry employees demonstrating outside their door. By spring, reform was all but dead. Rockefeller backed off, and the Kinzel plan was shelved.[107] That would have been the end of matters—had not Wilson, the lieutenant governor, leaned on Rockefeller to reconsider.[108] The governor was also feeling heat from bankers—his political base—and from the press. Rockefeller, who had long harbored presidential ambitions, understood that a pension mess at home would hurt his image nationally. In July, he convened a special session of the legislature and strong-armed it into enacting a compromise measure that would, indeed, reduce pension benefits for new employees. The cuts were piecemeal, and not nearly as severe as those advocated by Kinzel. Police and firemen were barely nicked. However, at transit and other departments, the age and service requirements were modestly increased—in transit's case the minimum age was hiked to fifty-five.[109] Also, new employees' pensions would be calculated on the basis of their last *three* years' pay, not just the final year.

Since the benefit cuts were aimed at future workers, they did nothing to shore up the city's immediate financial plight. And its financial picture was increasingly grim. Soaring pension expense was only a part of what afflicted the city, but it was a deeply representative part. New York had created a virtual welfare state—everything from subsidized transit fares to free tuition for 200,000 college students to its network of municipal hospitals. It was unsustainable. Lavish pensions were the apotheosis of the free-spending mentality that got it into trouble. And since monies owed to pension plans (unlike salaries or other current expenses) could often be deferred, the pension provided temporary cover for budget-makers. As Kinzel put it, New York City "use[d] pension underfunding as one method of balancing its operating budget."[110] When that no longer sufficed, the city began to patch its budget with short-term loans. Then, in 1975, lenders stopped the game, and the city ran out of people and institutions to borrow from.

In desperation, the state created the Municipal Assistance Corporation ("Big Mac"), chaired by Felix Rohatyn, to issue public bonds—hopefully more marketable now that Rohatyn, a respected banker-savant, was policing the city's budget. Investors, though, still refused to lend. And so the city could not pay its bills. In the first week of September, New York did not have the funds to pay employees, welfare recipients, hospitals, and others.

With default imminent, the city turned to its pension funds (including the ones for fire, police, the teachers, and the general fund including transit workers) as a possible lender of last resort. The funds invested $100 million in MAC bonds and enabled Gotham to limp into autumn.[111]

In mid-October, the city needed a further infusion to pay noteholders whose IOUs were coming due—on Friday, October 17, to be precise. The state was committed to advancing funds, but only if the city could also round up "outside" money. By Thursday, a day before the deadline, only one party to the rescue was missing: the teachers' retirement system. That evening, and again early Friday, the teachers' fund unexpectedly voted "no" on whether to purchase $150 million in MAC securities. Three of its trustees were former teachers—in history and in "home instruction"—and were, it seemed, philosophically disinclined to lend their pension assets to the public.

Hugh Carey, the governor, got word of this principled refusal just before 11 p.m., while attending a dinner at the Waldorf-Astoria. He left the hotel for his midtown office and, still attired in white tie and tails, went into overnight crisis mode, summoning top advisers, officials from MAC, and Richard Ravitch, a prominent builder who was acting as a Carey troubleshooter. Confronting the unthinkable, the group discussed their options if New York defaulted. Around midnight, Ravitch paid a call on Shanker, the defiant head of the teachers union, to stress that a default would be a calamity for all. Shanker was the one person with influence over the pension trustees, but he was bitterly upset that the state, which now had emergency authority over the city budget, had nixed the teachers' most recent contract. His meeting with Ravitch was inconclusive.

The next morning, noteholders went to the downtown Municipal Building to redeem their notes, but were calmly informed by city clerks to come back in the afternoon—by which time, they hoped, New York City might have some money. Meanwhile, the sanitation department put a halt on the distribution of paychecks. The financial capital of the world was about to go broke (though the teachers' pension fund would surely not). Carey now had relocated to Ravitch's Upper East Side home, where they, along with Simon Rifkind, the counsel for MAC, worked on Shanker one last time. Rifkind outlined the consequences of default in graphic detail. Did Shanker want to be the one to stop the world? The meeting lasted three hours. Shortly after two, Shanker begrudgingly—even resentfully, it seemed—stepped in front of TV cameras and announced that he would "advise" the trustees to invest the money. The city began redeeming its notes; the flow of money recommenced. The Federal Reserve Bank of New York delayed its Friday close to make sure the checks cleared.[112]

By investing $1.6 billion—about 20 percent of their assets—in the city's paper, the city pension funds eased the fiscal crisis at its worst.[113] Of course, this was money they had *received* from the city, by virtue of its reckless pension promises, and now were merely lending back. In reality, the city had never been able to afford those promises. The fiscal crisis merely proved it.

In the wake of the crisis, the legislature created another pension tier for employees hired after 1976. This second cut undid (outside of police and fire) a significant portion of the pension gains of the 1960s. At transit, the threshold for retirement was raised to sixty-two. Also, new employees would have to contribute 3 percent of their salaries. Even so, pensions in New York remained among the most generous in the country.[114] What's more, although the city slashed its operating budget, pensions (in the short run) were immune. Thus in 1976, the first year of fiscal austerity, New York's retirement costs reached a record $1.5 billion.[115] The fiscal crisis simply slowed the rate of accumulation and gave the city a chance to catch its breath.

Just as important for the future, the legislature outlawed collective bargaining on pensions and gave to itself the exclusive power to determine benefits. The idea was that this would keep public employers from giving away the store—that the legislature would be more vigilant. This took pensions out of the realm of negotiations where, at least in theory, bargainers responded to economic factors such as supply and demand. In the future, pensions in New York would be determined by politicians.

FOUR

ON STRIKE!

One day in the early 1980s, Barry Feinstein paid a visit to New York City mayor Ed Koch. Since the fiscal crisis, the unions had been obsessed with regaining their previous level of pensions. Although budget pressures were still intense, the city was doing better, and the danger of default was well past. Feinstein, the Teamsters official, thought the time was ripe.

Technically, he and other union leaders were no longer permitted to bargain on pensions, but nothing could stop them from making a kindly request of the state legislature. What Feinstein and the other unions wanted was to roll back some of the cuts imposed (on new employees) in 1976. Those new employees would in effect be penalized for receiving Social Security. But if the legislature acted, they would get both the federal and the transit pension. This was a very costly amendment. But the unions had been lobbying hard. They wanted their pension plum back, and the legislature, its memory of the fiscal crisis now beginning to fade, had agreed to give it to them. However, there was a problem.

Mayor Koch was fuming. He was outraged that the legislature could impose higher pension costs on New York City over the objection of the local government, and in particular its mayor, who felt the city couldn't afford them. Since Koch was powerless to stop the increase, he had resorted to his trademark tactic: complaining. He said the legislature was making a mistake of "tremendous" proportions. He spirited a letter ostensibly to the lawmakers, but really to the press, accusing Albany of returning to the "pre-fiscal crisis giveaway of pensions." He called it "an outrageous piece of legislation" and a "travesty."[1] For Koch, such talk was as routine as breathing.

But this time, there was a catch. Koch warned he was going to lay off city employees—cops, parks people, and so on—in the district of every legislator from the city who voted for the pension package. Then he would go public, very noisily, in each community, and announce, "Your legislator—Assemblyman Smith—is responsible for this. I had to lay off a cop on your street because Smith [or Jones or whoever] voted to raise costs."

This is why Feinstein was in Koch's office. "We have these pensions," Feinstein noted, referring to the proposed increases. "There is nothing you can do to stop them."

Koch listened.

"But I've been asked by the leaders of the legislature to see if I can satisfy you and get you to stop yelling," Feinstein said. The leaders of the legislature were Warren Anderson and Stanley Fink. They did not like Koch publicly embarrassing legislators, including Anderson and Fink. They wanted to deal with the pension quietly.

Feinstein offered to delay the increases by a month. Koch, for once, didn't say anything. Then Feinstein upped the offer to two months. Finally, the union leader said he could live with waiting an extra *four months.* The delay would save the city some money—but after that, of course, it would be on the hook to make higher contributions forever.

When Feinstein finished, Koch was still irate. Listening to Feinstein, the very same man who had once opened the drawbridges to protest a pension veto but now, having matured, had learned to work behind the scenes, and specifically to get the legislature on *his* side, made Koch want to scream all the louder. "I was so f——ing angry I wanted to kill him," he would recall. "I could have choked Barry Feinstein and sent his body in a box to the others." But Koch knew that if he did that, or rather, if he continued to squawk, Feinstein would withdraw his offer and the city would lose anyway. Koch made the deal.*[2]

The truth was that, new law or not, unions were slowly reasserting their muscle—a development that would have grave implications for the city's pension burden as well as for ordinary subway riders. Not surprisingly, the TWU led the charge. Soon after Koch took office, in 1978, transit workers began to agitate for a big raise (their first since the fiscal crisis). From the MTA's point of view, the timing was terrible. Subway service had reached an all-time low: trains were frequently delayed, the equipment was obsolete, and the stations were filthy. Then, in 1979, the MTA's chairman resigned. Facing the daunting challenge of rebuilding the system, and now the troubling prospect of labor unrest as well, Governor Carey looked around for a savior.

Ravitch, who had rescued the state's Urban Development Corporation and played a useful role during the fiscal crisis, was a natural choice. When Carey asked if he would like to run the MTA, the cautious builder made inquiries and discovered that morale among the workers was terrible and, what's more, whoever took the job might have to deal with a transit strike the following year. He told Carey he would do it anyway. Then he went to lunch with former mayor Wagner, who gave him a piece of advice. "This will be hard for you to follow," Wagner said, "but when you negotiate, make the union leader look good."[3]

Heeding Wagner's advice, Ravitch reached out to John Lawe, the Irish

---

*Teamsters officials later accused Feinstein of embezzling hundreds of thousands of dollars and living it up at the union's expense. The federal government brought noncriminal charges against him. Feinstein vehemently contested the accusations, which he said were politically motivated. He ultimately agreed to a lifetime ban from the Teamsters and repaid a loan of $104,000. In an odd twist, local officials would salute him as a stabilizing force in labor relations, and the governor would appoint him to serve on the board of the MTA.

immigrant and onetime bus cleaner who had risen to become head of the union. Lawe was of a younger generation than Quill and inclined to be reasonable. However, the local's membership was more fractious than ever. A nucleus of African American workers had been trying to unseat the leadership since the early 1970s, and Lawe's position within the local was tenuous at best. By 1979, the executive board was in the hands of a group of self-proclaimed black Maoists.[4]

With the latter controlling the agenda, and the union demanding a 30 percent wage hike (over two years) as well as pension improvements, Ravitch said nix. Privately, he asked Lawe, with whom he had established a good rapport, to meet him in secret at the banker's luxury apartment. The two worked out the terms of a deal—on the order of a 15 percent wage hike. (Given the high inflation of the era, this was reasonable but not extreme.) They agreed that neither would make it public, nor would Lawe disclose it to his colleagues.[5] Instead, they concocted an elaborate script for getting it past the local's executive board. Here was the plan:

Ravitch would present an offer to the board at 10 p.m. on March 31, 1980, the day the contract expired. He would emphasize that this was the MTA's "final offer" and, in a theatrical flourish, slam his hand on the table. Lawe would reject the offer and throw him out.

Then Lawe would turn to his board and say, "There will be a strike. But we shouldn't do it without putting an offer on the table. So we'll make one last proposal that the MTA will never accept." At this point, Ravitch would reappear, listen to Lawe's terms—the very same the two had worked out in private—hang his head as if in abject surrender, and agree.

That was the script. March 31 was Passover, and Governor Carey had catered a Seder meal for Koch and Ravitch (which the governor attended) at the St. Regis Hotel. Ravitch nervously played his part, sipping kosher wine while he waited for word from the Sheraton Centre hotel, the site of the negotiations. At 9:30 he got the call. When he arrived at the Sheraton, the scene was unruly. The board members had been drinking and were in a foul mood. Ravitch presented his "final offer" and was duly rejected.

But when Lawe suggested that they make a counteroffer, the board members angrily shouted him down. Some of them were drunk and the group was in no mood for a gesture of conciliation. At 2 a.m., without bothering to see if the MTA was truly done talking, the board declared a strike. Once again, millions of New Yorkers awoke to an immobilized city.

With the buses and trains ground to a halt, Koch paraded across the Brooklyn Bridge (it was an unwritten law that the mayor had to walk during a transit strike), denouncing the TWU as "unreasonable," lending moral support to footbound New Yorkers and urging them to support a hard line against the union. Though Koch was not a party to the contract, the city faced a series of negotiations with other public unions, and the mayor feared that if transit scored big gains it would have a ripple effect on the rest.

Governor Carey and Ravitch both worried that Koch's nonstop commentary was making it worse. The strike dragged on for eleven days. It ended when the MTA offered a 17 percent raise plus a cost-of-living increase—more than in the original, secret agreement. Koch fired an emotional parting shot, charging that though the city had won the battle in the "streets," the MTA had "lost it at the bargaining table."[6]

Actually, neither the union nor the MTA emerged from the strike feeling like a winner. The strikers were dealt a stiff penalty—two days' pay for each day of the strike, as well as a $1 million fine levied against the union. The net result was a deepening of mistrust on both sides. The agency tried to recoup its losses by getting the TWU to increase productivity (by eliminating work-rule restrictions, for example). Also, seeking to quell tardiness, absenteeism, and other morale-related problems, the MTA cracked down on discipline.[7] Union members seethed with resentment.

Even more worrisome, subway performance dipped to an all-time low. Cars were breaking down every 6,200 miles (the equivalent of only five trips around the system).[8] Aside from the effect on commuters, who suffered excruciating delays and were squeezed like cattle into the cars that *were* functioning, the breakdowns made life miserable for the workers in numerous small ways, as they navigated trains with sticky doors or malfunctioning intercoms and trod along catwalks with rotted or missing planks. Employees and passengers alike feared for their lives as incidents of crime in the subways soared to well above fifty a day.[9]

Ravitch proposed to fix the system with a massive infusion of capital. He adroitly maneuvered for a tax break in Washington and reached out to Albany for financing. Governor Carey, nearing the end of his tenure, was strangely aloof, so Ravitch courted the legislature. At one point, when his request for taxes seemed all but dead, he arranged for police cars to escort David Rockefeller, chairman of the Chase Manhattan Bank, to a predawn tour of the subways. The patrician banker gazed in disbelief at the decrepit underground rail network, in which workers were still routing some trains with ancient hand switches. Hurrying back to his office, Rockefeller called Warren Anderson, the state Senate leader, and told him, "You got to pass Ravitch's tax package."[10]

The MTA launched an $8.5 billion spending program, which centered on buying new cars and refurbishing stations. It also ditched its prior policy of deferring maintenance; from now on, Kremlin-style five-year investment plans would be the rule. But of course, the MTA's capital commitments created huge future obligations, just as its pension did.

Inevitably, the fare was raised. (From 1980 to 1995, the fare tripled, from 50 cents to $1.50, while the cost of living merely doubled.) Nonetheless, fare revenues typically covered no more than 60 percent of costs.[11] To cover the gap, the MTA relied on federal and local subsidies, and on monies dedicated by the state, such as a portion of the revenue collected from tolls and various taxes and fees. Transit was thus knit ever more closely to the local economy.

In the latter part of the 1980s, the city's economy boomed. However, the recovery was distinctly unequal. Investment bankers in red suspenders, the new princes of the city, amassed fabulous sums without, seemingly, making a commitment to the city's industrial base. LBO artists such as Henry Kravis hollowed out companies and garnered stupendous fortunes, and even ordinary bond traders began to boast of seven-figure incomes and pricey second homes. Meanwhile, bus drivers got by on $30,000 a year.[12]

With the exception of retired police and firemen, who received Christmas pension bonuses courtesy of the rising stock market, public-sector unions had little to crow about. With the fiscal crisis over, they naturally wanted a share of the spoils. In strict financial terms, such workers had *not* fared as poorly as many believed. Their salaries had more than kept pace with inflation, for instance.[13] However, public employees, who constituted a sizable portion of the city's middle class, did not share in the general feeling of prosperity, especially as once affordable neighborhoods were steadily priced out of reach by white-collar types. By the late '80s, civil servants were smarting to make up lost ground, and the 1989 mayoral campaign provided a showcase for their frustrations. Mayor Koch (the unions' frequent tormentor) was challenged in the Democratic primary by David Dinkins, the Manhattan borough president. As an African American, Dinkins had a natural affinity with the swelling population of black civil servants. Though the campaign had a racial overlay, Dinkins got a strong boost from public employees of all colors who were tired of being made to feel like the scapegoat for the city's problems. His triumph signaled that public employees were on the way back.

The union unrest brimmed over, as it always seemed to, at transit. A group of radicals with roots in the Black Power and New Left movements had been agitating for higher benefits. They were winning a following through their lively newsletter, *Hell on Wheels*, which spoke to employees in a more personal voice than the mainline TWU. It focused on benefits and workplace issues, such as child care and separate toilets for female workers, that resonated with the rank and file.[14]

By the early '90s, Local 100, which was feeling intense pressure from *Hell on Wheels*, began to fixate on restoring the "20/50" pension—that is, retirement after twenty years at age fifty. For all their radicalism, transit employees cared about the same issues as more moderate autoworkers: fringe benefits, health care, pensions. No union leader could ignore them.

Sonny Hall, the president of the local, learned this the hard way. In 1992, he secured a decent wage gain but gave a little ground on benefits by agreeing to a modest $10 copay for doctors' visits. Outraged members voted the contract down—humiliating their leader.[15]

Hall tried to retake the offensive on pensions. Since direct negotiation of pensions was prohibited, he had to go through the legislature. This worked to the union's advantage. In the difficult budget climate of the early '90s, employers such as the MTA proved to be hard bargainers, while politically sensitive legislators were a bit more pliant.

As Local 100 was preparing to go to Albany, two powerful unions—the corrections officers and the sanitation workers—each won pensions equal to half of salary after twenty years' service, similar to what they had enjoyed in the Lindsay era. Neither could claim a total victory, because employees would have to make additional contributions. Still, it was a big step, one that reestablished the notion of a pension after only a half-career.[16]

To buttress its case for a 20/50 pension, the TWU hired Jonathan Schwartz, formerly the chief actuary of New York City, to lobby the legislature. Schwartz, who in his former position had skillfully documented the heavy cost of pension benefits, sang a rosier tune as a union consultant, arguing that they would not be much of a burden after all. ("What people call actuarial science," Schwartz explained, "has elements of art.") The Republican-controlled Senate readily consented to the pension increase—perhaps because, if it was passed, the Democratic governor, Mario Cuomo, could be painted as a spendthrift. To save Cuomo the embarrassment of a veto, the Democratic-controlled Assembly refused to pass it.[17]

Hall proposed a more modest pension increase in 1994, when he argued that transit workers be allowed to retire at fifty-five (down from sixty-two) after twenty-five years on the job. This time, the legislature assented. As in the case of the sanitation workers, employees who opted to retire early would have to cough up higher contributions (5.3 percent of salary, instead of 3 percent). But for the second time since the fiscal crisis, the pension had been liberalized. Other municipal workers quickly demanded—and got—equal treatment.

At transit, the seesaw battle over benefits continued. Negotiating with Hall's successor, the MTA won a round in 1994, when the union agreed to a 1 percent deduction for retiree health care. This concession, too, was bitterly unpopular (and was soon rescinded). The new head of Local 100 was forced to resign. He was replaced by Willie James, a former bus driver and the local's first African American president. Given that two-thirds of the members were nonwhite, James's ascension was a significant milestone.[18] Nonetheless, he faced an immediate threat from the *Hell on Wheels* vanguard, whose adherents had upped the ante by organizing a political faction within the union known as "New Directions."

Dissident groups in American unions have rarely succeeded. Labor unions are not exactly beacons of representative democracy (many are corrupt), and even in honest ones ruling cliques have been able to work the system to remain in power. However, New Directions was unusually tenacious. In 1997, it came within a hair of unseating the local's president. James now realized that he had to win a big increase—preferably in benefits—to prevent the radicals from taking over.

THE CAST was also changing at the MTA, thanks to the election of George Pataki, a little-known state senator, as governor. MTA-watchers feared that Pataki, who was committed to lowering taxes, would cut back on its budget. However, subway improvements are politically popular (even if the taxes to pay for them are not). Pataki appointed E. Virgil Conway, a banker and close Pataki confidant, as MTA chairman, and Conway came up with a time-honored method of advancing Pataki's agenda *without* relying on taxes. That is to say, the MTA went on a borrowing spree.[19]

While this pushed the ultimate financing (that is, the debt repayment) into the future, the MTA had to make interest payments out of its ordinary operating budget. The combined effect of rising interest and rising pensions soon was to overload the portion of the MTA budget that was *fixed*. Both the pension and the debt saddled the authority with long-term commitments.

Pataki, however, could afford to be sanguine, as almost from the day of his election, in 1994, the stock market began an inspired climb. As pension assets soared, long-underfunded retirement systems were suddenly in balance. The bull market eroded the caution of pension actuaries (as it did that of many Americans). The actuaries began to take for granted that the market would *continue* to increase, giving rise to ever rosier forecasts and a consequent liberalization of plans.

This game was played all over the country. In many cases the "extra" money from stock market gains was spent on higher benefits. In California, for instance, state troopers were raised to "three percent @ 50"—a pension at age fifty equal to 3 percent of salary times the number of years served. Thus, after thirty years on the job, a trooper got essentially his full salary. When Social Security kicked in, he would be earning well above it. The fallacy behind such largesse, of course, was that the stock market could reverse course at any time. The higher pensions were forever.

Some jurisdictions chose to "spend" the surplus by reducing their pension contributions. California did both; at the same time that promised benefits were rising, cities and towns were putting *less* into state retirement funds. Illinois cut back on contributions with virtually no regard to actuarial need. In New Jersey, Christine Whitman, a Republican governor elected in 1993, relied on buoyant stock market predictions to finance hefty tax cuts, which were the centerpiece of her administration. Thus, on the eve of her reelection bid, in 1997, New Jersey borrowed $2.8 billion and advanced the funds to its pension system, on the convenient theory that its pension managers would make more in the market than the state paid out in interest. New Jersey even raised benefits. Meanwhile, Trenton achieved a sort of transitory budget balance by drastically cutting pension contributions. For three consecutive years, New Jersey's contribution to the Police and Firemen's Retirement System was *zero*.[20]

Similarly buoyed by the bubbly stock market, New York City's pension assets soared from $59 billion to $106 billion over the years 1995–2000.[21] There is a well-known principle in pension economics known as "smoothing." The idea is that, since the stock market fluctuates, pension plans should not assume that a rapid rise (or a sudden drop) will necessarily persist. Therefore, plans book only a small portion of their gains at the outset, and the rest (depending on whether the gains do in fact last) over a period of years. However, by 1999, the gains were pretty tempting. The city's brassy mayor, Rudolph Giuliani, who had defeated Dinkins in 1993, had managed tight budgets during most of his tenure. But now he was gearing up for a U.S. Senate bid and loosening up on the budgetary reins.[22] As spending increased, it was becoming evident that whoever succeeded Giuliani would have to deal with a deficit.

So Giuliani turned to the pension system for some extra cash. He did this by restarting the clock on "smoothing"—an accounting maneuver that allowed the city's retirement system to record *all* of its recent stock market gains, which naturally made the system look more flush. To his credit, Robert North Jr., the city actuary, insisted on a dollop of conservatism, and scaled back his estimate of future asset growth. But the net effect of these changes was anything but prudent: they permitted the city to halve its customary pension investment.[23]

In 2000, New York contributed only $700 million to the various city funds, down from $1.4 billion the previous year. Thus, in the short run, each city agency and employer—the fire department, sanitation, hospitals, and so on—reaped a tremendous saving. Transit's pension expense was pared to a mere $16 million, which was less than 1 percent of its payroll.[24] From a longer-term perspective, this was patently reckless.

A similar dynamic played out at the state level. The state pension fund (which manages assets for state employees and for those of localities other than New York City) is managed by the state comptroller, then the Democrat H. Carl McCall. *He* was preparing to run for governor, against Pataki, in 2002. McCall had enormous political leverage, as he determined how much various employers were required to contribute. With the state's fund brimming over, he dished out political chits, reducing contributions from school districts, cities, state agencies, and so forth to practically zero. Some districts were cut precisely to zero.[25]

As the highest financial officer in the state, McCall might have paused to at least consider whether the stock market, on which the system's present overfunding was based, was entirely dependable. He might have noted that the market had risen at an unprecedented rate, and that stocks now traded at a sky-high multiple of earnings—with the exception of many of the newly minted dot-com stocks, which had no earnings at all. There was no shortage of prophets forecasting a market correction or even a crash. If McCall, who was the sole trustee for a million workers and retirees, was not to temper his exuberance, and to conduct his office with at least a modicum of prudence, who was?

Certainly not the unions. Organized labor *supported* the move to reduce contributions. Though it might have seemed a selfless gesture for the unions to have excused employers from contributing to "their" funds, in fact it was cynical in the extreme. Since pension benefits were an inviolable obligation of the state, the financial condition of the funds was of no concern to the unions. One way or another the state would *have* to make good on their benefits.

And now, with employers enjoying a pension holiday, the unions demanded that the bounty be shared with the employees—that is, that they also be spared from contributing. This argument was deeply flawed. The principle of a defined benefit is that the employer promises a stated (thus "defined") pension and assumes the full risk of paying it. The very reason such plans exist is to relieve the employee of any responsibility for what happens in the market, or with other contingent factors—life expectancies, for example—that would affect the plan's cost. Since the employer assumes the full downside risk, it should also reap the savings.

New York City had already learned that straying from this principle could be costly. In the late '60s, it had promised retired cops and firemen the so-called Christmas bonus—a variable benefit tied to the return in the stock market. Eventually, this was converted into a straight bonus—paid regardless of what the city earned in the market.*

Now, not only was the city stuck, but other unions were agitating for the same plum. Early in 1999, Norman Seabrook, head of the corrections officers union, demanded that *his* members get the pension supplement. Seabrook was a buddy of Pataki's and regularly went to the races with the governor and

*By 2007, the supplement was worth $12,000 a year—paid in addition to the normal pension.

with Senate leader Joseph Bruno. Though that surely helped, it was Pataki's looming election battle against McCall that truly loosened Albany's purse strings. For political reasons, neither party could afford to say no.

Seabrook not only got the supplement, he went after "heart bill" protection (as in the case of cops, this would entitle members with heart ailments to the presumption of a job-related disability, and thus a pension equal to three-quarters of salary). Mayor Giuliani—who would have to pay for the higher benefit, rightly objected: "There is no valid medical study that has confirmed that a police, fire or correction officer's heart disease is a direct result of performance of duty."[26] No matter: the legislature approved, and Pataki signed, the increase. Subsequently, it extended heart bill status to sanitation workers and emergency medical technicians.

For good measure, corrections workers argued that employees with hepatitis, HIV, or tuberculosis should be entitled to a presumption that their conditions were, similarly, job-related. The city protested: "It will be virtually impossible to disprove the presumption and assert that the condition was not contracted in the line of duty."[27] It also warned that if the measure was enacted, firemen and cops would demand similar treatment. But Albany approved the bill. Then, as predicted, the firemen and cops got an HIV bill too. They also won back a cherished perk, as the legislature agreed to redefine their "final average salary" as their last year's pay.*

Most of these pension bills were passed by *unanimous* votes in the legislature. Consultants such as Schwartz were able to certify that, given the present surplus, increases would not require an appropriation from the budget. The prospect of a "free" entitlement made the legislators giddy. Pataki vetoed more of these bills than he approved, but the temptation to sign at least some was enormous. The unions contributed heavily to gubernatorial and legislative campaigns and simply could not be ignored. Transit's Local 100 spent $1.2 million on political donations and related expenses in 1999–2000 alone.[28]

---

*In 1973, when the legislature revoked this perk, a sanguine head of the PBA predicted they would win it back in twenty years. He turned out to be six years off.

New York State was hardly unique in such matters. Every statehouse in the country had been brought to heel, to a greater or lesser extent, by public-sector unions. However, New York's system was especially corrupt. Instead of bargaining for benefits with the agencies responsible for paying them, unions merely had to gain the endorsement of legislators and officials whose motives were patently political.

McCall made a pension cost-of-living increase a central part of his campaign. Older retirees, who had retired on small salaries, were living on pensions of less than $15,000, and for them an increase was justified. The city favored a one-time raise *only* for those who were most in need. McCall, however, was pushing for an across-the-board, annual adjustment for everyone.[29]

Not to be outdone, in 1999 Pataki threw a bouquet to the Civil Service Employees' Association, which represented 70,000 state employees. The state had offered a hefty wage hike but the contract remained unsigned. The union was fed up with its members' paying 3 percent of wages into the pension fund when the state was paying so little. So the governor proposed a sweetener: eliminate the contribution for anyone who had served ten years. The union snapped it up. Legally, of course, the parties weren't allowed to negotiate pensions, so they settled for a little artifice: a side memo in which they agreed to jointly seek the necessary legislation.[30] Pataki had to know that every other union negotiating with the state would demand the same, and they did.

The city unions came next. The first contract to expire, in December of 1999, was transit. In 1998, the union had managed to get the legislature to approve the 50/20 pension, but Pataki had vetoed it. The MTA was not having difficulty either hiring or retaining workers; thus, from its standpoint, sweetening the pension was unnecessary.[31] Nonetheless, Willie James, the head of Local 100, was under intense pressure from his members, including those in the rival New Directions caucus, to reclaim their lost benefits.

Seeking to exploit the precedent set by Pataki and the state employees, James held out for a rich settlement. "You're overfunded," the union chief kept saying. "What are you saving it for?" North, the city actuary, did not totally disagree. Given the pension system's flush condition, he advised the MTA that it could afford to lower member contributions.[32]

James snagged a 12 percent wage hike over three years, a very steep rise in an era of low inflation. But his big prize was in pensions. The MTA agreed to recommend to the legislature that it reduce the employees' contribution of 5.3 percent to a mere 2 percent—a significant saving. Thus, early retirement, which had been awarded to transit in 1994 on the condition that the workers pay for it, would—pending legislative approval—be theirs for free. Posthaste, James sped to Albany. Pataki had vetoed a pension bill the previous year, but now the climate was changing. As a Pataki aide recalled, "McCall was running. Stocks were doing well. The legislature was going to get credit; I figured: 'Why shouldn't we get some credit?' "

Pataki did take credit. In July 2000, the governor signed a package of legislation that amounted to the biggest pension hike since the Lindsay era. (Appropriately enough, the governor held a pen in one hand and a union T-shirt in the other.) The legislation cut contributions for state, transit, and city employees,* and, what's more, it partially indexed pension benefits to inflation—an unusual and costly plum. The cost of these changes over the ensuing decade was estimated at $36.5 billion. Pataki, McCall, and various legislators gushed that they had wrought an "historic" change, a "milestone," and so forth.[33]

None seemed to notice that the stock market had also hit a milestone, or, more aptly, a breaking point. In March, the bull market had finally snapped. In the subsequent three months, investors furiously unloaded tech stocks. By the time the legislature acted on pensions, shares in Amazon.com had plunged from 107 to 34 and the tech-laden Nasdaq index had tumbled 20 percent. The pension surplus that was the basis of the legislation was vanishing by the week, the day, the hour. But it was too

*Transit employee contributions were reduced to 2 percent of salary. City cops and firemen had their contributions cut by roughly half. State troopers did not contribute at all. Other city and state employees continued to pay 3 percent of salary for their first ten years, after which they contributed nothing.

late; the promises had been made. Giuliani abruptly canceled plans to cut the city's personal income tax and announced a hiring freeze.[34] The chill was on.

LOCAL 100 staged a disorganized election in November 2000 (while an equally disorganized contest was being held for U.S. president). In the prelude to the balloting, evidence surfaced that various union officers had cheated on their expenses. With the union in disarray, the members elected the New Directions slate, now headed by Roger Toussaint, a burly, stern-spoken native of Trinidad.[35]

The transit workers' new leader bore some superficial resemblance to Quill. Raised in a one-room house in a family of nine, Toussaint grew up amid a populace still seething at their former colonial overlords in Britain, which had relinquished the reins when Toussaint was a boy. As a youth, he was active in student protests and, on one occasion, arrested.[36] He emigrated to the United States and attended Brooklyn College, where he again became immersed in left-wing politics. Then he quit school to become a welder. In 1984, Toussaint joined the Transit Authority as a subway car cleaner—a poorly paid job that stoked his working-class consciousness. Within a year, he was promoted; however, he became incensed by what he deemed the MTA's arbitrary approach to discipline, as well as its insensitivity to the workers, and quickly became active in the TWU.[37]

By the mid-'90s, Toussaint was aligned with New Directions, and getting release time to do union work—investigating complaints, filing grievances, and publishing a newsletter that, in his words, was "extremely critical" of the Transit Authority. There is little doubt he was a thorn in the authority's side. In July 1998, a transit worker slipped and fell on a third rail, and was instantly electrocuted. Toussaint sped to the scene and made a videotape that he provided to the family's lawyer. Three months later the Transit Authority fired him. The case was convoluted, and involved whether Toussaint had faked a back injury (the TA spent long hours tailing him, without getting the goods). The MTA ultimately reinstated him but Toussaint's battle with the Authority raised his standing among the members, who instinctively favored rebels. However, Toussaint was less fiery than his image. In a comment that is also evocative of Quill, a union lawyer remarked, "It was always the rock throwers versus the cautious ones; Roger was cautious."[38]

Once in power, Toussaint sought to move New Directions toward the center. But he lacked his distant predecessor's talent for mockery, including self-mockery—a certain moral pliancy that had enabled Quill to sail with the current. Toussaint was righteous and grave; his sense of grievance was too acute. Full of high purpose, he proclaimed in his victory speech, "We have to be as accountable to the public as we are to members."[39]

Precisely seven weeks after Toussaint was elected, Conway resigned and Pataki appointed Peter Kalikow as MTA chairman. These two new leaders—Toussaint and Kalikow—would decide the fate of transit pensions and, ultimately, of transit service itself.

Kalikow was the scion to a real estate fortune started in Queens, just across the East River from Manhattan. H. J. Kalikow & Co. had been founded by his grandfather, a Russian immigrant who had scraped together the money to buy farmland in the years before World War II.[40] The Kalikows put apartments where the farms had been and struck it rich.

Peter attended Hofstra University on Long Island in the mid-1960s, where he got a degree in business administration and studied General Motors. After college, he went to work for his father, though in his spare time he opened a factory in Italy to produce a sports car he called the Momo Mirage. Alas, though Kalikow could sell it for $13,000, the cars cost him $20,000 to make. Kalikow went home.

Not unlike Donald Trump, another heir to a Queens developer, Kalikow had a yen to build sexier stuff than apartments in the boroughs. He convinced his father they should take a little risk, and in the late 1960s and early '70s the Kalikows started buying property in Manhattan. Peter went on to build luxury apartments, office buildings—even a hotel next to the World Trade Center. Some of it was highly speculative, but in the booming market of the 1980s everything he tried seemed to work.

With success, Kalikow grew increasingly brassy. He got buildings that stood in his way condemned, he evicted tenants, he beat back lawsuits. He was smart, but in an intuitive way as opposed to being analytical. He did not prepare for the possibility of a market downturn, or for failure of any sort. In 1990, the market did turn, and Kalikow was suddenly overextended. In 1991, at age forty-eight, he paid the speculator's price and was forced to file for bankruptcy. This was due to a truly reckless gamble—buying the city's afternoon tabloid, the *New York Post.*

Kalikow had become intensely interested in public service, and the failed investment in the *Post* exposed him to a fair amount of ridicule. Other papers gleefully reported that the bankrupt millionaire's assets included a trio of mansions and estates, as well an $8.5 million yacht and a collection of vintage Rolls-Royces, Maseratis, Ferraris, and other cars.[41] He owed his banks $1 billion and his public life seemed over.[42]

Kalikow, though, had the formidable advantage of a man who is too cocky to ever believe he is beaten. Also, the banks were quick to extend him new credit. Although he lost the *Post* and his hotel, he kept some of his real estate, including the Park Avenue skyscraper that was his signature building. As the economy recovered, he was soon riding high again.

Both before and after his bankruptcy, Kalikow sprinkled donations around to politicians, mostly Republican ones. In 1979, he and another developer had met over breakfast with Alfonse D'Amato, an officeholder and Republican Party stalwart in Nassau County. D'Amato told them he was going to run for U.S. Senate. "From which state?" Kalikow joked. But he agreed to serve as finance chairman for the campaign. D'Amato won, and after that the two became nearly inseparable.[43]

Ironically, given Kalikow's Republican ties, it was a Democrat, Governor Mario Cuomo, who launched his public career, naming him to the MTA board. In 1994, Kalikow backed Cuomo's opponent, the then obscure Pataki, who was a protégé of his friend D'Amato. Pataki won, and rewarded Kalikow by naming him a commissioner of the New York and New Jersey Port Authority, the agency that ran the airports, the bridge and tunnel crossings in the metropolitan area and, among other assets, the World Trade

Center. It was an important post but (prior to the attack on the Trade Center, anyway) not especially visible. In 1999, Pataki returned him to the MTA, this time as vice chairman. Two years later, he was moved up to chairman. This agency, which ran the transportation system he had ridden as a boy, was more to his taste. The subways and buses were highly visible. Kalikow would be responsible for moving eight million people a day. The political writers, remembering his adventure with the *Post*, were skeptical, to say the least. Kalikow was seen as a political novice, probably a dilettante. Worse, he was viewed as beholden to Pataki, and too close to D'Amato, who had a questionable record on ethics* and who, since losing his Senate seat, had become a high-priced lobbyist on MTA-related business.

The system that Kalikow inherited was physically much improved. Some $50 billion had been reinvested in the subways since the Ravitch era, and train cars now ran an average of 175,000 miles (145 trips around the circuit) between breakdowns. Dozens of stations had been rebuilt.[44] Also, subway ridership had resoundingly rebounded to its level of the early '60s.[45]

However, the financial picture was darkening. Pataki had eliminated the state's former practice of subsidizing the MTA's capital projects, forcing the agency to borrow ever more.†[46] The MTA's costs were also inflated by high-level influence peddling. In one notorious incident, D'Amato collected $500,000 for placing a single telephone call to Conway on behalf of a client hoping to remodel space for the MTA. The project ended up running hundreds of millions above budget.[47]

The full extent of ethics problems under Conway was not yet known (two MTA executives would later be fired when evidence surfaced that they had taken bribes).[48] But the MTA's image had been tarnished by the whiff of cronyism. Hopeful subway contractors contributed to Pataki cam-

---

*In 1991, D'Amato was rebuked by the Senate Ethics Committee for conducting "the business of his office in an improper and inappropriate manner," including allowing his brother to use his office for lobbying.

†From 2000 to 2004, the MTA received $16 billion in capital funds, with the primary sources being $8 billion in bond sales and debt restructuring, $5.8 billion in federal grants, and $460 million in city appropriations. New York State contributed nothing.

paigns as a matter of course, and the MTA's board was thick with the governor's pals. The appointment of Kalikow fit the pattern: a rich benefactor claiming his reward.[49]

But the pundits had underestimated Kalikow. He was determined to be a forceful, independent chairman—not a crony.[50] And he brought considerable political talents to the job. The secret of his charm was that he didn't hide his ego or apologize for his wealth. ("I don't take a salary," he noted a few years after becoming MTA chairman. "I paid $70 million in taxes in three years. Who the hell do I have to apologize to?")[51] His bankruptcy, which was born of his characteristic cockiness, had softened his roughest edges. "I thought I could do no wrong," he admitted later. "I was a victim of my own success—of my hubris."[52] Failure had given the new MTA chief a heightened awareness, a sense of financial risk.

By the time Kalikow took over, in early 2001, the MTA had more debt on its books than all but a few states. He was just settling into the job when, on September 11, the Trade Center towers were attacked and the world, for a moment, stopped. New York had an exceedingly difficult recovery. Business activity, including tourism, was greatly slowed. Moreover, the stock market's losses significantly deepened. The city's pension funds collapsed, from $106 billion to $78 billion.[53]

All this was devastating news for the MTA as well as for every department of the city, as they were all hit with steadily (and sharply) rising pension bills. Simply restoring the prior level of assets was no longer enough. The retirement system had in effect been thrice burned. Funds were depleted due to the low level of contributions during the late '90s. They had suffered drastic losses in the market. And their liabilities had been swollen by the hefty increases in benefits approved in Albany.

Michael Bloomberg, the new mayor, put the city on an austerity diet, but he was powerless to do anything about pensions, or about health care expenses that rose automatically with medical bills.[54] Bloomberg thus raised taxes on ordinary New Yorkers to pay for pensions. He served up an incredibly steep 18½ percent hike in the property tax. Within the year, every penny of the increase had been absorbed by the rise in pension costs.[55]

Meanwhile, Bloomberg asked North, the actuary, for ideas on overhauling the pension system.[56] North explored various alternatives, including switching the city from a traditional, defined benefit system to 401(k)s, which was the path being followed by many private employers. A few states around the country were contemplating such a switch, as a means of freeing themselves from pensions. North thought it was a bad idea. The original justification for public pensions—that they would deter employees from leaving—still made sense. Unlike employers in the private sector, who thrive on mobility, government employers such as schools, mass transit, and fire departments still depended upon *stable* workforces.

What North favored was retaining the present system but trimming its cost. Benefits should be lower; contributions higher. Also, given that people were living longer, it made no sense to be *lowering* the retirement age. Bloomberg agreed that cuts were warranted. However, such a step would, of course, require Albany to go along—unthinkable in the aftermath of the Trade Center attack, in which firemen and cops had died heroes' deaths. For the moment, Bloomberg did nothing.

Kalikow was not so timid. The MTA was still reeling from 9/11 and in 2002 the authority offered a bare-bones contract. Among other terms, it demanded that employees contribute an extra $1,000 each toward their pensions. The prickly Toussaint regarded the entire offer as insulting. Relations between him and Gary Dellaverson, the MTA's labor negotiator, turned chilly. Toussaint could not afford to disappoint his supporters (particularly those in New Directions), and the union prepared for a strike. With a shutdown looming, the mayor bought a bicycle as a sign to New Yorkers that they could pedal their way through a work stoppage. But Kalikow, for whom this was a first negotiation, was anxious to avoid a strike. Hours before the deadline, he got personally involved and sweetened the pot. He dropped the pension demand and improved support for health care. Toussaint, for his part, accepted a quite meager wage increase and agreed to productivity improvements. Thus a strike was averted.[57]

Kalikow decided that Toussaint was more reasonable than his troublemaker's image—a man he could work with. However, he was worried about the employees' rising fringe benefits. So was Dellaverson. The two began to think about ways of trimming costs in the next contract. In the meantime, Kalikow tried to fix his budget. The year after the labor settlement, in 2003, he bumped the fare from $1.50 to $2.00. Even with the increase, the MTA was anticipating huge deficits.[58]

Pataki, resisting calls for subsidies, said the MTA should simply get by with less.[59] However, its biggest expenses could not be trimmed. Pension costs were exploding, and so was interest. (The MTA's debt had doubled during Pataki's tenure to $21 billion.) And the MTA's continuing capital needs were huge—roughly $3 billion a year just for maintenance and upkeep. Within a few years, the agency projected, debt service, pensions, and other fringes would eat up 40 percent of its budget.[60]

As the MTA's fiscal trouble deepened, Kalikow began to prowl the corridors of Washington for increased subsidies—sloughing off criticism that a Republican should not be foisting such burdens on government. The MTA chairman would explain that mass transit was necessary for business, and therefore transit subsidies were good *Republican* policies. He would suck on a Tootsie Roll as he made this pitch, which made him seem boyishly earnest. Surprisingly, Kalikow managed to get nearly twice as much federal aid out of a reluctant Bush administration as the MTA had received during the Clinton years.[61]

He also began to pressure his patron, Governor Pataki, for a larger capital authorization than the governor, or the legislature, wanted. Then he implored the governor to raise the mortgage recording tax, the motor vehicle fee, and other state levies, and to earmark the extra money for the MTA. Appointed as Pataki's man at the MTA, Kalikow was becoming the system's advocate in Albany. Astonishingly, he got the new taxes he wanted. Next, after a bit of waffling, he opposed a plan, promoted eagerly by Pataki, to sell railyards owned by the MTA to the New York Jets for a football stadium. Kalikow declared that the Jets' offer was an "insult."

Though still a Pataki supporter, Kalikow had become more concerned with his own legacy. He wanted to leave the hundred-year-old subway system in better shape than he had found it—as he had not been able to do with the *Post.* Also, he had fallen a little in love with the subways: with the system's vastness and its centrality to the average New Yorker—and, naturally, with his role as its protector. Even the *New York Times*, which early in Kalikow's tenure had criticized the chairman for being a carbon copy of Pataki,[62] changed its mind about him. Seeming surprised that Kalikow, unlike his predecessor, was willing to challenge the governor, the *Times* observed that he had been "better known as a Republican donor and heir to a real estate business than as a forceful voice in civic affairs. . . . But in recent months, Mr. Kalikow has become a far more forceful advocate for the system than Mr. Conway was."[63]

In 2004 and early 2005, Kalikow made some painful decisions. He deferred the plan to build a new subway line on Second Avenue (a dream of subway architects for decades), as well as other expansion projects. Also, he proposed eliminating bus routes, cutting back on late-night subway service, and other service cuts.

Kalikow, therefore, approached the 2005 contract talks with a feeling that *he* had already made some sacrifices. He had raised the fare, he had pressed for new taxes, he had given up, at least for now, on expanding the system. The TWU would also have to give. And the workers, he maintained, had little to complain about. A typical bus operator earned $63,000 (those close to retirement earned in the neighborhood of $75,000, and sometimes more, depending on their overtime). Even a low-ranking cleaner was paid $51,000.[64] Kalikow thought of his workforce as among the privileged—blue-collar workers with middle-class incomes.

Although this could sound patronizing from someone who tinkered with Ferraris for a hobby, Kalikow's analysis was basically correct. The average high school–educated worker in the New York area earned $29,000; a motorman earned more than twice as much.[65] Thanks to its high wages and benefits, transit perennially had a long list of job applicants and razor-thin turnover (only 4 percent a year). Subway jobs were *good* jobs.

Since the MTA was beating its budget projections, thanks to the resurgent city economy and a real estate boom, Kalikow was prepared to offer what he considered a decent wage improvement. But the benefit structure was out of line. In particular, he wanted to cut back on pensions.

The pension obligation was simply staggering. Transit contributed $381 million, or 14 percent of the payroll, to the city pension funds. By 2009, the bill was expected to nearly double, to $620 million—more than four times the total of a decade earlier. Health care cost the authority an additional $410 million, and it too was rising at double-digit rates. And transit workers contributed only 2 percent of their salaries for pensions and nothing for health care. Meanwhile, they as well as spouses and dependents got full medical coverage including vision and dental—for life—with free generic drugs and a minimal $15 copay on doctors' visits.[66]

To Kalikow, this plush coverage inescapably evoked the example of GM, whose precarious condition and ever deeper losses had become front-page news. Kalikow repeatedly told a fellow board member that the automaker's troubles derived from its pension and health care obligations. "It scares the s—— out of me," the developer said.[67]

What Kalikow didn't understand was why nobody else in the city was doing anything about it. The MTA's predicament was hardly unique. The fire department shelled out $490 million for pensions just in 2005. Within a few years, its pension expense was projected to rise to an astounding $760 million—78 percent of its payroll.[68] Health care for retired firefighters would raise the total to more than 100 percent. Incredibly, taxpayers would be paying as much for retired firemen as for active ones.

Overall, the city's pension bill had soared from $695 million in 2000 to $3.67 *billion* in 2005. This figure was projected to nearly double *again* by 2009.[69] (Other cities in the state were also dealing with alarming increases.) And while cities were paying more, the employees were paying considerably less.[70]

To Bloomberg's immense frustration, soaring pensions and other fringes undercut his efforts to control the budget. Though he had kept wage growth to the rate of inflation, the total budget, thanks to pensions and health care, was growing far more quickly. By 2005, fringes accounted for a third of the city's labor costs. Within a few years they would amount to *two*-thirds.[71]

Just as the United States could not escape ever higher Social Security and Medicare bills, the city was becoming hostage to pensions and health care. It's true that neither New York State nor the city had a budget crisis. What they had was a budget precariously balanced thanks to the highest tax rates in the country,[72] and to a booming real estate sector. It was unlikely, and presumably undesirable, that the city could keep raising taxes. And sooner or later, the real estate market would cool (or so economists kept saying).

In 2005, political and civic leaders began to talk up the case for pension reform. The city's Independent Budget Office warned of a growing danger from pensions, and the Citizens Budget Commission, a private group, called for an end to traditional pensions and for sharp cuts in the city's lavish health care package.[73] The CBC concluded that New York's pensions were far more generous then they needed to be; once again, many public employees were earning (including Social Security) more in retirement than on the job. No one in the private sector enjoyed such a pension. New York's pensions were rich even compared with those at General Motors, the gold standard of private benefits. In 2004, a freshly retired municipal employee with thirty years' experience drew a pension of, on average, \$42,000—20 percent more than his counterpart at GM.[74] And unlike the case with the retired autoworker, when the city clerk or subway maintenance man began to collect Social Security, *his* pension would not be reduced.

Statehouses around the country, which once had followed New York's lead, were, in a tentative way, beginning to retreat from such costly guarantees. California governor Arnold Schwarzenegger was pushing a referendum to move the state from pensions to 401(k)s, and Alaska and Michigan had already closed their pensions to new employees. Other states were letting employees choose between defined contribution plans and traditional pensions. On the other hand, some states were so far behind in their pension bills that they had yet to propose a remedy at all. In New Jersey, the reckless Whitman gamble had backfired due to the market crash, leaving the state's pension system $25 billion in the red.[75]

In New York City, it was an open secret that Bloomberg wanted to rein in pensions.[76] However, he shied away from pressing the issue.

As for the legislature, it seemed not to have noticed that the stock market had fallen. It continued to pass dozens of pension sweeteners (most of which were duly vetoed) every year. In 2003, it approved (by votes of 148–0 in the Democratic-controlled Assembly and 62–0 in the Republican-led Senate) a 20/50 pension for transit. The MTA asked Pataki to veto it, and he did. His main objection, as stated in his veto message, was that the MTA, as well as the mayor, "contend that this type of enhanced benefit should be the subject of mutual agreement through collective bargaining." This patent attempt at passing the buck ran counter to the spirit of the law that restricted pension amendments to the legislative process. In 2004, the legislature reapproved the transit bill, which Pataki, in identical language, again vetoed.[77] This subtly encouraged Toussaint to press ahead. He reckoned that if he and the authority could reach a pension deal, the governor would sign it.

For internal reasons, Toussaint needed a fat settlement. The scantiness of the gains in 2002 had left members with a sour aftertaste, especially as the MTA's revenues rebounded. Also, Toussaint's high-handed management style had alienated many of his supporters. Rather than empower the rank and file, as the purists in New Directions had hoped, their goateed leader had micromanaged Local 100 and concentrated power in the president's office. He was suspicious of his members and incapable of taking advice. He fired his most able lieutenant, a Yale grad named Marc Kagan, merely for expressing discontent with a provision of the 2002 contract.[78] Meanwhile, Toussaint resisted peace overtures from the union's old guard, who still dominated the TWU (the parent organization). Mistrusted on both left and right, Toussaint was dangerously isolated within his own union.

While Kalikow approached the negotiations as a chance to rein in pensions, Toussaint, in view of his weak political position, needed to seal the pension enhancement that had eluded him in Albany.[79] The pressure for a big settlement increased considerably in the fall, when the MTA (which received a portion of the taxes on commercial property transfers as well as on mortgages) disclosed rather sheepishly that it would reap a huge, unexpected surplus, approaching $1 billion, thanks to the continuing boom in real estate. Kalikow had to explain that the bull market in property was *temporary,* and that once it cooled, the agency still expected very large deficits. This did not go over well with the union, especially when the MTA earmarked a small portion of the surplus for holiday-season fare cuts—giving riders (but not employees) a Christmas gift. Toussaint hit the roof. If previously the forty-nine-year-old union chief had been suspicious, now he was apoplectic. His troops were ready to strike then and there.

The contract expired a minute after midnight on the morning of Friday, December 16. In mid-October, Dellaverson sent Toussaint a new contract. The terms called for future transit workers to get a pension only after thirty years' service, and only at age sixty-two, instead of the present 25/55 arrangement. Also, they would have to contribute 3 percent of their salary, instead of 2 percent, to pensions, and make a small contribution to health care as well.[80] Since no present employees would be affected, Kalikow figured that the concession would be no big deal. He could not have been more wrong.

Toussaint replied that both the pension and the health care benefit would have to *increase.* As to future employees, he snapped that he would not sell out "the unborn." In the next few weeks, he proclaimed, repeatedly, that defending the unborn was a matter of "principle."

As strained as that sounded to Kalikow, it accurately reflected the feelings of Toussaint's members. Benefits were the ticket to, and a symbol of, a middle-class lifestyle they had never quite obtained. Transit workers still did dirty jobs, and they still bristled from the tight supervision of their MTA overseers. Indeed, the tension between bosses and workers had not greatly subsided since Quill's day. Employees called in sick an average of thirteen days a year, a number that suggested a high degree of passive resistance or shirking (or both). Also, the authority issued 17,000 disciplinary notices (one for every two workers) a year. To many nonwhite employees, these frequent reprimands reeked of plantation justice. Retirement and medical benefits not only made the job tolerable, they made it halfway respectable. To give them up would be to retreat to a darker era.

By early December, Dellaverson was seriously worried about the lack of progress in the negotiations. His biggest concern was that Toussaint was not in command of his executive board, and thus wasn't in a position to deal. When Dellaverson proposed that they submit to arbitration, Toussaint balked. The labor leader was painting himself into a corner, publicly insisting he would not make concessions on the pension.

Basil Paterson, Toussaint's cool-eyed lawyer, also was worried. Paterson, a former deputy mayor and state senator from Harlem, had advised or negotiated with just about all of the city's unions at one time or another, and was known for his dogged willingness to keep talking until, somehow, he got to an agreement. What concerned Paterson was that he did not have a clear sense of Toussaint's goals. The fraternity of New York labor leaders was similarly mystified. Toussaint was demanding richer benefits in addition to annual 8 percent wage hikes—clearly, the other leaders felt, an unrealistic target.

On December 7, Dellaverson sweetened his offer on wages to 5 percent over two years. He repeated that the retirement age had to be lifted to sixty-two. Toussaint once again insisted that he would not sell out the unborn—a charged phrase that seemed to link pensions to the abortion issue. Three days later, on the Saturday before the deadline, transit workers jammed the Jacob K. Javits Convention Center, where they voted to give the board of Local 100 authority to strike. The Reverend Jesse Jackson was on hand, implying a civil rights connection to the union's grievances. Toussaint, barking through a megaphone, rallied his members with a cry of "No contract, no work!" They erupted in cheers and waived red bandanas.[81]

Though he seemed to be egging them on, Toussaint was actually stalling for time—trying to satisfy the rabble while desperately searching for an alternative to striking. His secret wish was that Kalikow would come to the rescue again. There was a well-honed myth within the union that the steely Dellaverson was to blame for their troubles. Paterson tried to get Kalikow involved in the talks, but the developer, who was wise to the union's strategy, curtly said, "No back channels. Gary is doing this."

The talks were held in the MTA's suite, on the thirty-third floor of the Grand Hyatt hotel. The MTA usually had several bargainers at the table; the union six or seven. A coterie of the union's board members was often milling around the halls, putting added pressure on Toussaint. Periodically he would go outside and greet supporters and say a few words to the press. Kalikow, who was camped in a separate suite, fought off boredom as he waited for reports from Dellaverson, munching on club sandwiches and staring at the television. When the sessions ended, often late in the evening, Kalikow would sneak through secret exits and slip past waiting reporters to his chauffeured Lincoln Continental.

Local businesses—retailers in particular—were terrified by the prospect of a strike over Christmas. The Partnership for New York City, an organization of local CEOs, reached out to Paterson and suggested that he bring his client around. Thus, on the Monday before the deadline, Toussaint met with a delegation of pinstriped executives. Terry Lundgren, the $3.5 million a year chief executive of Federated Department Stores, was in the uncharacteristic position of having to plead with a onetime track maintenance worker from Trinidad. Lundgren, whose own pension was worth a minimum of $738,000 a year, told Toussaint that transit pensions were not worth striking over.

Stores such as Macy's and Bloomingdale's, which Federated owned, realized a large portion of their annual sales over the Christmas season, Lundgren noted. Their employees as well as their customers depended on mass transit. A strike would cost them—and the city—dearly.

Toussaint graciously conceded the point. However, he noted, his primary concern was Local 100. He talked about the union's desire for respect, and went over the contractual issues, emphasizing that the MTA's pension and health care terms were unacceptable. The businessmen came away disheartened, especially when Toussaint brought up the touchy subject of Dellaverson, whom he accused of lying and of ruining any chance of meaningful bargaining.

Actually, Kalikow was just as adamant on the pension issue as his negotiator was. Kalikow was *fixated* on pensions. Dellaverson, if anything, was more flexible, because he understood the subtleties of managing a workforce. Unlike some would-be reformers, he did *not* want to abolish the pension, which he recognized was vital for hanging on to employees. He simply thought fifty-five was an unaffordable, and unjustifiable, age at which to grant retirement.

Toussaint suspected that transit was being used as a stalking horse for the mayor or possibly the governor, as part of a grand attack on government pensions. A true child of labor, Toussaint detested the thought of giving in on pensions, which he equated with surrender to the ruling class. He told an interviewer, "There is a certain drumbeat and bias to roll back the gains of the middle class and the working-class people. That's part of the agenda of the right wing of this country, which we intend to fight tooth and nail."[82]

The power structure had failed to convince him with Monday's genteel business meeting. On Tuesday, a Brooklyn judge, granting a request of the state attorney general, Eliot Spitzer, formally enjoined the 33,700 subway and bus workers from going on strike. The Bloomberg administration joined the fray with a suit seeking punitive fines against Local 100 and its members. The mayor kept the heat on in private, getting word to Dellaverson that he did not want the MTA to pay too dearly for peace.

The union countered with rallies in all five boroughs. Toussaint, along with the ubiquitous Reverend Jackson, the Reverend Al Sharpton, and various nontransit labor leaders, gathered outside the Grand Hyatt on East 42nd Street. Waving a copy of the city's suit, Toussaint thundered in his best imitation of Quill yet, "If Mayor Bloomberg wants to know what we think about this lawsuit, I'll show you," and tore it to shreds. For a moment, it was possible to hear in his lilting cadence an echo of the real Mike Quill gleefully exhorting, "An *injoonction* can't run a subway."[83]

On Wednesday, negotiators met for four and a half hours. The MTA upped its wage offer to 6 percent over twenty-seven months. Otherwise, they made no progress. Toussaint continued to plead for Kalikow to make an appearance. Bloomberg warned that a strike would cost the city's economy upwards of $600 million a day and issued emergency instructions for a walkout. Governor Pataki chimed in, warning of "dire consequences" for strikers. Though the threatened strike was little more than twenty-four hours away, the governor was nowhere near the city and, indeed, was en route to New Hampshire to test the presidential waters. The *Wall Street Journal* called on Pataki to prove his mettle by "stand[ing] up to the transit workers union that is threatening to ruin New York City's Christmas."[84] But as far as the governor was concerned, it was Kalikow's ball game. The local press generally sided with the MTA. According to polls, most New Yorkers opposed a strike, but transit workers were solidly in favor.[85]

Thursday was foggy and cold. New Yorkers made last-minute arrangements: contingency plans for getting to—or skipping—work. TWU members gathered outside the Grand Hyatt, less in anticipation of a settlement, it seemed, than to celebrate the expected cessation of service. Toussaint, his close-cropped beard showing a dapper streak of gray, sauntered outside and, leading the crowd in a rehearsed chant, asked for guidance should the MTA fail to make a "fair" offer—to which the multitude gleefully shouted, "Shut it down!"[86]

Inside, the bargaining was going slowly.[87] As the afternoon wore on, Paterson, who was painfully aware of the legal penalties that would befall his client, kept urging the parties (on both sides) to keep at it. Dellaverson gave a little ground; the union stood pat. Toussaint was increasingly argumentative; Dellaverson, peering from behind his wire-rimmed glasses, thought he was under enormous pressure. In the evening, as if afraid to abandon his constituency, Toussaint ducked out to give a press conference. Some militants led by John Mooney, the union vice president for station workers, tried to storm the podium. Toussaint's security guards bodily shoved him aside while Toussaint kept talking and tried to appear calm. He returned to the conference room in an agitated state. Then Dellaverson saw Toussaint on television, ripping into the MTA. Dropping his customary detachment, Dellaverson bolted downstairs to give the media *his* version.[88] It was now well after 10 p.m.; the deadline was less than two hours away. At 11 p.m., Kalikow joined the bargaining and faced Toussaint for the first time.

With the sixty-three-year-old chairman at the table the pace quickened. The MTA upped its wage offer to 9 percent over three years. Kalikow noticed as midnight struck that Toussaint did not leave the table: an encouraging sign. At 2 a.m., they were still thrashing out the MTA's demands for concessions on benefits. Kalikow conferred with Dellaverson in private and then cut the health care demand in half. That left the pension.

Kalikow sensed that the moment for reaching a deal, so long elusive, had perhaps arrived. He made a final concession: employees could continue to retire after twenty-five years' service. However, he insisted on raising the minimum age to sixty-two, which had been his main goal all along. "It's only for the future," he noted. "Nobody working now will lose a penny."

The invitation to punish the next generation made Toussaint bristle. He would *never* sell out the unborn. He and his aides, their patience exhausted, made ready to leave. Kalikow's spirits sagged; he had thought they were close. Trying to rekindle the momentum, he made a patronizing speech, telling Toussaint that a strike wouldn't hurt him or the rest of the brass at the MTA; it would hurt the "little people": "the shoeshine boys and the guys who work in the luncheonettes, the chambermaids, the small business guys." Trying to disarm him with a dose of humility, Kalikow added, "I'm begging you; don't walk out." Toussaint barely replied. Exasperated, Kalikow said, "Roger, if you strike you go to jail."[89]

Toussaint said Rosa Parks had gone to jail; he could too. Kalikow got a little hot. He had a cherished memory of Martin Luther King Jr., who had spoken at his graduation at Hofstra, and he did not like Toussaint trying to claim the moral high ground. At 4 a.m., the union delegates left. They did not say whether the strike was on or off.[90]

In the predawn light, Toussaint and his entourage groggily made their way to union headquarters, on West End Avenue. Rousing the members of the executive board, who were sleeping on cots or draped over chairs, Toussaint gave them the details of the MTA's offer. Members were angry and shouted that Toussaint should not have let the deadline pass. The chance to strike was gone; the morning trains were rumbling. After a raucous meeting, they voted to reject the authority's offer and set a new strike deadline, for a minute after midnight Tuesday.[91]

To the city, it felt like the briefest stay of execution. Department stores on Friday were empty; shoppers had taken no chances. Bloomberg, who had spent the night in the city's crisis bunker in Brooklyn, darkly observed that the MTA's offer was more generous than it could afford.[92] Toussaint and Kalikow kept up the flow of rhetoric. Each invoked the larger struggle. Kalikow said the MTA was like "every business and government in this country . . . seriously clouded by the extraordinary growth in pensions and health-care costs." Toussaint, drawing an opposite moral, said, "Working people and people of good faith will look at what's going on with General Motors and the stripping of health care for tens of millions of Americans, and the taking away of the hard-earned pensions of retirees, as an outrage."[93] Eighty-four years after the IRT's first, threadbare pension, subway benefits had become a national metaphor.

On Saturday the parties held a light bargaining session. Union shop stewards, taking no chances, circulated instructions on how to safely shut down the subways.[94] Monday morning, the union began a limited strike against two private bus companies in Queens. This sent an SOS to the seven million New Yorkers who daily relied on the subways and city bus lines. At 10:45 a.m., the bargaining teams reassembled at the Grand Hyatt. They were down to their final day—again.

Dellaverson was feeling pressure from the city (which was thinking about its own upcoming labor negotiations) to hold the line. For Toussaint, the pressure was unceasing. He was already being ridiculed by members for having kept the talks going. One longtime employee, airing her thoughts on the Internet, declared that postponing the deadline had been an "embarrassment." Another opined that there was no point in talking to the MTA, which stood accused of cooking its books to hide its surplus.[95] Toussaint doubted that *any* agreement would satisfy such members.

The MTA offered yet a steeper wage hike—3½ percent a year. That would lift a bus operator to $70,000 in the contract's third year. The authority threw in a twelfth paid holiday, for MLK Day. The union failed to counter. It occurred to a labor observer that there was no give-and-take to the discussions; no flow. With time slipping away, Toussaint ordered everyone in the union's suite out except for a labor movement official who was there as a sympathetic observer. With the official expecting a high-level strategy session, Toussaint inexplicably accused him of befriending a former TWU rep with whom Toussaint had quarreled. The astonished laborite said, "Roger, I'm here to work for *you*." It struck him as a dark portent: the sky was falling and Toussaint was focusing on internal politics.

By early evening, representatives from the other New York unions, including the umbrella AFL-CIO, had converged on the Grand Hyatt. Publicly, they offered support for Local 100. Privately, they were desperate to ward off a strike. Seeing Kalikow in the halls, Randi Weingarten, the teachers union president, declared, "It's important that we settle this." The developer shot back, "I made them a good offer."

At the bargaining table, Dellaverson suddenly dropped the MTA's demand, which was at the crux of the dispute, that new workers not retire until sixty-two. Instead, he had a new condition: workers could go out at fifty-five, but they would have to contribute 6 percent of their salary to pay for it.

Dellaverson was hoping that this reformulation would get the talks moving, but Toussaint exploded. The notion of paying extra—6 percent instead of 2—for what the union had already won infuriated him. The meeting broke.

Paterson decided that if anyone was going to cut through the impasse it would have to be the union's chief adversary: Dellaverson. No one else had his encyclopedic knowledge of the contract (or his brilliance). Paterson took Dellaverson into a private room. He said, "Gary, nobody is going to make this deal but you."[96]

Dellaverson had a brainstorm. He began to thrash it out: normal retirement would be at sixty-two, as the MTA wanted. But the employees would also get a 401(k) account. The authority would throw in 1 percent a year; the employees could invest the same or—if they chose—more. When they reached fifty-five, they could use the 401(k) money to buy extra years on their pension, enough to retire by their late fifties or possibly even at fifty-five. The MTA wouldn't *guarantee* the outcome, nor would it shoulder all of the burden. But transit employees still could plan on a youthful retirement.

Paterson smiled. He had to admit the idea had merit. Dellaverson thought he had found the sweet spot: a guaranteed pension but with some sharing of the risk. It was not turning the clock back to the days of Santo and the Reds, when the transit workers got essentially nothing, nor would it expose the authority to the open-ended hazards that had crippled GM. It was the sort of deal that each side could live with, and (though Dellaverson wasn't thinking about this) possibly other employers in America as well. He and Paterson went back to the conference room and Dellaverson's idea was vented. The MTA made another concession. They were fingertips apart, but the "unborn" would still get nicked and Toussaint wouldn't allow it. He began to shut down, like a man who knew his fate.

A little after midnight the union delegation caucused; then it left for headquarters. Toussaint, giving a summary of the talks, weighed in in favor of a strike, though he acknowledged that it would entail serious risks. Others pleaded for time. Michael O'Brien, the president of the parent TWU, noted that each negotiation had produced a better offer, so the sensible thing to do was to keep talking. "Talking is cheap," he noted. "Strikes are costly."

The vote was tabulated at 1:15 a.m.: plenty of time for the trains to finish their runs and drop off passengers (though most New Yorkers had taken care to arrive at their destinations much earlier). By 3 a.m., the trains were safely in the yards. At just that hour, Toussaint announced that the union had voted "overwhelmingly [though not unanimously] to extend strike actions to all MTA properties." For the third time in forty years, the famous New York City subways had been silenced.

Toussaint could take momentary solace from having placated some of his more strident members, such as the train operator Harry Harrington, who was "overjoyed to be striking against this miserable management," and who voiced the hope they would all get fired.[97] But soon Toussaint's organization would be hit with a contempt citation and $1 million a day fines. He also faced the opprobrium of much of the city. The *New York Daily News,* unsatisfied with mere court citations, editorialized with its trademark New York bluntness, "Throw Roger from the Train!"[98] Kalikow also was furious at Toussaint, who he felt had betrayed him. Later he would reckon that fixing the pension system was more difficult than he had imagined.

Schools opened late on Tuesday and classrooms remained half-empty. Manhattan streets were eerily quiet. Rather than snarl the city in much-feared traffic jams, people in the outer boroughs and suburbs had stayed home. The winter weather was thankfully mild.

Mayor Bloomberg, as to be expected, walked or rather bounded across the Brooklyn Bridge. Attired for his trip in a leather bomber jacket and stone-washed Levi's, the mayor lashed out at the union leadership for having "thuggishly turned their backs on New York City and disgraced the noble concept of public service." The first part of his comment was to be much rehashed by those who took offense at Bloomberg's use of the modifier "thuggishly"; little was said about the other part, "the noble concept of public service." It had been a long time, of course, since the phrase "public service" carried the clarity of purpose, much less the dignity, that it had in LaGuardia's day. It was the sort of phrase that rolled off the tongue, an unobjectionable cliché; most listeners barely paused over it. But it was there, in the meaning of public service, its rights and its responsibilities, where the meat of the pension dispute was to be found.

New York, at very least, had dealt with the issue openly. The city had raised taxes to pay for pensions and then, finally, it had said enough. There were governments in many other jurisdictions that utterly lacked such courage. For them, pensions would truly be a recipe for disaster.

Part III

DEBACLE IN SAN DIEGO

FIVE

FINEST CITY

There is a San Diego brewing in every community.

—Carl DeMaio, *local government consultant*

By the time the New York subways screeched to a halt, pensions were nationwide news. But worse than the debacle in New York—even worse than the ruin of the auto industry—was the storm in San Diego, where a pension scandal bequeathed a fiscal, a legal, and a political nightmare. In San Diego, pension abuse flowered into its fullest form. As in New York and other jurisdictions, powerful labor unions were for years able to wring higher benefits from weak politicians. But excessive benefits were only a part of the problem. The greater temptation—the "moral hazard"—was the latent risk that government would thrust the expense onto a later generation. In other towns, pensions had put "the future" in peril; in San Diego, that future had arrived. Nowhere else would the consequences of pension abuse be so painful.

By summer 2005, the municipal pension fund was $1.7 billion in the hole—a debt equivalent to $6,000 for every San Diego family of four.[1] Public employees were being laid off; plans for a new, state-of-the-art downtown library had been shelved; swimming pools had been closed; hours at existing libraries had been curtailed; an after-school program for kids had been gutted, as had maintenance of the sprawling parks network, formerly one of the prides of San Diego. Some 60,000 potholes had gone unfilled.

The city had no audited financial statements, therefore no bond rating and no access to Wall Street—a condition it had endured for approximately two years, a streak of fiscal misery virtually unmatched in municipal finance. The mess was under investigation by a slew of watchdog agencies, including the Department of Justice, the Securities and Exchange Commission, the City of San Diego, as well as a special investigative team headed by the former SEC chairman Arthur Levitt.

As if all this scrutiny wasn't enough, San Diego's government was, at midsummer, rudderless and adrift. The mayor had resigned. The city treasurer who had presided over the pension scandal had resigned. The auditor had resigned. Six trustees of the San Diego City Employees' Retirement System had been charged by the local district attorney with violating the state's conflict-of-interest statute, a felony.

The national press had taken to referring to San Diego as "Enron-by-the-Sea," a testimony to its financial, and also its moral, unraveling. But just as the real Enron was not so much an exception to corporate misbehavior as an extreme case, San Diego, too, was but a heightened version of the common hazards of public pensions.

The immediate cause of the debacle was that the city was chronically short on cash—but then, the same could be said of almost any government. The deeper cause was the extreme reluctance of local politicians to close the gap by levying taxes. In New York at least, when the boom ended and the bill began to come due, the city was willing to raise taxes and to cut services. It was willing to *pay* for its benefits. That is what the subway strike was about; New York realized that pensions bore a cost, and the transit agency, through the person of Kalikow, resolved to hold the line.

San Diego, though, had a very different political culture. It was not historically a union town like New York. San Diego was Republican to the core—home terrain to both Richard Nixon and Ronald Reagan. (Reagan, who made a point of ending each of his campaigns in San Diego, called it his "lucky city").[2] If the residents of this deeply conservative enclave mistrusted government, they simply *despised* taxes.

To a succession of San Diego mayors and city officials, therefore, pensions held a particular allure. Being short on cash, these officials (over a period of many years) connived to avoid making the required and necessary pension contributions. In effect, they tapped the pension fund for every purpose that might appeal to politicians—park maintenance, policemen's wages, new fire trucks, subsidies for sports teams.

This is what hard-pressed pension sponsors from General Motors to the state of New Jersey to United Airlines have always done—they cheat on contributions to satisfy present needs. As Roger Toussaint might say, they rob the unborn. Except that in San Diego, the abuse was deliberate and repeated in the face of mounting evidence that the retirement system was in trouble.

All of this directly flouted local law, and never could have occurred but for another aspect of the city's culture—its endemic corruption. San Diego has a long history of scandals, among the most significant of which occurred in the early 1970s, when C. Arnholt Smith, a prominent supporter of President Nixon, was implicated in the then largest bank failure in U.S. history, and convicted of embezzlement. The embarrassment caused the Republican Party to drop San Diego as the venue for its 1972 convention. Hoping to erase the taint, Pete Wilson, the mayor, adopted a new slogan, "America's Finest City." The slogan stuck, but the scandals continued.

San Diego was a close-knit town—a big city in which local officials functioned like a cozy board of directors. Businessmen seeking tax breaks had open entrée to City Hall, and political back-scratching was a way of life. City officials were beholden to the public unions, and the union chiefs kept a close thumb on the local retirement board (a nominally independent body that was supposed to protect the interests of the retirees).

These alliances were critical to the unfolding drama; thus, City Hall was permitted to shortchange the pension system and to use the unspent monies to cover the holes in its budget. The unions winked at the underfunding—in return for which they were rewarded with higher benefits. And so every nest was feathered: pension benefits were hiked, the budget squeeze was alleviated, the politicians' obligations were conveniently deferred.

The fiscal demands on the government had risen, in part because the unions had obtained a stronger foothold, and in part because San Diego, riding a tide of growth in the Sunbelt, had emerged (by the end of the twentieth century) as America's seventh largest city. San Diegans may have loathed paying taxes, but they demanded and needed government services all the same.

And its form of government was particularly unsuited to delivering them. San Diego was governed by a city council, one of whose members included the mayor—by design, a "weak" mayor. The council delegated executive functions to a staff of bureaucrats led by a city manager. Real power was vested in the local business interests, of which the *San Diego Union-Tribune* has been paramount. (Its editor in the 1960s was Herbert Klein, who doubled as press agent in Nixon's campaigns and ultimately was his White House director of communications.) For practical purposes, the reigning authority was the Chamber of Commerce, an arrangement that may have been reasonable when San Diego was more or less an oversized hacienda in between Los Angeles and the Mexican border, but it was unsuitable for a metropolis of 1.2 million.

Many government services were simply unprovided for, as evidenced by the legions of homeless who wandered unattended in the downtown business district. The disconnect between San Diego's need for government and its reluctance to pay for it meant that officials were forever having to improvise—to find the unspent funds, to access the buried account. That it wound up pillaging the pension system seems, in retrospect, almost inevitable.

THE CITY OF SAN DIEGO is shaped like an oil can, with the spout jutting northeastward into rolling hills and plunging canyons that are dotted with affluent subdevelopments. On the western edge of the can lies La Jolla, a spectacularly picturesque seaside community ensconced in a crescent-shaped bay. The southernmost part of the city is detached from the rest, looking as though the can had sprung a leak; it borders on Mexico and is largely Hispanic. Just above it, and fronting the harbor, is downtown San Diego, home to City Hall, the courts, and the pension system.

The roots of San Diego's problem lie hundreds of miles to the north, in the state capital of Sacramento. More precisely, they lie in California's system of popular referendums, which leaves localities as well as the state especially vulnerable to democratic passions. In 1978, Howard Jarvis, a onetime advance man for Herbert Hoover, succeeded in placing on the ballot Proposition 13, which rolled back the property taxes collected by local governments, critically reducing their revenues. Specifically, it limited property taxes to 1 percent of assessed values, and limited increases in the assessed values to 2 percent per year.

Passed overwhelmingly, Prop 13 was a political thunderbolt. It reverberated far beyond the state, sparking a national revolt against high tax rates. In California, cities and towns suffered a devastating loss of revenue—just over 50 percent.[3] And the effect endured. By 2000, schools in California were receiving $600 per pupil *less* than the national average, compared to $600 above the average in 1978.[4] A perhaps unanticipated result was that localities furiously began to look for other sources of revenue.

It was soon after Prop 13 that San Diego began, slowly but methodically, to tinker with the local pension system, formally known as the San Diego City Employees' Retirement System (SDCERS), which administers pensions for 14,500 or so public workers and retirees. Pete Wilson, mayor at the time, was a fiscal conservative who had set his personal sights on Washington. To win higher office he had, of course, to please his constituents, but he was loath to overload the city budget, and in any case Prop 13 greatly limited his options.

Wilson, though, found a cheap way to dispense some goodies via SDCERS (the acronym is pronounced "S.D.-SIRS"). In 1980, he and the rest of the city council fashioned a novel plum. They decreed that in any year in which the system earned more than 8 percent on its investments, half of the so-called surplus would be distributed to pensioners. (This became known as the "13th check," similar to the Christmas bonus awarded to New York City firemen.) The 13th check was predicated on a seriously flawed actuarial premise. As in the biblical tale of Joseph and the Pharaoh's dream, bountiful harvests should be stored for the inevitable years of lean, not consumed when the harvest is in. But by the time the lean years arrived, Wilson would be long gone from San Diego.

Wilson next tried to reach directly into the pension fund to, in effect, lend the city cash, but a local judge raised such a fuss that the idea was dropped.[5] Still eyeing retirement contributions as a potential life raft, Wilson took the extraordinary step of withdrawing San Diego from the federal Social Security system (it remains one of the few cities that is outside the system). Wilson no doubt figured that San Diego would reap a saving, as it was spared from having to pay its share of the federal payroll tax. However, the city employees, who now lacked Social Security protection, naturally demanded a heftier pension from the city and also retiree health care.

Praised for keeping government small, Wilson won two terms in the U.S. Senate and in 1990 was elected governor. This, approximately, is when the hard times in San Diego began. The immediate fiscal pressures stemmed from an upheaval in the political system. At the time, the councilmen who ran City Hall were elected "at large," or on a citywide basis. This limited the influence of minorities, who could have prevailed in district elections but not over the entire city. It also minimized union influence. The council, though officially non-partisan, resembled an exclusive and virtually self-perpetuating club. Members would frequently resign before their terms expired, so that the mayor, conveniently, could pick their successors.

In 1988, a local attorney named Michael Aguirre initiated a voting rights suit, contending that at-large voting discriminated against minorities. A litigator with the physique and temperament of a spark plug, Aguirre had a passion for the underdog. Nearly always, he had represented the little guy—voting rights plaintiffs, retirees, migrant workers. But his real interest lay in politics. His suit shook up the city, and following a referendum, the at-large system was scrapped. Henceforth, eight of the nine council members (all but the mayor) would be elected by individual districts.

This seemingly modest reform ushered in revolutionary changes, as it splintered the city into political fiefdoms. Southern San Diego became a Mexican district, the Sixth District was working-class, and so forth. Also, the districts were small enough so that five thousand or so votes could swing an election. This gave special interests—including the public employee unions—a political clout they had never had, somewhat on a par with business interests.

The unions began to contribute more to political campaigns, with discernible effects at the polls. Naturally, councilmen felt more pressure to raise employee salaries, and to respond to other interests. But though government spending began to rise, the council still refused to tax. Unable to raise revenues through conventional means, the city balanced its budget with mirrors and one-time expedients such as selling land, some of which had first been granted to California from the king of Spain (a nonrecurring revenue source, to be sure).[6] Its budget woes worsened when the country suffered a recession in 1990 that hit California especially hard. The following year, after the Gulf War, the defense industry went into a nosedive, eviscerating San Diego's tax base.

Once again, the city turned to the pension fund to ease the crunch. In 1991, it played a little game—actually a couple of games—with SDCERS's accounting. First, it convinced SDCERS to switch to a more liberal method of computing its pension liability, a maneuver that reduced the city's annual payments in the short run. It also extended the repayment period for its liability over a new thirty years (the equivalent of granting the city a fresh mortgage on its pension debt). This reduced its bill even more. However, the trustees who presided over SDCERS demanded a favor in return. And they got it: the city significantly increased benefits.[7] In effect, the trustees could say to the beneficiaries, "Though there is less money in the fund now, more will be coming your way later." But the fact remained that San Diego had set a dubious fiscal precedent, borrowing from the future to avoid a short-term squeeze, and offering a carrot to get the trustees to look the other way.

The state government, which was experiencing budget problems of its own, was hardly more virtuous. Once installed in Sacramento, Governor Wilson (perhaps fondly recalling his raids on SDCERS) brazenly shortchanged the California Public Employees' Retirement System, a big state pension system. The fund sued him, but meanwhile, the state went about deliberately underfunding its pension plan by some $1.36 billion.[8]

Wilson generated even more problems for San Diego in the early '90s when he, along with the legislature, began to siphon property tax revenues from cities and counties to the state. This cost San Diego on the order of $30 million a year—a crippling loss.[9] From then on, the city government was chronically short of cash.

Just as San Diego was absorbing this blow, it elected a new mayor, Susan Golding, an ambitious politician with a demonstrated ability to dodge potential landmines. Golding had launched her political career in the late '70s, when she was appointed to a vacant council seat by then mayor Wilson. Her husband, Richard Silberman, a politically connected and wealthy financier, spent a bundle to help her get elected to the county board of supervisors, after which Silberman frequently called on the county government for personal favors. Subsequently, he was convicted of money laundering. Golding divorced him, and in 1992 was elected mayor.[10]

Despite the shortage of funds, Golding unveiled an expensive agenda, featuring headline-grabbing projects such as a new library and an expanded convention center. Shoring up the retirement system was not high on her agenda—to be fair, in those years, save for the occasional breast-beatings of Alan Greenspan about the looming Social Security deficit, pensions were ignored by most of America. Golding, in any case, was popular with local businessmen; she had a vision for moving San Diego forward, for attracting new industries and completing the city's evolution as a big-league destination for culture and sports. She was intemperate with doubters and seemed to regard the financing of her schemes as little more than a detail.

Golding turned the funding side to her wizardlike city manager, a ramrod-straight ex-Marine named Jack McGrory—or rather, Golding ordered McGrory to figure out how to pay for it all. The indispensable cog in an overburdened machine, McGrory kept lists of the projects dear to the elected council members (including the mayor) and separate ledgers of the available city funds. These he somehow managed to bring into balance. No one quite understood how he did it, and that was his secret. He moved expenses around, shifted personnel, offset one account against the other. A favorite McGrory tactic was to charge the water or sewer departments for laying pipes under city streets, which effectively transferred costs from the general fund to water and sewer (which had the power to assess fees).[11] Council members complained they didn't understand his machinations, that he never explained the budget (the complexity of which one member likened to that of a Leonardo da Vinci drawing), but the truth was they were happier *not* knowing what McGrory was up to.[12]

When McGrory reached the limit of even his resourcefulness, he would beg the council for tax increases (which required a referendum) and/or higher usage fees. The business establishment, invariably led by the *Union-Tribune*, almost always thwarted him. Whereas businesses in nearby Los Angeles paid a fifth of 1 percent of their receipts for licensing fees, those in San Diego contributed one-*fiftieth* of 1 percent. Similarly, residents in L.A. paid $137 per capita as a utility tax; those in San Francisco $97, and in Santa Ana $75. San Diegans paid *zero.* Despite its appeal as a tourist haven, hotel room taxes were among the lowest in California. Homeowners in San Diego did not want to *pay* to have their garbage hauled away, and so, unlike virtually every other municipality on the planet, the city did it for free. Nor did the city impose on its snug denizens the indignity of parking meters along their miles of pristine beaches. Overall, the revenue collected by the city amounted to only 2 percent of household income—the lowest ratio of any big city in the state. Since the average was

3 percent, San Diego was forgoing fully a third of the revenue that presumably was available to it.[13]

Golding needed some other revenue source, and the reader will guess that she turned to SDCERS as the most practical option. Shortchanging the pension fund *always* seems expedient, because future beneficiaries do not have a voice. And what other option did Golding have? San Diego already was coping with a threadbare level of public service. It had fewer cops per capita; it spent less on upkeep per each acre of park; it made fewer repairs on its streets, highways, and storm drains than any city in the state.[14] (Frustrated bureaucrats occasionally twisted the official slogan, referring to their hometown as "America's *Cheapest* City.") So badly outmoded were its sewers that it was under a federal mandate to improve them.[15]

Further cuts would have been highly unpopular. And Golding, who was hoping to use the mayoralty as Wilson had—as a springboard to the U.S. Senate—knew that to propose new taxes was political folly, even if economically it was the soundest course. Due to demographic shifts such as the aging of the workforce, the city's pension bill was rising, but writing a bigger check to SDCERS was unlikely to win her many votes. Therefore, in the spring of 1994, she made a startling suggestion: that SDCERS give the city a one-year "holiday" from contributing to pensions at all. The SDCERS board promptly and properly rejected the idea.[16]

The next year, Golding again attempted to "save" money by skimping on the pension fund. Given some of her other priorities, stiffing SDCERS was a revealing choice. Golding had attended the recent Super Bowl in Miami, to cheer on the San Diego Chargers, and after the game she flew home with Alex Spanos, the team's owner. After this apparently aphrodisiacal experience, she began to talk up the need to improve the aging, city-owned Jack Murphy Stadium—the better to lure a Super Bowl to San Diego and to dissuade the Chargers from leaving town, which is what Spanos, a real estate mogul, was threatening to do.[17] McGrory quietly worked out a deal (rubber-stamped by the city council) under which the city would pay for any unused football tickets, up to an attendance of 60,000, and thus ensure Spanos a guaranteed purse.

With such added burdens as the Chargers, the city could hardly afford the tab for pensions, or so Golding and McGrory maintained. It seemed a small matter, they argued, to skim a little from SDCERS, whose assets totaled $1.3 billion. No matter that its liabilities were even larger; to a city manager with a budget to meet, a pension liability seems far off indeed.

And now, the city's tone became more insistent. Ed Ryan, the city auditor, warned that without a concession from SDCERS the city would be forced to slash police and fire budgets. That was a clear threat. The SDCERS board heatedly debated Ryan's demand, with one member rightly objecting that the pension fund did *not* exist for the purpose of bailing out the city, much less its football team. However, when an auditor says he needs a break, boards find it hard to refuse. It voted 7–6 to reduce the city's pension contribution, pending an approval from the board's lawyer.

SDCERS's fiduciary counsel was a San Francisco law firm, Morrison and Foerster. *It* recognized that the underfunding would violate the city charter, which required the city to make contributions at a rate consistent with the actuarial calculation, and the law firm said so plainly.[18] As far as the 1995 budget process was concerned, that ended the matter.

But the idea of chiseling the pension fund was now on a very high burner. And so SDCERS dismissed Morrison and Foerster, presumably to seek a "second opinion" more to the city's liking.

Why would the retirement system cashier its counsel when it had demonstrated both competence and courage? The explanation, at least in part, lies in the deeply conflicted composition of the SDCERS board. Three of its trustees were City Hall employees who represented the city manager, the treasurer, and the auditor. Additionally, four trustees were selected by the mayor and the council. In short, while it was in SDCERS's interest to remain as flush as possible, it was in the city's interest to *minimize* its contributions, and the board was controlled by the city. Indeed, the three trustees who worked at City Hall had an intimate, day-to-day involvement with the city's budget.

Going into 1996, McGrory knew that the required pension contribution would be rising again. He was facing a real budget squeeze, which was especially awkward given that Golding was up for reelection. She was hankering for the new library, a nature preserve, daytime care for tots and after-school programs for teenagers, more police officers. And with Spanos, the Chargers owner, still whining about the team's home, Golding was preparing to float a $60 million bond issue to pay for a stadium expansion, luxury boxes and so forth. Spanos, as it happened, was also a major Republican fund-raiser, a fact of considerable interest to Golding, who was now laying the groundwork for her Senate bid. To bolster her chances, she also wanted San Diego to host the 1996 Republican convention (its first since the lost convention of 1972). But the convention would further drain the city's coffers. McGrory simply did not have the money to pay for everything on Golding's gaudy agenda.[19]

Golding surely did not want to ask the voters to pay for it.* The rest of the country, and in particular the Republican Party, seemed to be catching up to San Diego in terms of its dislike for taxes, and Golding was a politician in glorious harmony with the moment. In her otherwise expansive State of the City address, she boasted of having further *cut* taxes. With regard to the proposed library, she chirped that the council had "figured out a way to pay for it, and adopted a plan to build it—all without raising taxes."[20]

With such promises afloat, McGrory knew that squaring the budget would be impossible. To make matters worse, the city had to negotiate new contracts with its labor unions. But maybe—just maybe—that spelled an opportunity. The most powerful union was Local 145, representing the firefighters. Local 145 was run by Ronald Saathoff, a forty-eight-year-old fire captain and decorated Vietnam veteran. Other than McGrory himself, Saathoff had more clout with the city council than anyone else in San Diego. Conveniently enough, he was also a trustee on the pension board.

---

*After she retired from politics, Golding admitted to the *Union-Tribune,* "They [the city managers] are right about us approving new programs without new revenues, but they don't have to go to the electorate."

Saathoff was not a firebrand labor leader in the manner of a Mike Quill. Rather than trying to fight the establishment, Saathoff had tried to co-opt it. Having been president since 1980, he was deeply versed in union matters and, significantly, he was an expert on the particular complexities of pensions. Many of the trustees shied away from the details; Saathoff reveled in them. A high school graduate who owned a car wash with his father, he was self-taught and determined. Slender and well proportioned, he had a Roman bearing and an air of authority. And the greater his mastery of pension details, he found, the more he could intimidate those who found the intricacies of pensions overwhelming—including the other pension trustees.

The city's move to district elections was a gift to Saathoff. It gave the firefighters, as well as the other public unions, their first real influence over the city council. Saathoff used this gift wisely. He learned to soften his approach and to cultivate business and political friends downtown.

Meanwhile, the firefighters worked the streets. Candidates favored by Local 145 would wake to see firemen at fund-raisers on their behalf, firemen at bake sales, fire helmets emblazoned with messages of support. Saathoff used his influence in a very intelligent way. Formerly, when business interests lobbied for a favor—say, lower development fees—labor unions would oppose them. Saathoff's approach, as a union official put it, was, "Why embarrass them? Let's work with them and get a piece of the pie."[21]

Saathoff knew that, given everything else on the city's plate, 1996 would be a tough year for bargaining. He didn't necessarily object to the agenda the mayor was promoting—the Chargers, the convention, and so forth. He just wanted the firefighters to get their slice.

Early in the year, McGrory drafted a budget fix that he figured would appeal to Saathoff. It was the boldest attempt yet to duck the city's pension obligation. Basically, it would reduce the city's contribution below the actuarial rate for a period of ten years. During that time, the city would "save" as much as $15 million a year, or a total of $110 million, though of course the money would have to be paid later. In return for shortchanging the system—this was the carrot—McGrory offered to raise the unions' pensions.

McGrory rationalized that the pension fund, which was earning good returns in the stock market, was in better shape than the city.[22] Given that Governors Wilson and others had shortchanged their state pension systems, his plan did not seem so outlandish. However, by offering the four city unions an explicit quid pro quo—a sweetener in the form of higher benefits—McGrory had crossed a serious line. He was not just asking for a favor; he was literally trying to buy the unions' acquiescence.

But the unions would not settle cheap. In a brazen letter, Ann Smith, the lawyer for the municipal employees association, snubbed McGrory's offer and warned that the union would accept nothing less than "a vast improvement in the retirement formula."[23] Smith tried to feign a deep fiduciary concern, as though she was truly upset that the city was "tampering with funding methods." She added that it would require a "yeoman's effort" to overcome her, and her members', misgivings. By yeoman's effort, she meant a bigger payoff than McGrory had proposed, or, as she put it, "gains [that] are clearly respectable." This was patent blackmail. Left unstated was the inconvenient fact that if Smith were truly worried about funding levels, higher benefits would be counterproductive, since they would increase SDCERS's liability. Higher benefits wouldn't *compensate* for the underfunding, they would aggravate it.

McGrory duly improved his offer. He now proposed a *one-third* increase in the multiplier used to calculate municipal workers' pensions—a staggering raise.* The other unions also got hefty raises. The uniformed services (police and fire) would now be able to retire, after thirty years, on a pension equal to 90 percent of salary—a level unheard of in industry (save for the unpardonable pensions of many CEOs).

---

*Pensions were calculated as a percentage of employee final salaries. For municipal employees, the formula had been 1.48 percent × the number of years served. McGrory's plan raised the multiplier to 2 percent.

And the formula improvements were just for starters. To further entice the unions, McGrory promised to:

- Increase the 13th check.
- Let employees buy (as it turned out, at a steep discount) extra years of service, and thus qualify for a greater pension than they had earned.
- Let employees eligible for retirement continue to work and earn a pension simultaneously—a form of double dipping.[24]
- Have SDCERS cover retiree health care.

Such improvements would cost the city dearly. Presently, the SDCERS actuary calculated that to stay current on its obligation, the city had to contribute 8.6 percent of its payroll a year. After the benefit hikes, the tab would vault to 11 percent. But McGrory, of course, wasn't intending to *pay* the full tab. According to the terms of his underfunding scheme, the city would pay only a little over 7 percent. This would further increase the liability in the following year, when the actuarial cost would rise to 12 percent. Each year of underpayment would exacerbate the deficit in the next. The plan was fiscal lunacy on its face.

McGrory had to sell it to the council—which would be committing to higher pensions forever—but the council wanted peace with labor and the plan had Saathoff's backing. And McGrory was a consummate salesman. He assured them it was a "package deal," meaning if the city didn't get a funding break, it wouldn't be on the hook for the higher benefits.[25]

The SDCERS board was a tougher sale. Essentially, McGrory was asking the trustees to waive their duty to keep SDCERS financially sound in order to accommodate a labor negotiation. A couple of the trustees heatedly protested, with one wondering how the city would be able to come up with $100 million later if it couldn't pay a much smaller sum now.

The board's new fiduciary counsel, a Denver attorney named Dwight Hamilton, warned that McGrory's plan raised "red flags," and fretted that it would shift the pension liability to future taxpayers.[26] But he didn't say outright that it was illegal. The actuary, Rick Roeder, also waffled. The two advisers needed but a tiny encouragement: a face-saving.

McGrory came up with a clever mechanism to reassure them: a failsafe mechanism known as a "trigger." Presently, the retirement system was 92 percent funded (that is, 8 percent underfunded). As McGrory described the trigger, if SDCERS fell another ten points—to precisely 82.3 percent, which is a pretty anemic level of funding—the city would immediately be required to make a big balloon payment. It was uncertain how *much* it would owe—at least $25 million and possibly more. The arrangement was akin to a homeowner promising to make bigger payments if he fell behind on his mortgage. It was patently illogical; if he fell behind, even normal payments would be a burden. But the trigger gave the scheme the patina of security: it was a "failsafe," a "guarantee."[27]

Conny Jamison, the city treasurer and also a board member, was still dissatisfied. But Jamison was in a tough spot; as treasurer, she worked for McGrory, the plan's author. He accused her of not being a team player and menacingly added, "I hope you'll support me on this."[28]

The trustees considered the revised plan at the end of June 1996. Saathoff argued strenuously in favor of the plan.[29] The other trustees waited to hear from Hamilton, the lawyer, and Roeder, the actuary. Pension advisers are typically unsung, but they have moments, at least potentially, of quiet heroism. Nothing but the absolute truth will do, and they cannot allow either peer pressure or a desire to please to corrupt their opinion. Neither Hamilton nor Roeder was up to it. Each gave a grudging okay and the resistance collapsed. By a vote of 8–3, the board approved its own underfunding. In July, the council kept its part of the bargain, passing the new, higher pension benefits without discussion.[30]

The Republican convention the following month was a smashing success. The city (flush with unspent pension dollars) was able to show conventioneers its best face. The unions pitched in with the Chamber to spruce up the city, and visitors who thought of San Diego as a sleepy haven for retirees discovered it had gleaming skyscrapers (and swaying palms), too. James Brady, on assignment for *Parade*, likened San Diego to a second Eden—one that fell only "just short" of the original. Bob Dole, the nominee, doffed his cap toward the host city or at least toward its governing ideology, as he promised in his keynote speech no fewer than twenty-four times that if elected he would cut taxes. He was presumably unaware that San Diego had defrayed the convention's cost by shortchanging its public retirement fund.

WITHIN A YEAR, the California Court of Appeal ruled that Wilson's underfunding of the state system in the early '90s had violated the constitutional right of employees to an actuarially sound pension.[31] Arguably, San Diego was also in violation.[32] But no one challenged it. The city's timing was fortunate: the stock market was booming, and SDCERS's investment portfolio was soaring. McGrory, seeing a chance to go out on top, left the government for a lucrative job in private industry.

Two years later, Golding strong-armed local business leaders to support yet another sports project—a new ballpark for the San Diego Padres. The baseball stadium had the Golding trademark: an elaborate vision, combining sports and real estate development, that would be financed with bonds to be repaid well in the future. The proposal was expensive and encountered strong opposition, as well as numerous legal challenges.

Meanwhile, the mayor was having trouble with Spanos, the Chargers' owner. Once the city floated bonds to pay for renovating the football arena, renamed Qualcomm Stadium, Spanos, in effect, double-crossed the city by raising ticket prices.[33] Attendance flagged, leaving San Diego on the hook for millions of dollars a year in unsold tickets, which it distributed gratis to children. In addition, the city was stuck with debt service obligations on the stadium bonds of $5.7 million a year.[34] The "ticket guarantee" was ridiculed as a costly fiasco; it ended Golding's senatorial hopes.

But with the stock market continuing to boom, the city was under pressure to raise pension benefits again. Legislators are naturally accustomed to making short-term accommodations; a tax may be levied and then, when circumstances change, rescinded. Police forces can expand and contract with the level of crime. The trouble with hiking pensions is that the benefits are immune to cyclical fluctuations; they never go away.

But as in New York State, politicians in California regarded the bull market as an excuse not only to raise benefits but also to reduce contributions. In California, home to the dot-com industry, stock market mania was at a peak. Gray Davis, who was elected governor (with strong support from public unions) in 1998, inherited a budget surplus. He sharply cut pension contributions and simultaneously pushed through bills to increase benefits. The higher benefits trickled down to localities as well.

It is one thing to demand a wage hike every year or couple of years; a regular pension improvement is something else. Public pension benefits are typically set at a percentage of final salary; therefore, employees *automatically* get pension raises the longer they work and the more they earn. Sweetening the formula amounts to a raise on top of a raise.

In March 2000, though, SDCERS was forced to raise benefits when it settled a lawsuit brought by a group of retired employees who claimed their benefits had been miscalculated. The settlement was extremely costly,* and given that it was the second major hike in four years, some respite from further increases was presumably in order. But by the spring of 2000, the height of the dot-com bubble, considerations of prudence were demonstrably passé. In the first few months of 2000, a newly minted tech stock was *doubling* on its first day of trading every other day, a speculative orgy that seemed to suggest, especially in California, that any public commitment could be underwritten by some future rise in the market.[35] Moreover, 2000 was a local election year. The unions, which were better organized, and better funded, than in previous campaigns, were pushing for higher pensions.

The council considered the issue in September—two months before various of its members stood for reelection. Saathoff got the firemen an-

---

*The claim was that "final salary" improperly excluded the value of various benefits such as sick leave and vacation. The settlement raised future pension benefits by a total of $186 million.

other boost; his troops could now claim their 90 percent pension at age fifty, rather than, as before, age fifty-five. In other words, they would enjoy essentially a full salary for half of their expected adult lives without doing a stitch of work. Not even Walter Reuther would have thought it possible (or feasible). The cops got more as well, and the city council passed a big hike for its *own* members, including Golding, who was retiring. Each of these hikes, of course, increased the system's future liability.

By the time the increases were enacted, the stock market was well off its highs. There was mild disquiet as the mayoral election neared, a sense among the city fathers that the extravagances of the recent past needed to be tempered: the fiscal house put in order. The promise of the Golding era had begun to wilt. The Chargers' ticket guarantee had cost the city $5 million over the past year, an expense that outraged ordinary San Diegans. As for the Padres' stadium, construction had been suspended following revelations of corruption involving a councilwoman with close ties to the team's owner. The much-feted, and sorely needed, library had not advanced beyond the blueprint stage. "Confidence in the mayor and City Council has ebbed ominously," opined the *Union-Tribune.*[36] But the pension was not a particular concern, and the downtown business leaders, who had always called the shots, fancied they had found the perfect antidote to the profligate and undisciplined '90s. They had in mind a mayoral candidate who was cautious, deliberate, judicious—he was in fact a superior court judge.

Richard Murphy was fifty-seven, a conservative Republican like his mentor, the former mayor Wilson. Murphy was modest, more comfortable forging consensus than grabbing the limelight. He was a family man, a churchgoer who tended to the choir loft, neatening it before the services. He loathed disorder and was painstakingly methodical. A native of Chicago, he had gotten an MBA at Harvard and gone into banking, but it didn't take. He got another top-drawer degree, this time from Stanford Law School, and joined a San Diego law firm. The mystery to his career, given his intellect and résumé, was its failure to really ignite. He made a point of scheduling a weekly lunch with a potential campaign donor, but for years he didn't run for anything bigger than the city council. Once, in the '90s, he was all set to run for Congress, but disappointed friends by changing his mind. In 2000, when he put his hat in the ring for mayor, a sympathizer warned him, "You backed off once. You won't get another chance."[37]

True to his organizational bent, Murphy proposed "Ten Goals" for San Diego's future. With Murphy it couldn't be nine or eleven; it had to be ten. Among these, he had in mind an ethics commission to elevate the character of local government, and also a blue-ribbon committee to study the state of city finances and, indeed, to determine how to pay for the other items on his list, such as the library and finishing the ballpark. This was vintage Murphy: commissions and committees as a prelude to action. The *Union-Tribune* was wary of his indecisiveness but endorsed him anyhow.[38] In Murphy's favor was his personal rectitude, his distance from the political fray, and from special interests such as labor unions. He won handily.

By late 2000, when Murphy was installed in office, San Diego's fortunes had noticeably turned. Valerie Stallings, the implicated councilwoman, resigned and pleaded guilty to a pair of misdemeanors for accepting gifts from John Moores, the Padres' owner. Moores was cleared by a U.S. attorney, who explained helpfully, "It is not a crime to give gifts to public officials."[39]

Improbably, Donna Frye, a throaty, perpetually sunburned surf shop owner who had become disgusted with the city's discharges of sewage into the ocean, which she said were poisoning surfers, ran for Stallings's vacant seat and won—giving the Democrats their first majority on the council. Of more immediate moment to the new mayor, the market and the national economy cooled considerably, putting the pension fund on shakier ground.

SIX

PENSION PLOT

A retirement board's duty to its participants and their beneficiaries shall take precedence over any other duty.

—Article XVL, Section 17, California State Constitution

Murphy picked nine people for his blue-ribbon panel to study the city's finances. Richard Vortmann, president of a local shipbuilder, took charge of reviewing SDCERS. Vortmann was a shrewd choice. A strapping, six-foot-five industrialist, he had long experience with unions and knew the risks inherent in pensions. On first glance, he thought SDCERS was in okay shape. But as he probed deeper, he realized that benefits in San Diego were far richer than those in the private sector and that, even after a long bull market, the city's plan was underfunded. By the end of August, he had decided that SDCERS needed an intensive, top-to-bottom review.[1]

Less than two weeks later, September 11 upset America's equilibrium and—not least—shook the country's financial footings. The surprise attack reminded Wall Street of what it had too long denied—that in finance risk is ever-present. For financial instruments such as pensions, which reach far into the future, the potential risk is nearly incalculable. General Motors had learned this slowly; San Diego discovered it in an hour.

The economic fallout from September 11 hit San Diego hard. Already reeling from the dot-com crash, the city suffered a painful loss of tourism revenue, along with the collapse of its holdings on Wall Street.

For the moment, there wasn't much that pension sponsors could do besides hunker down, hold expenses flat and hope for the best. It was the prudent course; in the wake of the attacks, one could say it was the patriotic course. It is, therefore, fairly remarkable that on September 18, a mere week after the attacks, Saathoff, the firefighters' president (who was also a SDCERS trustee), began to push for another increase. More astonishing still, this increase would benefit just one person—Saathoff himself. At present, his pension was to be calculated on the basis of his firefighter's salary from the city, but he also received a stipend from the union. If *both* salaries were considered, it would raise his benefit enormously, from $86,000 a year to $116,000.[2] That is a truly gold-plated pension (recall that a retired autoworker's pension is only about $36,000).

To get his pension plum approved in the next round of labor negotiations, which was scheduled for the spring, Saathoff needed to plant a seed now. He was in an enviable position, being friendly with the folks at City Hall, and with utter lack of shame, he floated the idea of his special perk while the Trade Center was still smoldering.[3]

But the officials—even though favorably disposed toward the union leader—were growing concerned about SDCERS. On October 11, Cathy Lexin, the city's chief of human relations, emailed Terri Webster, the assistant city auditor. In the subject line of the email, Lexin typed, "EEEK." She was worried because SDCERS's investment earnings had fallen sharply—by 70 percent, to be precise—even *before* the terrorist attack.

Both Lexin and Webster were pension trustees as well as city officials—a highly conflicted position. While each sat on the pension board, their primary responsibility was to the city. They knew that if SDCERS's funding were to fall to 82.3 percent (the "trigger"), the city would be required to inject a massive dose of cash. And the city couldn't afford it. In December, as SDCERS's investments continued to sputter, Webster shared her mounting worries in an email to Larry Grissom, the SDCERS administrator:

Larry

Oct statements showed $15.4 m loss on sale of stocks and a total monthly loss of $7m bringing YTD [year to date] earnings at Oct 31 2001 to only $14.1 million compared to $107 m last year same time. A 87% decrease. !Eeek!

Sincerely,

Sleepless in San Diego[4]

Grissom's staff was losing sleep as well. City employees by the score were exploiting the special sweetener added in 1996, buying extra pension credits on the cheap. Since the price had been set so low, employees with, say, only fifteen years' tenure were getting pensions corresponding to twenty years' service. The city was virtually giving its retirement credits away.

Early in 2002, the city officials exchanged more bad news about the flagging performance of SDCERS and the likelihood that it would not be able to fund benefits out of its earnings. "These are SERIOUS consequences and needs [sic] attention," Webster warned.[5]

It would be one thing if the officials dealt openly and honestly with the problem—as a public issue that needed airing—but as a matter of expediency and also of habit, they preferred to handle pension matters behind closed doors. If the public learned that SDCERS was in trouble, there would be pressure on the city to return to full funding. Then it would have to cut spending someplace else or—heaven forbid—raise taxes.

Therefore, the blue-ribbon report, scheduled for release at the end of February, posed a worrisome public relations problem. A draft version of the section on pensions, authored by Vortmann, was highly critical (informally it was dubbed "the 'sky is falling' version"). The timing was also awkward, as San Diego was due to sell bonds for its new baseball stadium. City officials were worried that a negative blue-ribbon report would hurt the city's credit rating and jeopardize the sale of the bonds.[6]

The officials—in particular the auditor and assistant auditor—made a concerted effort to water down Vortmann's findings. The rest of the blue-ribbon panel, which was stacked with Murphy's cronies (six had contributed to his campaign), went along.[7] Under heavy pressure, the fifty-eight-year-old executive agreed to tone down his report.

This was an ominous step—not just because full and open disclosure is as vital to good government as it is to a healthy stock market, but because, once set, the habit of concealing the truth is hard to break. One reads with dismay the conspiratorial email from Webster, the assistant auditor, in which she noted approvingly that Vortmann "did in a small way improve his language." The bureaucrat coolly added, "[W]e gave a good shot at changing him . . . he just didn't fall for it all."[8]

On February 11, the SDCERS actuary reported more bad news. He revealed to the staff that the plan's funding ratio had fallen from 97 percent in June 2000 to 89.9 percent in June 2001 (the date on which its fiscal year ended). By now—early 2002—it was assuredly lower. In cash terms, the unfunded portion of the SDCERS liability had mushroomed from $69 million to $284 million. Webster saw the figure and winced.[9]

The public, of course, remained completely in the dark; indeed, to the outside world, San Diego was the picture of health. The city completed the sale of the ballpark bonds, and a few days later, *Reason*, a West Coast journal advocating libertarian politics, presented San Diego with a management award. Carl DeMaio, a Newt Gingrich protégé who was representing *Reason*, shook Murphy's hand and the two were photographed with satisfied smiles. Yet even as DeMaio was stepping off the elevator at City Hall, someone who had been in the audience approached him and said, "I can't believe you gave them that award." Over the next two weeks, DeMaio got a handful of calls from people who maintained that the city wasn't being candid about its finances—about SDCERS in particular.[10]

On the very day Murphy was getting the award, Vortmann was fretting that the funding level at SDCERS had dropped to the vicinity of 85 percent—perilously close to the trigger level of 82.3 percent. "This is a rather big issue," he noted to a fellow trustee. He added, in a second email, "I get a very strong sense of 'game playing' or 'ass covering' by the Actuary."[11]

But Vortmann, who had been named to the SDCERS board, and had a growing awareness of its troubles, was uncomfortable about his own role in sanitizing the blue-ribbon report. The final version did warn that the city's pension expense was growing at a rapid rate (at $68 million, pensions were already one of the larger items in the city budget, which totaled $710 million). It also noted that San Diego was deferring some $300 million in maintenance on streets, sidewalks, traffic signals, and the like. But the report did not strike a sufficiently urgent tone. It concluded that San Diego was "fiscally sound," and that, of course, was the lead sentence in the next day's *Union-Tribune*.[12] Even worse, it said the pension was 97 percent funded. That was no longer true (indeed, it was twenty months out of date), and Vortmann and others who had helped to write the report knew it.[13]

Vortmann was franker when he met in executive session with a subcommittee of the city council, including the mayor and the auditor. He presented a worrisome chart showing that pension expenses, which had been equal to only 8.8 percent of the payroll in the early '90s, had soared to 14.1 percent by 2001. "That is very troublesome for any business," he said, "particularly when it is, as I said, a non-discretionary item."

Byron Wear, a councilman, blurted out, "It sounds like we have our own version of a Social Security scandal here."

Ed Ryan, the auditor, objected, "It's not a scandal at all."

Since the councilmen had no thought of fixing the problem—which would have required them to either raise taxes or impose budget cuts—Wear suggested that they resume the discussion "later." The mayor had thus far been silent, but at the suggestion of a postponement, he jumped into the fray and seconded the idea.

The group resolved to hand off the issue to the city manager. Though the blue-ribbon report had been *Murphy's* idea, its findings, even toned down, were simply too hot for him to handle. Thus the mayor and the council—the one group with the power to raise revenue—resolved that they should wait for the city manager; that is, they should do nothing.[14]

THE CITY MANAGER, Michael Uberuaga, was quieter and less charismatic than his predecessor, McGrory. He was less a financial wizard than a bureaucrat eager to satisfy City Hall. Uberuaga and his staff were already grappling with the looming issue of the pension trigger. They had concluded that the city did not have the money to make a special balloon payment.[15] Webster, the expressive assistant auditor, referred to the trigger as a "time bomb" that could sink the city's bond rating, thereby increasing its borrowing costs and setting San Diego on a downward and ever steeper financial spiral.[16]

Meanwhile, a *Union-Tribune* reporter had begun to sniff around the story. Grissom, the SDCERS administrator, correctly guessed that his masters at City Hall would not want him talking. He slavishly queried Webster, "Is there any 'party line' for me to communicate?"[17]

THE CITY OFFICIALS' one hope lay in the upcoming labor negotiations. Strange to call it a hope, because the firefighters and the other unions would be demanding raises. But negotiations are two-sided. The officials began to wonder whether the city could offer *something* to the unions in exchange for being released from the pension trigger. This was like trying to disable the fire alarm at the first sign of smoke. The trigger had been created precisely to make sure that SDCERS did not get into trouble, and now the city wanted out of it.

A group at City Hall began to flush out the idea of increasing pension benefits in exchange for leeway to make lower contributions. This was an exact redo of the underfunding plan that McGrory had engineered in 1996. Bruce Herring, the mercurial deputy manager and a former assistant to McGrory, strenuously advocated this approach. As far as Herring was concerned, the 1996 accord had achieved its aim of buying the city time.

Why not try to strike the bargain again? One might as well ask, why not do it forever and never pay the bill?

THE CITY OFFICIALS quickly reached a consensus that dealing with the unions was their only way out. The job of crafting a deal was given primarily to Lexin, a fifty-one-year-old high school–educated career public servant. Lexin was not only the lead labor negotiator for the city but one of a handful of people who put together its budget. She was dependable if cocky and rather abrasive. Nothing in her experience would have alerted her to the singular hazard of underfunding the pension (namely, that future generations would have to pay for it forever). Even if it had, Lexin had risen through the ranks by doing what her superiors told her. Her bosses—especially Herring, the deputy manager—were now insistent that the trigger be scotched. So Lexin, with help from Webster as well as from Saathoff, began to draft a proposal to—once more—increase pension benefits.[18]

The pressure for a deal accelerated in mid-March when, in a closed briefing, the city council heard the worst news yet: if the trigger were detonated, it would require the city to pay at least $40 million a year. Possibly, the bill would be as much as $75 million—far more than what the council had anticipated and, indeed, far more than it had.[19]

Two days later, when the mayor and the council subcommittee met in private, Murphy acknowledged that the pension problem was "serious." But again, he found reasons for waiting rather than acting. The city was in the midst of negotiations with the unions, and the mayor, like the city manager, preferred to let the talks run their course. Rather than fixing the problem at the source—that is, the city's overextended budget—the officials were hoping to defuse the trigger by cutting a deal with Saathoff.[20]

SDCERS's condition worsened even as the talks progressed. The stock market was plummeting again, due to the revelations of scandal at Enron and other corporations. By mid-April, Grissom estimated that investment losses in 2002 would cause the system to breach the trigger and fall to 80 percent funding. This only enhanced Grissom's conspiratorial frame of mind. Sharing the doleful outlook with Webster, he implored her, "Please treat this as confidential for the moment . . . haven't shared with any of the other Board members yet." Incredibly, the SDCERS administrator was keeping vital information from his own board.[21]

Had the officials paused even for a moment, they would have realized that each benefit hike (though designed to alleviate some temporary hardship) merely exacerbated the long-term problem. But that very day, April 16, the city council authorized the labor team to negotiate new benefit improvements. The city's negotiators were quite explicit that the hikes were to be offered *only* in exchange for getting funding relief.[22]

Such a quid pro quo was highly improper. Pension trustees have a duty to protect the integrity of their systems *unconditionally.* It is not to be bargained away in return for benefits or money for potholes or anything else.

When word reached Vortmann that new benefits were in the works, the executive was horrified. Agonizing over his prior failure to speak more candidly, he wrote a frank letter to his fellow blue-ribbon members in which he admitted:

> I have a growing and daunting concern that we possibly did our City a disservice by not ringing a very loud bell that:
>
> i) the City's fiscal health is not what it appears,
> ii) there are serious problems,
> iii) their solutions will be painful in terms of reduced services and/or increased taxes and fees.[23]

Vortmann sent a copy to the mayor's senior policy adviser, Dennis Gibson, who passed it along to Murphy's chief of staff. If Murphy saw it, he never responded.[24]

IN ORDER TO BECOME LAW, benefit increases in San Diego have to go through a series of approvals at the city council. Councilman Jim

Madaffer had been elected with the strong support of the firefighters, and in May he returned the favor by offering a motion for the so-called Presidential Leave benefit that would let Saathoff combine his two salaries and rake in the larger pension.

There was an open question about whether it was legal.[25] SDCERS was chartered to provide benefits to *city* workers based on their *city* salaries. Nothing in the local laws authorized the system to pay benefits on wages paid by a union.* When the city's personnel director had the temerity to question it, Madaffer slavishly ordered him, "Just do it!" Saathoff's plan was coming up trumps.

The council then approved a package of pension hikes. This was a preliminary vote—a final vote was still pending—but the eye-opening truth was already evident: to "cure" its ailing retirement system, San Diego was going to further strain it by hiking benefits! The package, which included the Saathoff benefit as well as increases for various of the employee groups, was dubbed Manager's Proposal 2, or MP-2. (The 1996 accord, which had reduced funding and attached the dubious "trigger," was now to be known as MP-1.)

By far the most expensive feature in MP-2 was a hike in the multiplier used in calculating benefits for municipal workers, the city's largest union. On a combined basis, MP-1 and MP-2 raised the formula for these workers by an astonishing *two-thirds*—all at a time of financial distress.

In another carefully crafted plum, MP-2 raised the benefit ceiling specifically for employees hired before age twenty-four—a small group that happened to include Webster, the official who had helped to draft it.[26] This was pension plunder on its face.

---

*Technically, the Presidential Leave benefit was awarded not just to Saathoff but also to the presidents of the police and municipal unions. However, the latter two did not receive *any* city salary. They had been contributing part of their union pay to SDCERS all along, with the expectation of receiving a pension based on the formula for employees in their respective unions. The legality of this arrangement had been questioned, but the city had, informally, gone along with it. The resolution implementing the Presidential Leave benefit provided that all three union heads could count their combined salaries, but as only Saathoff got a salary from the city, he was the only one to receive an economic benefit. The only effect on the other two was to codify, and perhaps to sanction, benefits they already expected to receive.

The council hardly cared; to be rid of the trigger it would pay any price. But city officials *were* concerned about whether SDCERS would fulfill its end of the bargain, by relaxing the trigger. They were counting on Saathoff—who, they believed, controlled the board. "[We] especially need Ron behind releasing the trigger *since he runs the show at [SD]CERS*," Webster emailed with characteristic bluntness.

Mike McGhee, a city negotiator, reassured Webster via e-mail that Saathoff knew exactly what was expected of him. McGhee replied, "I assure you that Ron is well aware of the contingent nature of the benefits."[27]

McGhee was a good source, because he had previously sat on the other side of the table, as a negotiator for Saathoff and Local 145, illustrating the cozy relations between the city and the union. However, even allowing for San Diego's rich web of conflicts, it is remarkable that the city officials were putting so much faith in Saathoff's ability to deliver the board. The city, after all, was negotiating labor contracts covering thousands of employees that would hinge on the board's agreeing to waive the trigger. And until the end of May, when the city manager made a formal pitch, the board had not even been consulted on it.[28]

Of course, not all of the SDCERS trustees were in the dark. The board was effectively split between appointed trustees, who were deliberately kept out of the loop, and those who represented City Hall or the unions. The latter were decidedly in the know. Indeed, to the union reps and bureaucrats on the board, the existence of MP-2 was an open secret. Three of them (Lexin, Webster, and Saathoff) had essentially *written* it.

One of the outsiders, a financial consultant named Diann Shipione, was palpably unhappy about this blatant division on the board, though her concerns were not as yet focused on MP-2. Shipione had written an accusatory letter to the mayor, asking for an audit of SDCERS and charging that its hired consultant, Callan Associates, was picking investment managers in return for favors rather than on the basis of merit. This was a rather serious charge.[29]

However, SDCERS's long-term investment record had been good.[30] And as Shipione's tone was unnecessarily strident, her criticisms tended to be dismissed. The other trustees suspected that she was a mouthpiece for her husband, Pat Shea, who was a wealthy lawyer with close ties to the Republican Party and had been a classmate at Harvard Business School of George W. Bush. In San Diego, the Shea-Shipione wedding had been a political event, attended by Mayor Golding and presided over by the then judge (and future mayor) Murphy.[31] After they were married, Shipione was appointed to the board of a small endowment and, a couple of years later, to the retirement system.

By 2002, Shipione was challenging every aspect of how SDCERS operated. She asked some good questions, but her tone was relentless and unsparing, as though a dark secret were hidden in every drawer. This turned off the other trustees and some of them openly mocked her.

However, the board could not make light of criticism from Rick Roeder. The actuary had wilted in 1996, when he had approved of MP-1, but he seemed determined to resist the new assault on his client's funding. On June 12, Roeder, who had been asked to evaluate MP-2, delivered a scorching critique of it. He pointed out that the board's only job was to supervise the retirement system—not to accommodate labor negotiations. In addition, he observed, the system's funded ratio was one of the lowest in California. This seemed to leave little room for waiving the trigger, much less for raising benefits further. In sum, Roeder declared, "What the City proposes is outside the norm for generally accepted actuarial funded policies."[32] Herring, the deputy manager, was furious at Roeder. He blurted out, "You're an actuary on the edge!"

Next up was Robert Blum, a San Francisco attorney who was SDCERS's latest fiduciary counsel. Blum was similarly critical, though his opinion was shrouded in lawyerly caution. In an unsigned letter, he warned that waiving the trigger could be viewed by a future court as "not a proper exercise of the Board's fiduciary responsibilities." Cutting through his dense legalese, Blum had delivered a clear warning.

Yet the officials, as if driven by some fatal instinct, forged ahead. Lexin alerted the mayor and the council that the situation was becoming dire. Given that (a) the new benefits were contingent on the board's waiving the trigger and (b) Blum seemed to be balking on giving his blessing, MP-2 might fail. In that case, she warned, not only would the city be liable for the unaffordable balloon payment, it would probably have to renegotiate its contracts with the unions.[33] Little by little, the pension mess was consuming the entire city. It didn't seem to dawn on the officials that their so-called solution would only create a bigger mess.

The SDCERS board met again on June 21. The day before, it received a letter from Michael Aguirre, the securities lawyer who had filed a voting rights suit against San Diego's electoral system, and who seemed to get involved, one way or another, in most of the city's high-profile disputes. Aguirre's letter urged the board to reject the underfunding plan and contained the ominous language, "This letter is written in the hopes of avoiding a lawsuit." He said he was representing a client whose identity could not be disclosed for fear that the client would suffer "retaliation."[34]

Aguirre's furtive client was one of the trustees—the discontented Shipione.[35] Aguirre was good friends with Shea, Shipione's husband. Despite their political differences (Aguirre was a Democrat), both were iconoclastic lawyers who liked to tilt at the establishment. They had once worked on a utilities case together and, like everyone else who came into contact with Aguirre, Shea had been amazed by his energy. Aguirre was known for writing briefs—even for calling other lawyers—well after midnight. He would go to sleep with his books and papers scattered around him and commonly rose at 3:30 a.m. According to a colleague, "his mind never shut off." What Aguirre lacked was a cause. He had recently run and lost for district attorney—his fourth failed campaign. Then Shea called and told him about the troubles at SDCERS.

The suggestion of pension abuse struck a chord with Aguirre, whose biggest case to date had been representing victims of a multimillion-dollar pension fraud.[36] SDCERS, he knew, was potentially much bigger; it could get him back on the front page. The five-foot-seven, two-hundred-pound litigator, the grandson of an immigrant prizefighter, crackled with barely controlled fury as he warned the board that approving MP-2 would be a costly mistake.

WHEN THE BOARD met in private, the trustees, who naturally were not eager to be sued by Aguirre or anyone else, asked the city for indemnification. Shipione sensibly asked why the board didn't simply leave the present funding arrangement in place. If the city couldn't pay what it owed now, what reason was there to think it could do so later?

Herring, the deputy city manager, gave a revealing answer: "It will not be easier nor desirous [to pay later]," he replied—"just necessary." He was anticipating that the city would suffer yet another revenue shortfall from the state, which was suffering its own budget woes.[37] This is the problem with all delayed pension schemes; they leave the fund vulnerable at the worst possible moment—when the sponsor is also hurting.

Though the city's budget problems were real, they should have *remained* the city's problems, not the retirement board's. Police and potholes were properly the responsibility of the taxpayers—not of pensioners. Getting to the nub of it in a letter to his fellow trustees, Vortmann reckoned, "The problem is very simply that the City does not want to pay currently for what they want to give the employees."[38]

On the Monday after the SDCERS meeting, Blum, the outside counsel, happened to be speaking at a seminar in the Bay Area on public pension negotiations. A veteran pension expert (he had helped to draft ERISA in the '70s), Blum was in an expansive mood, and his San Diego experience was on his mind. He warned that pension trustees were not always the ideal fiduciaries that the textbooks described—especially when "the president of the union sits on [the] board." Now he told a little story:

> So here's another example. We have had circumstances in which benefits have been increased through negotiation, and the deal was explicit. The deal that the negotiators brought to the retirement board was, we're going to give these increased benefits . . . on the condition that you "stabilize" the contribution rate for the agency. Stabilize is a euphemism for "reduce." You had a retirement board that really, really wanted to do this.

Blum evidently had deep misgivings about this board:

> By the way, that precise deal is being revisited right now because the structure, as we have learned in bad times, was doomed to fail. Now we are dealing with what I consider to be a failed structure.[39]

While Blum was waxing eloquent on San Diego's doomed structure, Saathoff was still trying to jack up his benefit. That same day, he held a protracted meeting with Grissom, the pension administrator. In truth, Grissom was a little awed by Saathoff. After the union leader left, he emailed Lexin about the status of Saathoff's special benefit. Lexin, sniffing out the source, replied, "TELL RON TO COOL HIS JETS."[40]

The next Sunday was June 30, the date on which SDCERS closed its books. The system would turn out to be underfunded by an eye-popping $720 million. Though the figures had yet to be calculated, Grissom, as well as the city officials, knew that the numbers would be grim.

Saathoff, meanwhile, was furiously thinking of ways to revise MP-2 to mollify the board's advisers. At the board meeting of July 11, he offered a fig leaf to amend the plan, but one that kept the "practical impact" of the underfunding scheme unchanged.[41]

The meeting dragged on for two and a half hours. Shipione and Vortmann couldn't understand why the board was still considering the plan, which had been all but rejected in June. They asked question after question trying to derail it. Lexin grew increasingly anxious, as though her job were on the line. "If you don't approve this—" she blurted out threateningly, then stopped in midsentence. Blum and Roeder were asked for their opinions of the revised proposal. The advisers wavered. Roeder gave confusing answers; he seemed to have tired of doing battle.[42]

Even with Saathoff's changes, the proposal would allow the city to continue the underfunding until at least 2009. Also, as the trustees knew, waiving the trigger was part of a quid pro quo: the city council would do its part by enacting new benefits. But there was one thing the outside trustees *didn't* know. Saathoff had omitted to tell them about his Presidential Leave benefit (the one that would net him an extra $30,000 a year). This was a blatant and calculated bit of deception, as the knowledge of Saathoff's plum might have roused the trustees' dormant sense of propriety.[43]

The board voted 8–2 in favor of MP-2, contingent upon approvals from its actuary, Roeder, and from its lawyer, Blum, following which the board would have to vote once more, in November.

Grissom, who knew Blum well enough to exchange emails with him about women, cars, and fishing, worked on him over the summer and into the fall.[44] Blum gradually came around. There is no convincing explanation, other than that he was tiring of offering resistance. He had the necessary virtue but not the backbone. So eager was Blum to please, he also began to work on Roeder. In fact, Blum offered to draft the actuary's letter *for* him.

By mid-September, to judge from a Blum communiqué, the lawyer had stopped thinking critically and was, in fact, busily engaged in contriving a convenient out. Thus, he wrote of the letter that he was drafting for Roeder, "it is highly dependant [*sic*] on what rick will say in writing and I am trying to find words that will both give him comfort and give the board what it needs."[45] Blum had given his honest opinion in June and the board had ignored him. Now he wished to be done with it.

The inexorable progress of MP-2 got no coverage in the *Union-Tribune* or anywhere else, enhancing Shipione's feeling that she was fighting it alone. Actually, a retired city bureaucrat and former SDCERS board president named James Gleason was tracking the story by gleaning what he could from the public notices. In August, Gleason wrote to the mayor and to the board urging them not to repeat the mistake of the first underfunding plan. Predictably, he got no response and, for the moment, Shipione remained unaware of him.[46]

SAN DIEGO had asked Kelling, Northcross & Nobriga, an advisory firm, to study the city's budget, and it happened to deliver its report at the end of the summer, as the pension plot was reaching a climax. According to

KNN, San Diego was seriously undertaxed compared to other cities in the state, which should have suggested to *somebody* in City Hall that there were potential revenue sources in San Diego other than the pension fund. The list of the top twelve cities in California, ranked by revenue raised per capita, made this eminently clear:

San Francisco	$2,343
Santa Clara	$1,110
Oakland	$916
Santa Barbara	$817
Los Angeles	$754
Irvine	$666
Long Beach	$630
Sacramento	$598
San Jose	$560
San Diego	**$545**
Anaheim	$509
Santa Ana	$439[47]

The study identified ten fees or taxes that San Diego could tap for revenue, and the amount it could hope to generate (substantial, in some cases) from each. But taxes remained taboo and the study was shelved. The city was simply obsessed with getting the board to release it from its promise to hold to the 82.3 percent funding threshold, and the pension board, despite having been warned by its lawyer, was on the verge of going along.

Late in October, the city council voted for the second of three times on Saathoff's special benefit. Saathoff was on the cusp of building a political machine; his former legislative aide, Michael Zucchet, was running for the city council and would be swept to victory in November with the strenuous support of the firefighters. It was hardly a surprise that the council quickly ratified Saathoff's perk.

Still to be corralled was Roeder, the actuary. In late October, Blum, who seemed to have completely forgotten his own prior objections, sent Roeder a draft of the agreement with the city. "[R]emember the letter we need from you?" he prodded. "[W]e now need to have it signed. a copy is attached."[48]

However, Roeder still had qualms. "Hmmmmm, [he replied] thinking about this I do not want to have anybody think that we advocate a method, which, in total, would have over a decade of subsidized [underfunded] rates."[49] But of course, they would be advocating just that.

Blum replied impatiently, even a bit menacingly, "You had signed off on this exact language before. So lots of people would be very unhappy if you are unwilling to sign off on it now."[50]

And with that, Roeder completely caved. "I can live with the language just not optimum," he wrote back cheerily. "No huge deal at my end."[51]

Even while giving his grudging okay, Roeder acknowledged that "[t]he higher the City's contribution levels, the better the funding status of SDCERS." Indeed, he admitted, "From a pure actuarial viewpoint, it would be best to hold the City to the existing Manager's Proposal and the 82.3 percent trigger."

It is fair to ask, what other viewpoint besides a purely actuarial one was Roeder expected to give? Nonetheless, the tortured actuary had wriggled himself into a position from which he could deliver a minimally favorable verdict; namely, that if the board was set on approving MP-2 in *some* form, this version was reasonable.[52]

Roeder's metaphysical exertions were no match for those of Blum himself. *His* favorable opinion, which ran for fourteen pages, was a triumph of professional plasticity. It has virtually no analysis, even under the lengthy section titled "Analysis." Blum gives a history of the case, he devotes a page to the *Wilson* decision (which established the right of Californians to a secure retirement system), and he somehow arrives at the conclusion that in approving MP-2, the SDCERS board would be reflecting "consideration of the principles set out in *Wilson*," which is not the same as saying it would be consistent with *Wilson*. He cites the actuary's opinion, rather disingenuously since Blum himself had drafted it. But—good attorney that he is—Blum could not ignore the actuary's statement that full funding would indeed be "best." Here is where he does his heavy lifting: "We recognize, as does the Board's actuary, that higher City contribution levels than required under the Agreement [MP-2] would provide better financial protection to SDCERS. . . . However, we also recognize that the board engaged in extensive analysis of the issues."

Blum seems to be saying that since the board has thought about and debated the matter, its decision—any decision?—would suffice. As the board is relying on Blum, for him to cite the trustees' deliberations was an abject circularity.[53]

When the board met, on November 15, Shipione spoke bitterly against MP-2. Saathoff, who had yet to mention his promised special benefit, strenuously argued in favor. Roeder, still searching for comfortable terrain, said he hoped the board would never enter into another such deal.[54] Given that his signature was on this one, it was an empty gesture. His one duty was to provide strict actuarial advice and he had failed at it.

Even with the advisers on board, the trustees needed a push. Elmer Heap, a deputy city attorney, said the city council would consider granting the trustees immunity.[55] He was like a priest offering absolution before the crime is committed. The trustees kept arguing, especially Shipione. The mood was contentious. Vortmann thought the scheme was wrong but he had given up—he felt it was preordained. MP-2 was approved with only Shipione and the policemen's rep voting no.

Three days later, the city council met in open session. The agenda included three measures on the various facets of MP-2. The public, for the most part, was wholly unaware of them (the premeeting publicity was about a measure to fund the library). The pension items, therefore, had been placed in the "consent" agenda—meaning they were considered uncontroversial. Even the council members knew little of the details. When it came to SDCERS they were accustomed to trusting the city manager, even though the pension was the rare issue that could potentially bankrupt the city.

Items in the consent agenda are voted on without debate, and this is what Murphy wanted. However, any citizen has the right to pull items from the consent agenda. And Shipione pulled them. This aroused the attention of a single council member—surf shop owner Donna Frye.

In a written statement, which was framed as a letter to the mayor, Shipione described MP-2 as the fruit of conflicts of interest "on the part of City and Labor representatives that sit as Trustees." She added, "It gives the appearance, if not the reality, that the City 'bought' votes on the Retirement Board." Shipione also fingered the council for its political cowardice. By delaying full funding until 2009, the council would be deferring the burden until, precisely, the year that term limits would force the council and the mayor to retire![56] They would literally leave the problem to their successors.

When Shipione rose to speak before the council, she was nervous and trembling. Facing the mayor who had presided at her wedding, she denounced the pension proposal as "almost corrupt"—a phrase she had carefully considered. She also laid into the pension board and city officials. Saathoff followed with a rebuttal; he was far more polished.[57]

Murphy, who loathed such public displays, was hoping to move to a vote—but Frye wanted to hear more. She was intrigued by Shipione, whom she saw as a kindred spirit, and asked the city to respond. Lexin thus had to defend the plan; she said San Diego's budget pressures "gave the City little choice."[58] But even for a supposedly lofty purpose, a violation of a retirement system is still a violation.

The council voted 8–1 in favor. It approved the new pension benefits, the continued underfunding, and immunity for the trustees. MP-2 was now law.[59] According to the next day's *Union-Tribune*, "A financing plan for $312.3 million in library improvements was approved by the San Diego City Council amid growing concern over the city's finances." The article did not mention SDCERS.[60]

But news of MP-2 traveled fast. A reporter with a local business journal, the *Daily Transcript*, was intrigued by Shipione's use of the word "corrupt" and asked her for an interview. The paper published a news article as well as an op-ed by Shipione. Lamont Ewell, the assistant city manager, had to say *something* in response. Lexin drafted a memo, which Ewell signed, charging that Shipione "omitted, slanted and misrepresented the facts."[61] Actually, it was Ewell and Lexin who were distorting. Dissembling the events of the past six months, their letter managed to suggest that the board's action to waive the trigger was "separate" from the city's labor negotiations.[62] The record clearly showed that they were linked.

On December 26, Roeder reported on SDCERS's latest balance sheet. It revealed a shocking deterioration. As of the previous June, the system's funding had plunged to 77.3 percent—well below the agreed-upon threshold.[63] Only now there was no trigger to force the city to restore it. Presumably, few San Diegans were paying attention the day after Christmas. One who assuredly did notice was Gleason, the retired board president who had tried to derail the underfunding plan by writing to the mayor in August. After the summer, he had lost sight of MP-2, and figured that it had been scuttled. Sometime in December, he learned the truth. Gleason immediately called a local attorney who specialized in pension cases, Michael Conger. Conger was in Oklahoma for the holidays. Gleason sent an urgent email: "Mike, they are under-funding the pension plan. They can't do that."[64]

When Conger returned to San Diego, he worked with exceptional speed. He debriefed Gleason, researched SDCERS's funding history, and in mid-January filed a class-action lawsuit with Gleason and another retiree as the named plaintiffs. Conger sued the entire cast of plotters: the city, SDCERS, and the key trustees. After six years of deliberate underfunding, the machinations of the pension board were to be scrutinized in open court.

SEVEN

THE BILL COMES DUE

Conger plunged his tiny law office into the *Gleason* case. He had two principal claims—that the city was violating the local charter by failing to make pension contributions at the actuarial rate, and that some of the trustees had violated section 1090 of the California Code, which makes it a crime for a public official to participate in the making of a contract in which he or she has a financial interest.

Though technical in nature, the lawsuit was a threat to the entire artifice that had been propping up City Hall. If Conger could force the city to restore full funding, it would unravel the convenient lie on which San Diego had been figuring its budget. Its tax base, its ability to pay for libraries and sports teams, and everything else would be affected. Its elected officials could suddenly be vulnerable.

More than any other government program, pensions are a test of political character. They are a bargain with the future: a statement about the value that a city places on its workers. When the bargain is corrupted, the whole society is affected. Its sense of equity is destroyed, and with it the people's faith in their leaders and their institutions.

Such an unraveling was hardly foreseeable when Conger began the litigation. The pension mess was a thicket of details. It did not have the public's eye, and Conger was but a lonely lawyer—a sole practitioner battling the entire city establishment. He remortgaged his house twice to finance the litigation; meanwhile, no money was coming in.

Early in 2003, Conger wrote the city attorney and pleaded with him to settle. He was turned down flat. Then Conger started filing more suits—one brief after another. His aim was to get the retirement system to recognize that, though nominally a defendant, it (along with the retirees) was the *victim* in the case. In practical terms, he wanted the board to switch sides and help him to force the city to restore full funding.[1]

Trying to quell the barrage of lawsuits, Michael Leone, an outside attorney hired to defend SDCERS, pleaded with Conger to "stop throwing cherry bombs."[2] What Conger couldn't know was that Leone basically agreed with him. In his view, his client (or at least its board) was in the wrong. Its deal with the city was both indefensible and contrary to its own interests. Only in the upside-down world of SDCERS would a pension system conspire with the sponsor to deprive *itself* of contributions.

By early March, Leone and his partner, Reginald Vitek, were urging SDCERS to drop its opposition to Conger and file a counterclaim against the city.[3] Save for Shipione, the trustees gave the lawyers a cool reception. They were hardly about to abandon MP-2, which after all was their creation.

At this point, Vitek and Leone came to an important realization. The trustees' *personal* interests were in conflict with those of SDCERS. The lawyers threatened to quit the case unless the board recused itself from directing the litigation. After some jawboning, a compromise was worked out, but the essential conflict of interest remained. SDCERS continued to oppose Conger's suit, and to maintain that MP-2 had been absolutely proper—even though its own attorneys had reached a diametrically opposite view.[4]

As with other besieged organizations, the retirement system's instinct when under attack was to stonewall. It worried not only about Conger's legal cherry bombs but about attacks in the court of public opinion. The pension staff tried to keep discussion of the case to a minimum; the *Daily Transcript* called it San Diego's "dirty little secret."[5] As the in-house attorney for SDCERS directed in a memo, "The present strategy is to stress [the] importance of privilege."[6] That meant keeping all information under wraps. The board increasingly skirmished with Shipione, whom they suspected of leaking. In a foolish pique, the board president even took out an ad in the *Union-Tribune* accusing an unnamed party (clearly Shipione) of behaving like "Chicken Little."[7] In point of fact, Shipione was looking prophetic. By mid-2003, SDCERS's funding ratio had plummeted to 67 percent—this for a system that had been almost fully funded three years earlier.

As its financial position weakened, the plight of SDCERS was beginning to create fiscal problems for the city. Local executives were fretting about its possible effect on business. San Diego, like other cities, was also coming to grips with the fact that it had a massive retiree health care liability, estimated at $1 billion. What the city fathers hungered for was some leadership on these issues at City Hall. But Murphy was passive and ambivalent. He didn't defend the underfunding—but he didn't move to correct it either.

The cloud over City Hall darkened in the spring, due to a tawdry political scandal. Three city councilmen, including Michael Zucchet, the former firefighters' lobbyist, had accepted campaign gifts from a strip club owner, allegedly a bribe for promising to repeal the "no-touch" law. The three proclaimed their innocence and, for the moment, retained their seats. However, the prospect that a third of the council would be serving while under federal indictment, added to the trouble at SDCERS, gave rise to fears of generalized corruption, as though all of official San Diego was for sale.

Where the government was not corrupt it was simply ineffective. Nothing so demonstrated the point as the mayor's pained deliberations with regard to his own future. In one bizarre month, Murphy announced he would run for reelection in 2004, then changed his mind, saying he preferred to focus on the problems of the city, then, after supporters pleaded with him to reconsider, declared he was back in the race. His lack of resolve dismayed ordinary citizens. San Diegans did not like expensive government, but they liked (or so they were discovering) weak government even less. The impression of irresolution was confirmed when the Chargers, who had not enjoyed a winning season in eight years, demanded a *new* stadium, without which they were threatening, again, to pull up stakes. Characteristically, Mayor Murphy created a task force to study the issue. Taking a definite stand seemed beyond him.

Edward Fike, a retired *Union-Tribune* editor, was so agitated that he called on Murphy and urged him to get a grip. "There is a tsunami approaching that is going to take you and all of us down," he warned.[8]

Fike urged Murphy to fire the city manager. Murphy replied that he had to get past "stripper-gate" (the Zucchet scandal) and the Chargers mess before considering changes. Soon after, a delegation from the Chamber of Commerce implored the mayor to enlist *its* help. Murphy spurned them, too. The mayor increasingly relied on a single adviser, his chief of staff and former campaign consultant, John Kern, to set his agenda, and his view of the city was increasingly blinkered.[9]

Murphy was particularly ill suited to dealing with the pension crisis. He preferred to act only when the facts were resolved neatly in a bow, and SDCERS was anything but. His instinct in such cases was to dither—especially when, in late summer, Zucchet and the other two councilmen were indicted. The only action Murphy took with regard to SDCERS was to create yet another deliberative group, a "Pension Reform Committee."

WHILE CITY HALL seemed stalled, Conger was trying to force it to move on the *Gleason* case. He hit on a clever tactic. Municipalities are required to make full disclosure to the investors who buy their bonds (just as are corporations). In July, Conger reviewed a trove of the city's disclosures, many of which contained the assertion, "The state legislature requires us to fund our retirement system at the actuarily determined rate."[10] In other words, the city was implying to investors that San Diego was current on its pension obligation—a blatant untruth. For Conger, this was a secret bullet.

In August, Conger and the city started settlement talks. By then, Conger had discovered some twenty-one bond offerings with suspect language. He didn't, as yet, reveal his discovery to the city. But he mentioned it to Gleason, and Gleason shared it with Shipione.[11]

Shipione, too, had been poring over the city's financial records, often at home or at the gym on her stationary bike. One disclosure statement was of particular interest—in September, the city planned to sell $505 million of bonds for improvements in its sewer system. The lead underwriter was UBS Financial Services, Shipione's employer. Perhaps prompted by Gleason, Shipione reviewed the prospectus for the sewer bonds and spotted a seeming error in the description of the pension liability. She brought the error to the attention of Grissom—as well as to Orrick, Herrington & Sutcliffe, the law firm that handled the city's disclosures.[12] Bit by bit, the collateral damage from the pension system was spreading.

While Shipione was outing the faulty bond disclosure, she was also writing to the chairman of the San Diego Port Authority and disparaging SDCERS's financial records.[13] At this point, it is hard to disentangle Shipione's legitimate concern over SDCERS from her fury with the board. Her relations with the other trustees had deteriorated to open warfare. She was missing meetings, talking out of school, and regularly accusing her colleagues of ignoring their duty. Though she was not always wrong, her accusations were draped in self-righteous fervor, as though she were the lone honest trustee and a victim of the others' persecutions. She even called them "criminals." Roeder took her aside and said, "Diann, try not to make this personal." The city trustees (Lexin most of all) despised her.

Even among SDCERS staffers, presumably a less conflicted group than the board, Shipione had few friends. She accused the staff—money managers, people who ruled on claims, and so forth—of incompetence and dishonesty. As a sign of her isolation from the system, she regularly challenged its decisions to deny disability claims to retirees. A few of these claimants were patent liars, such as a fireman who claimed to have been injured by the bouncing of the fire truck all the while he was competing in triathlons. Other cases were more nuanced, involving employees who claimed to have suffered job-related injuries, the exact origins or severity of which were often unclear. Shipione invariably took the employee's side; what's more, she treated them less as claimants than as martyrs, sometimes hugging them in front of the board and offering "apologies" for her colleagues' rulings as though they had been deliberately prejudicial. She was a most trying and fragile trustee—after meetings she often burst into tears—yet she had a way of being right when it counted.

The sewer bonds were scheduled to go to market the second week of September. The day before the bonds were to be priced, Shipione shared her concerns with her manager at UBS, which of course was the underwriter. Her boss called New York. Before San Diego knew what hit it, UBS had postponed the underwriting. San Diego insisted that its mistakes were trivial; however, regulatory "mistakes" are not so easily put right. Orrick, its counsel, insisted that the city undertake a review of its past disclosures, and it soon became clear that the problem was larger than the city had let on.[14] In the meantime, San Diego was locked out of bond markets. Like a contagion, the pension scandal was infecting everything it touched.

As 2004 (an election year) drew near, City Hall was increasingly eager to resolve potentially damaging litigation. In December, San Diego offered to settle the *Gleason* case. Its offer was woefully inadequate. Incredibly, under the terms of the offer, which had been crafted by Herring, the deputy manager, SDCERS would have received *less* in contributions than under MP-2. The "settlement" offer was in fact the city's same old game of trying to perpetuate the underfunding.[15]

Conger was on the verge of taking it.[16] There is no good explanation for why, except that he was a solo attorney who hadn't been paid in a year, and he may have misjudged what the plan was worth. But Vitek and Leone, the outside SDCERS attorneys, saw through the ruse and urged the board to reject it.

Herring was furious. "Why are you raising this now for the first fucking time?" he screamed at Vitek.[17]

Determined to ram his settlement through, Herring took the extraordinary step of writing directly to the SDCERS board members. He claimed they had been kept "out of the loop" by counsel—a brazen attempt to divide the board from its own attorneys.[18]

As if shocked out of an unconscious slumber, SDCERS finally realized what it had at stake in *Gleason.* As the lawyers had been saying, SDCERS was the victim—and had been all along. It promptly rejected the city's offer. "Then we started going after the city in a classic adversarial sense," according to Leone.[19] After seven years of being shortchanged, the retirement system had awakened.

The litigation reached a climax just before Christmas. An attorney for the city, hoping to nullify Conger's basic claim, stated in court that San Diego was *not* required to contribute at the actuarial rate.[20] This was a pivotal mistake—the one Conger had been waiting for. Remember, he had all those bond disclosures in which the city had been saying just the opposite.

Conger pointed out the inconsistency to the judge. The litigator played like Columbo, the television detective. "I'm a little confused here," Conger said, as if it were a great mystery to him why the city would say one thing about its pension liability to investors and tell the *Gleason* court something else.[21]

The city had no good answer. In February, it agreed to a settlement—this time a fair one. In its next installment (in June) it would contribute $130 million to SDCERS, $45 million more than a year earlier. After that, contributions would be set at the actuarial rate—about $170 million. Just in case the city was unable to pay, SDCERS was awarded trust deeds on huge tracts of city property as collateral, including the parking lot at Qualcomm Stadium.[22]

Although the *Gleason* settlement in theory stopped SDCERS from deteriorating further, the damage already done to the system was severe. Indeed, its unfunded liabilities had soared to $1.4 *billion.*

Taking a longer view, since the mid-1990s, when Mayor Golding had started cheating on the city's pension obligations, the unfunded liability had soared from 22 percent of its payroll to an incredible 215 percent.[23] And of course, the city's now much-higher benefit levels could not be rolled back.

But the *responsibility* for the pension had shifted. Thanks to the *Gleason* court, the daunting obligation was now the burden of the city. Thus, pension expenses, formerly only 5 percent of the general budget, soared to approximately 20 percent. With SDCERS squeezing out other agencies for funds, the pension debt exploded as a political issue.

Michael Uberuaga, the city manager, declared that San Diego faced a fiscal crisis; he called for sharp budget and payroll cuts. This put Murphy, who faced a primary on March 2, in a difficult spot. Murphy was running against Ron Roberts, an uninspiring county supervisor whom he had defeated in 2000, and two other contenders. He dearly wanted to win 50 percent of the vote so as to avert a runoff in November. But the mayor was battered by a series of humbling plagues, almost biblical in their grim foreboding. Two scorching wildfires blazed out of control, exposing the inadequacy of the city's firefighting equipment, following which heavy rains produced one of the worst sewage spills in years. Then, early in 2004, the city admitted it was guilty of having issued dozens of false and misleading bond disclosures (most of them relating to the pension system).[24] Honest bookkeeping being the coin by which Wall Street does business, Standard & Poor's cut San Diego's credit rating a notch and Fitch Ratings downgraded it by two notches.

Struggling to do *something* in response, the city fired its outside auditor. Ed Ryan, San Diego's veteran inside auditor, resigned as well.

Yet no matter how hard the mayor tried to contain the damage, it kept spreading to new and more ominous fronts. In February, Carol Lam, the U.S. attorney, opened a criminal investigation into MP-2. The SEC began a probe of the city's disclosures. Before long, fourteen officials received federal subpoenas, and the FBI began to prowl through the city's files.

Hoping to seem cooperative, San Diego hired Vinson & Elkins, a Houston-based law firm, to both conduct an internal review into its past disclosures *and* to represent the city before the SEC.[25] Yet this showed a basic lack of comprehension of the true source of San Diego's woes. By asking a single law firm to play the roles of both ombudsman and advocate, the city was creating the potential for a new conflict of interest.* Neither Murphy nor the city manager had grasped that such conflicts on the pension board had been the system's original sin. Nor did they quite appreciate how corrosive such conflicts were—how they poisoned the well of trust.

Murphy won the primary but fell short of 50 percent, meaning he would have to face the stubborn Roberts again. Now sixty-one, the mayor loathed the thought of another campaign. Murphy had a Methodist's love of service, but the scent of the rabble repelled him. He did not have the common touch.

And his grip on the city was weakening. After the primary, Uberuaga, the city manager, resigned. KPMG, the city's new auditor, remained dissatisfied with the condition of the city's books and refused to sign off on its audit. Thus San Diego could not tap bond markets, and had to delay much-needed sewer and water projects. Fiscally, the city was frozen.

The pension mess, by now, had attracted a swelling (if oddball) chorus of critics: Aguirre, the left-leaning attorney, Councilwoman Frye, and Shipione. The most unlikely was Carl DeMaio, the Gingrich protégé who two years earlier had presented Murphy with a good-government award,

*Vinson & Elkins had already shown itself to be obtuse on conflict-of-interest matters. As outside counsel to Enron, it had blessed the notorious ring of self-dealing partnerships that had led to Enron's collapse.

and since then had become disenchanted with City Hall and launched a cloak-and-dagger investigation of its inner workings. DeMaio began to hold nearly weekly press briefings that amounted to potshots at City Hall. A political zealot with intense, gleaming eyes, he accused the city manager of concocting a budget with phantom revenue and exposed what he said were wasteful and lavish expenditures.

Murphy could slough off DeMaio as a political opportunist, but he could not face the voters without a plan for retiring the pension debt. He tried to take the high road, saying he would wait for the report of his Pension Reform Committee. The committee said the city should contribute $200 million (even more than was required by *Gleason*) a year. This was too much for Murphy. He wouldn't fire cops and firemen to bail out SDCERS (nor would he raise taxes).[26] He was still unwilling to impose sacrifices on the voters—the flaw from which the pension scandal had been born.

Murphy proposed that San Diego simply issue bonds (that is, borrow) to pay off its pension debt, but for a city that lacked an audited financial statement, this was a fanciful idea. As Roberts, his challenger, pointed out, "They can't even issue bonds right now."[27]

Murphy rejoined that Roberts, as a San Diego County supervisor, was hardly one to be throwing stones. San Diego County *also* had a serious pension-funding problem.[28] Murphy's point was that pensions were everybody's problem, not just the city's. Of course, he was right. No less than the governor, Arnold Schwarzenegger, was waging a war against state employee unions to phase out pensions for new state workers. This battle was occurring in various forms in a half dozen other states as well.

But San Diego had a *particular* problem. Murphy could not escape that. As if to underscore the point, in June, SDCERS sued Blum, its hapless fiduciary counsel, for malpractice. Blum instantly settled for $15 million.

Then Aguirre, the tireless litigator, declared he was running for city attorney, with a mission to investigate the pension mess. In some ways, this took Aguirre back to his beginnings. Early in his career, he had been a prosecutor for the assistant U.S. attorney in San Diego and directed a probe of pension racketeering. Then, in the late '70s, he had been assistant counsel to the same Senate subcommittee from which, during the 1950s, Robert F. Kennedy had investigated the labor rackets and Jimmy Hoffa. Bobby Kennedy was Aguirre's hero. Like his idol, Aguirre was happiest when he was pursuing some perceived injustice—preferably one with societal overtones. Once, when the United Farm Workers were sued by a lettuce grower, Aguirre had rushed to Yuma, Arizona, to take up the case. The suit had the potential to bankrupt the union, which represents the poorest of migrants. Aguirre told the jurors, "You are being asked to judge history." The UFW lost, but won on appeal.[29] Aguirre thought the pension scandal had similar historic overtones. San Diego was a parable of America as his generation—the baby boomers—began to retire, and as companies and communities chafed under the demands of caring for them. Pension abuse was the cutting edge issue he had been looking for. He promised that if he were elected he would dig, and dig deeply, into the unfolding pension scandal.

TO MURPHY'S great discomfort, it was his own Pension Reform Committee that fully focused the mayoral election on SDCERS. The committee understood that conflicts of interest had undercut the board's judgment, and it made a truly sensible recommendation: cut the board from thirteen to seven members with none of them city officials or union reps. Needless to say, this proposal was highly unpopular with the unions.

Saathoff immediately denounced it, as did the powerful municipal workers union. Rather quickly, this dampened the city council's enthusiasm for reform. "The sad thing is these are serious problems," Lisa Briggs of the taxpayers' association told a reporter. "As soon as you turn these into political issues, all rational dialogue seems to disappear."[30]

Murphy opted for a hollow compromise. He proposed a thirteen-member board with independents comprising only a slim, one-person majority. Given the ability of insiders such as Saathoff to exercise greater than proportional influence, this was scarcely a reform at all.

Before the council voted on the proposal (which would go on the November ballot), Councilman Zucchet, the former firefighters' lobbyist and now a defendant in the pending bribery case, added a clever amendment banning financial advisers from serving on the board. Zucchet's amendment would affect only one current trustee: Diann Shipione.

Thus a measure intended to cleanse the board of the trustees who had orchestrated MP-2 was instead twisted so as to exclude *only* the trustee who had most vocally opposed it. "It's an interesting conclusion that everybody gets to stay on this board—unions, city people, retirees—except me," Shipione, in a rare moment of understatement, observed.[31]

Saathoff and his union quickly repaid the favor and endorsed Murphy for reelection. This left the clear impression that the mayor had cut yet another deal. With the SDCERS deficit now estimated at a mind-numbing $1.7 billion, it was no longer clear that the city could stay afloat. For practical purposes, the election now became a referendum on the pension scandal.[32]

Aguirre proposed that San Diego file for bankruptcy. The real author of this idea was Pat Shea, who had made a name for himself (and also $3 million in fees) representing local government agencies during the 1994 bankruptcy of nearby Orange County.[33]

Though San Diego's losses were not as sharp as Orange County's, bankruptcy had a superficial appeal; it proffered *some* sort of closure to San Diego's season of torment. In the first national story on the crisis, the *New York Times* dubbed San Diego "Enron-by-the-Sea," which seemed to reinforce the notion that San Diego was close to a collapse. The newspaper quoted Aguirre, who said that any corporation that had behaved like San Diego would be delisted from the stock exchange. John Kern, Murphy's chief of staff, sounded downright Hooverish on the mayor's behalf, insisting that San Diego was "on a sound fiscal footing."[34]

Aguirre turned out to be the more prophetic. Two weeks later, Standard & Poor's suspended its rating on San Diego's bonds—a rare event and about as close as a municipality can come to being "delisted."

IN MID-SEPTEMBER, the electoral campaigns paused for the much-awaited report of Vinson & Elkins. It turned out to be a sweeping critique of San Diego's pension practices. However, the law firm was more mixed in its appraisal of the city's disclosures. Although it found that San Diego's public reports had been deficient and often misleading, it did not find evidence of *willful* violation of securities laws.[35] As V&E was also representing the city before the SEC on this very point, its conclusion set off a firestorm over the simmering issue of the firm's independence.

KPMG, the city's auditor, had been withholding its audit until it could determine if any laws had been broken; it quickly decided that the V&E report failed to settle the question. Steven DeVetter, KPMG's partner in San Francisco, fired off a blunt letter to San Diego's assistant city attorney. "Unfortunately . . . we do not believe [V&E's] statement."[36]

The practical impact of this professionals' quarrel was serious. KPMG would not complete its audit and San Diego remained shut out from capital markets, preventing it from raising money to build firehouses or complete federally ordered wastewater upgrades—or anything else. The city now faced a hornet's nest of regulatory troubles.

With its fiscal crisis deepening, the city council voted to put on the ballot a measure to increase the hotel tax. Ironically, though the pension scandal made the potential revenue critical, it darkened the prospects for approval. Voters were wary lest their taxes be "wasted" on gold-plated pensions, and two well-heeled opponents—Doug Manchester, a local hotelier, and DeMaio, the right-wing consultant[37]—played on their fears with an alarmist antigovernment campaign.[38] As for Murphy, though the hotel levy was the one concrete measure that might have saved his budget, he stuck with the safe course for a San Diego politician and urged the voters to reject it.

Murphy was lucky to be running against a weak opponent. Roberts tried to score points by endorsing bankruptcy—a reckless step that helped

Murphy to keep his core supporters in the business community. For all his faults, Murphy was personally likable; he had promoted downtown development, he had built the Padres' stadium. And he got more support than he could have hoped for from Saathoff and the firefighters, who spent $100,000 on ads attacking Roberts.[39]

Nonetheless, entering the final month, Murphy was trailing in the polls.

Kern, his chief of staff, was deeply worried. Hoping to spark the mayor's campaign, Kern had lunch with Councilwoman Frye, for the purpose of recruiting the onetime surfer to the mayor's cause. A fifty-two-year-old recovering alcoholic with a voice silted with tobacco, Frye was an unlikely ally for the fastidious mayor. Earthy and coarse, she hugged perfect strangers and would show up at council meetings in blue suits with big floral pins and hammer away with questions. Murphy would nervously tap his watch and implore her, "Mrs. Frye, take it off line." He liked to hush up discord, whereas Frye was hopelessly uncensored.

When Kern proposed that Frye hop aboard the mayor's campaign, Frye replied, "I'm thinking of running myself."

Kern let out a nervous laugh. "You should endorse Dick," he said.[40]

But the notion that Frye might enter the race as a write-in candidate was suddenly alive. Her supporters beseeched her to run, and on September 30, she announced. At City Hall, reporters mobbed her.

Frye was in some ways a perfect choice for a city hoping to recover its faded grace. Her life story read like a tawdry miniseries: beach girl leaves home, gets work as a short-order cook, marries badly, takes to drink, is allegedly abused as a wife, divorces. But then the tides turn: she meets a big-time surfer, remarries, operates (with Skip, her husband) a surf shop, becomes an environmentalist when Skip and his buddies repeatedly suffer from (she thinks) the effects of polluted water. And then some inspiring episodes: Frye tilts at corporate Goliaths; she pushes the city to investigate impurities in drainwater discharges and gets the state to pass a law that requires monitoring of coastal waters.[41]

As a councilwoman, Frye connected with ordinary citizens as neither

Murphy nor Roberts could dream of. Her campaign had something of the frenzied character of a rock fest. She cheerfully promised that she would put an end to cronyism and to backroom pension deals.

However, Frye's candidacy split the anti-Murphy vote. Ironically, it gave the mayor his best shot at winning. The election was incredibly close. With a third of the precincts counted, the *Union-Tribune* reported 35.3 percent of the vote for Frye, 32.6 percent for Murphy, and 32.1 percent for Roberts. It was obvious that San Diegans had registered a profound desire for change. Aguirre was elected city attorney and a proposition to transition to a "strong mayor" form of government was approved. So were two reforms of the pension system, though their effect was negligible. Predictably, the hotel measure met the fate of previous proposals to raise local taxes and went down to defeat.

As the votes for mayor were tallied, Frye retained a slim lead and the San Diego establishment, so used to controlling the city, was seized by panic. Then, after two and a half weeks, the registrar closed the book. Frye received an amazing 160,805 write-in votes to 157,459 votes for Murphy. Alas, state election law required write-in voters to inscribe their candidates' names on the ballot *and*, also, to darken an oval bubble beside it. And 5,551 of those who voted for Frye had neglected to darken the bubble. The registrar refused to count them; Murphy had squeaked in.*

No sooner was the election over than a fracas erupted at the pension board—which met in Shipione's absence and voted to exclude her from private sessions, on the grounds of her repeated leaks (which she denied). If necessary, they agreed to call the police to escort her out. "Citizen's arrest of Shipione weighed. Contingency not used in pension board fight," the *Union-Tribune* breathlessly reported.[42]

The significance of this juvenile squabbling, and of Murphy's questionable victory, was that the epicenter for resolving the pension scandal was

*The San Diego League of Women Voters sued on Frye's behalf. The judge ruled that people who failed to shade the oval "did not vote." In writing Frye's name they were merely "augmenting" their ballots.

shifting. The catalyst for reform would be neither the mayor nor the hopelessly divided SDCERS. It would be the newly elected city attorney.

TRADITIONALLY, THE OFFICE of the city attorney served the *government* of San Diego. It was the city's advocate in court, and was chiefly occupied with defending the city against lawsuits. Aguirre had a very different notion—that the office should represent the *people* of San Diego, even people who were suing the city. Since KPMG, the auditor, had requested an inquiry into whether city officials had committed illegal acts, Aguirre thought he had a mandate to look into the actions of city officials.[43]

Aguirre's instinct when involved in a case was to sue everyone in reach. He talked a thousand miles a minute, more or less ignoring the other party and directing the conversation where he wanted it to go. After his election, he ran into a city councilman named Scott Peters in the parking lot behind City Hall. Aguirre said, "Scott, I'm really looking forward to working with you on this pension stuff."

Peters, like most officials, was wary of Aguirre. But all he said was, "That's great, Mike."

"But Scott," Aguirre continued, "you have to do what I say."

A bit surprised, Peters said, "Mike I'm sure you have ideas and I have ideas. We'll work together."

Aguirre said, "No, Scott. You have to do what I say. If you don't I can't protect you from being indicted." Peters was stunned and understandably outraged.[44]

But to Aguirre, all of official San Diego was at least a suspect in the pension disaster. He quickly informed SDCERS that, as the system's lawyers were compromised, *he*, Aguirre, would serve as SDCERS's counsel. (The SDCERS board utterly refused to go along with him.)[45] Then he advised the city council members that they should hire *personal* lawyers.

Peters, the unfortunate councilman whom Aguirre had bullied in the parking lot, replied that it would be too expensive. If it turned out later on that any of the members had a conflict (meaning, if any of them were implicated) they could get their own counsel, Peters suggested.

Aguirre said, "No, everyone has a conflict. The council members should get their own attorneys."[46]

By this time, official San Diego was terrified of Aguirre. City Hall greeted him with an information blackout. It ordered Vinson & Elkins, which was continuing its investigation, to report to the city manager instead of, as in the past, to the city attorney.[47]

Not that this slowed Aguirre down. In December, the newly confirmed official sent an assistant attorney, Robert Abel, to City Hall to oversee the work of Vinson & Elkins. Abel saw boxes and boxes of files labeled "SDCERS" that hadn't been delivered under the federal subpoena.

When Aguirre heard about the files he exploded. Invoking his customary profanities, he ordered Abel to go back and seize every document that mentioned SDCERS. Abel returned to City Hall, but now the city officials had summoned a private attorney who refused to grant him access.[48]

Eventually, they cut a deal. Aguirre was allowed to haul out the boxes (twenty-five in all) as long as they remained under seal. But once he had the files, he allowed Shipione to ransack them.[49] He rationalized that since Shipione was a trustee, she should have access. Shipione went through the files as if she were possessed—tipping over cartons, spilling papers on the floor. Aguirre let Shea go through the files too. Meanwhile, he installed a padlock on his door and got into a spat with the chief of police when the latter refused to grant him police protection.

Not yet in office a month, Aguirre was at war with the pension system, the city manager's office, the council, and the local police. He was preparing to file lawsuits against every aggrieving party he could think of and doing it all under the, to him, luxurious light of reporters and television cameras that Aguirre, now fifty-five and finally a public servant, so desired. Though his tactics were heavy-handed, they fulfilled a worthy purpose. San Diego's government had flitted around like a bat intent on avoiding the sunlight for far too long. Now its people would learn the truth.

Aguirre divulged the results of his probe in serial fashion. In January 2005 he startled San Diegans with the publication of a sixteen-page brief bearing the improbable title "Interim Report No. 1 Regarding Possible Abuse, Fraud, and Illegal Acts by San Diego City Officials and Employees." Soon, all of San Diego was awaiting his reports like the next installment of *Harry Potter.*

Though sketchy on details, "Interim No. 1" homed in on a pivotal moment of the pension scandal—the failure of the blue-ribbon report to come clean. "Had the public known that the City faced the very real prospect of having to pay hundreds of millions of dollars into the pension plan," Aguirre allowed, "would the City have proceeded with its plan to increase employee pension benefits?"[50]

Aguirre's staff nervously tried to tone down his incendiary prose, which only fueled his fire.[51] While Murphy was trying to calm the city, Aguirre was working to raise its temperature—to push the drama to a climax. He so spooked the pension trustees that the board (exclusive of Shipione) took the extraordinary step of suing Aguirre to prevent him from turning over the files he had seized to the SEC and to the Justice Department.[52]

On February 9, Aguirre published "Interim Report No. 2." This one was a shocker that meticulously chronicled the pension plot—lurid emails and all. Aguirre accused Murphy and the council, and many others, of keeping San Diegans "in the dark" about the condition of the retirement system. He laid out the duty of fiduciaries according to the California Constitution—and accused both the council and the pension board of violating that duty. Most seriously, he presented evidence to suggest that the mayor and the council had authorized bond disclosures "that the Mayor and City Council Members knew to be false."[53]

City officials from the manager on down were furious at Aguirre for personalizing his attacks. A councilman likened Aguirre to Joe McCarthy. Even the usually mild-tempered Murphy was spurred to anger and threatened to sue.[54]

Had Aguirre and the other officials not remained a part of the same government, a civil war might have ensued. But they all had to be concerned with the failing state of the city's finances. San Diego was desperate for credit, access to which depended on satisfying the auditor, KPMG, that all evidence of wrongdoing was flushed out. As San Diego had gotten conflicting opinions from Vinson & Elkins on the one hand and Aguirre on the other, the city hired yet another investigator, Kroll Inc., to reconcile the two. Kroll recruited a high-profile regulator—former SEC chairman Arthur Levitt—to be part of a three-person "audit committee" to supervise the inquiry and serve as a single point of contact for the SEC.

The hope was that with Kroll on board, the various investigations would be consolidated and (quickly) completed. But Aguirre and Kroll immediately got into a nasty turf battle. (Aguirre ultimately sued Kroll's attorney.) And official San Diego was not quite ready to cooperate. As late as March 2005, City Hall had yet to fully comply with year-old federal subpoenas. Local officials were summoned to the federal building and warned, presumably, that obstruction charges could follow. Similarly, the pension board voted *not* to hand over documents sought by the feds. Aguirre fumed that the board was "completely out of control" and moved to throw it into receivership.[55] The pension mess was leading San Diego to the brink of civil anarchy.

Aguirre's third report contained a splendid suggestion: that the council enact funding rules similar to those mandated by ERISA for private pension sponsors.[56] Aguirre had hit on the beginnings of a solution to the entire problem of public pensions—hold them to the same or similar regulations as corporations.

But Murphy was simply too swamped by the escalating demands of the budget crisis to consider such a far-reaching reform. The mayor was trying to get the unions to agree to a pay freeze and also to benefit cuts for new employees (the same medicine that General Motors was prescribing for *its* workers). He was fretting over how to fund the library and sorely needed firefighting equipment. He had replaced the pension board with new trustees (Shipione was out, as was Saathoff). And Murphy was pushing ahead on the transition to a "strong mayor" form of government. Though personally ineffective, he had the sense to see that the mayor of

America's seventh largest city should be more than a coequal on the city council.

However, events were moving faster than he was. Donna Frye was preparing a recall drive to force the mayor from office.[57] As Murphy's approval rating had fallen to less than 10 percent, this was a serious threat. Aguirre, whose rating was 53 percent,[58] said the mayor should simply resign.

It was at this troubled juncture, in April 2005, that *Time* magazine, in a cover story on America's big-city mayors, named the likable judge with the sterling résumé as one of the U.S.'s three worst mayors. It was a devastating blow. Murphy was a decent man, but he had never shown the courage to confront the city's pension genie, and it had turned his mayoralty into a nightmare. Eight days later, on April 25, he announced his resignation, to become effective in the middle of July.

Three weeks after this blockbuster announcement, the district attorney filed conflict-of-interest charges against six former pension trustees, including Saathoff and three city officials: Lexin, the human resources chief, Webster, the assistant auditor, and the city treasurer. Sometime later, a federal grand jury indicted Saathoff, Lexin, Webster, pension administrator Grissom, and another official on conspiracy charges stemming from MP-2.

Aguirre, who by summer had published six "interim" reports, spun them into a lawsuit against former trustees and pension officials. *His* case sought the unthinkable: a rollback of pension benefits prior to the enactment of MP-1 and MP-2. Typically, pension benefits are immutable; they can never be rescinded. However, Aguirre argued that the two underfunding deals in San Diego were illegal and that, therefore, so were the benefits that flowed from them.[59] This was a novel and also a difficult case.

BY THE NATURE of the beast, pension fiascos cast long shadows. The effects reach far into the future, and perhaps inevitably, so did the attempts to adjudicate responsibility. The defendants (in the civil as well as the criminal actions) vigorously disputed the charges. The various cases turned not so much on the facts—which were not in dispute—but on whether MP-2 fit the applicable definitions of a crime or of a civil offense. SDCERS was eventually forced by a federal judge to turn over a trove of its papers, but the lawsuits multiplied, and San Diego labored for a long while without resolutions to either the indictments or the civil actions.

Regardless of what the courts decided, San Diego was in the throes of a budget crisis that was the pension scandal's true offspring. In the aftermath of the debacle, library and after-school hours were shortened, the social services budget was slashed, swimming pools were closed, plans to provide wheelchair access to beaches were mothballed, and a program to feed AIDS patients was reduced by the equivalent of 25,000 meals. Capital projects such as the downtown library and new fire stations were put on hold, and head counts were reduced across the board.

San Diego was unlikely to solve its budget crisis overnight, but it did not have to wait to change its political cast. Mayor Murphy had anointed Councilman Zucchet as the deputy mayor, and thus the person in line to succeed him pending a new election. This was a most unfortunate choice. Zucchet was a product of the firefighters' lobby, an organization as tainted as any in the pension scandal. Moreover, he was under federal indictment and, as Murphy's exit neared, was awaiting a verdict.

Zucchet succeeded Murphy on July 16. Approximately forty-eight hours later, a jury ruled he had conspired to collect campaign gifts in return for changing strip club regulations—and convicted him of extortion.* That ended his "reign." As a city clerk wondered aloud, "So, who's the mayor?"[60]

San Diego was now in the hands of the city council, as close to rudderless as a democracy permits. Eleven hopefuls jumped into the race for mayor, in a special election at the end of July. The predominant theme of the campaign was that government had created the city's problems and ought to be shrunk down to size. One of the candidates, Pat Shea, said the city should file for bankruptcy. A libertarian entry wanted to privatize the

---

*In 2007, the conviction was overturned.

fire department. Another candidate, who owned a Harley-Davidson dealership, said the city should spend "profits" instead of taxes, though how the city would get its hands on profits without taxing people was unclear. The candidates studiously avoided mention of a study by a local think tank that found that San Diego could raise $250 million annually, easily enough to pay the pension bill, by raising taxes just to the average level of California's other big cities.[61] As a perceptive correspondent for the *Los Angeles Times* observed, "If a visitor from out of town wandered into a recent debate among leading candidates for mayor, he or she might have come away thinking San Diego is one of the most overtaxed, overregulated cities in the nation."[62]

The exception was the one candidate who thought she already should be mayor—Donna Frye. Much to her advisers' chagrin, Frye refused to rule out tax hikes. She finished first by a wide margin anyway. But since she won less than a majority, Frye faced a runoff in November against the second-place finisher—for weary San Diegans, the fourth mayoral election in eighteen months.

Frye attracted a formidable team of advisers; they sensed that the moment for electing a Democrat, even a loose-haired environmentalist, might have arrived. Her challenger was Jerry Sanders, a former police chief, more recently head of the local United Way. Sanders was a moderate Republican. The son of a cop, he was less hostile to government than the Republican ideologues were. He had supported tax hikes in the past, though he was careful to avoid doing so now.

Frye campaigned for "openness"; Sanders for "leadership." While each slogan addressed a failing of the Murphy years, Sanders's was more soothing to established San Diego. Frye was a change agent; Sanders promised to run a tighter ship, but not to turn it upside down. Also, Frye was (to downtown San Diego) worrisomely close to Aguirre. Though unions supported her, business rallied for Sanders, which enabled him to outspend his charismatic opponent by three to one.

What little chance remained to Frye was buried by the *Union-Tribune,* which relentlessly savaged her as a would-be taxer. Her platform was anything but radical. She proposed to ignore the new pension benefits, on the basis that the deals were illegal, and if that failed (that is, if a court ordered the city to pay them) to raise the sales tax by half of 1 percent.

In San Diego, even this was too much. The *Union-Tribune* excoriated Frye for advocating the *possibility* of a tax hike. While conceding that the city was facing "a fiscal emergency of staggering proportions," the newspaper intoned, "Our guess is, the unhesitating response of most San Diegans would be not only no, but heck no." This was blatantly demagogic; indeed, it mirrored the attitude of politicians who, in refusing to pay the bills for benefits they had enacted, had brought San Diego to its current pass. Taxpayers would *have* to pony up. The only question was whether it would be today's taxpayers or tomorrow's.[63]

Sanders won handily. He had no magic fix—nor did one exist—for a decade of pension shenanigans. San Diego still had no access to bond markets and, as the mayor-elect observed, "I can't print money." But Sanders took a sensible first step: he used San Diego's portion of a giant settlement between tobacco companies and the states to chip away at the pension liability. And Sanders, who was not a man to be trifled with, restored a sense of authority at City Hall.

He inherited a SDCERS that was in brutal shape. On the date of Murphy's resignation, the average funded ratio of the retirement plans of the ten largest cities in California was 94 percent; in San Diego it was 66 percent. SDCERS's condition was greatly aggravated by employees who had purchased pension credits for time they had not really worked—an astonishing 13,000 years' worth of extra credits that would be on the books for a lifetime.[64]

The city's benefits were *not* the highest in the state—that distinction went to liberal San Francisco. However, because of the San Diego system's poor level of funding, the city's burden was bigger by far. Pensions cost 26 percent of payroll in San Diego compared to 14 percent for the ten largest cities.[65] Adding insult to injury, San Diego had been saddled with costs amounting to $25 million and counting for the various investigations. That alone would have paid the pension bill when McGrory first ducked it a decade earlier.

As for the various officials who helped to craft the underfunding deals, many moved on to other jobs and all would benefit from gold-plated retirements fattened by their own machinations. Uberuaga, the hapless city manager who spearheaded MP-2, got a lifetime pension (after having worked for San Diego for a grand total of six years) of $55,000 a year.[66] McGrory, the wizardlike city manager in the '90s, did even better—a pension of $86,000.[67] And Bruce Herring, the long-serving deputy manager who helped to orchestrate both MP-1 and MP-2, retired in 2005, with an incredibly rich pension of $144,000 a year.*[68]

Among those who battled to stop the underfunding, "Columbo" Conger got the bonanza he deserved. Though his claim for a $10 million fee was rejected by the court, he collected $3.1 million—a tidy reward.[69]

Diann Shipione was toasted by the press for having blown the whistle on MP-2, and honored with a public service award from the League of Women Voters. But public recognition did not seem to bring her peace. She distanced herself from various proposals to help SDCERS regain its footing, and when the idea was aired of her rejoining the board, she balked and weirdly proposed that the entire system be "disbanded."[70]

Late in 2005, Shipione appeared in a black suit to testify in pretrial hearings against her former colleagues. She looked nervous and fragile. The former trustees in the dock—the defendants—fixed her with stares that may best be described as hateful. The defense attorney grilled her, and as Shipione replied—often evasively—the defendants mockingly rolled their eyes. Shipione began to sniffle and then to openly sob. She seemed utterly alone.

---

*Thanks to the provision in MP-1 that let employees accumulate benefits while working, Herring also collected a lump sum of more than $300,000.

Among the political insiders who were habitués of the county courthouse, Michael Aguirre had made even more enemies than Shipione. He continued his breakneck pace—quarreling with the city council and the pension board, as well as with Vinson & Elkins, KPMG, and even with the distinguished Arthur Levitt. He filed a pointless suit against Orrick, San Diego's bond counsel, whose only crime was to have been deceived by San Diego. He tried to grab the additional job of SDCERS lawyer and was rebuked by a judge. He fought with, and fired, one of his best attorneys, and suffered an exodus of lawyers who were exhausted or fed up with his mood swings and accusatory tirades. He was unable to slow down, even between 2 and 5:30 a.m., which was the time he allotted to answering his mail.

But Aguirre wisely chose not to fight with the new mayor, who became his ally for a while, and this afforded him the capital to continue his crusade for honest pensions. Most of Aguirre's suits did not accomplish anything, at least in a narrow legal sense. And Aguirre surely did not measure up to the politicians he revered, and whose photos adorned his office—Bobby Kennedy and FDR and Winston Churchill—but in his rare moments of calm, Aguirre could gaze out on a resplendent San Diego Bay and reflect that he had accomplished something. He had convinced the SEC not to punish San Diego—presumably because the agency was satisfied with Aguirre's self-flagellations on the city's behalf. He had educated the people to the dangers of living off the pension fund. And he had revealed to them their own recent history. It was a saga of greed, conspiracy, and political cowardice—as Aguirre wrote, one that sparked "the worst financial crisis in the history of the City of San Diego."[71]

It is a cautionary tale—especially for pension sponsors and politicians in other overobligated and underfunded towns, cities, and states. If only public servants heed it, there need not be a San Diego "brewing" in every community.

CONCLUSION: THE WAY OUT

America is sitting on a retirement time bomb. Companies such as General Motors are fading fast and governments such as the City of San Diego are overrun with obligations. As the population ages, the problem will only get worse. Clearly, retirees need to be taken care of. But the solution cannot be to ruin once great firms or to impoverish whole cities and future taxpayers.

In the private sector, pension failures have been running at record rates since the beginning of the twenty-first century.[1] Many of the steel, airline, and textile companies have already been forced into bankruptcy. Thanks to its intolerable level of pension and health care benefits, the auto industry is shrinking beyond recognition. Delphi and numerous other parts firms are in bankruptcy. The auto manufacturers are struggling to stay afloat. In 2007, after the events chronicled in this book, Chrysler was sold to a private equity concern, Cerberus Capital Management, which went deeply into hock to buy it. And General Motors offered a buyout package to every one of its unionized workers—an unprecedented attempt to escape from its past. Once an army of nearly a half-million, its workforce shrank to 74,000. Then, late in 2007, the UAW called a nationwide strike against GM and its patient CEO, Rick Wagoner, over the festering issues of job guarantees and health care. Wagoner and Gettelfinger, the UAW president, settled the strike with a revolutionary pact, similar to the Plan B discussed in chapter 2, under which GM would transfer more than $30 billion to a special trust, to be managed by the UAW—and finally be freed of its crippling health care liability. Ford and Chrysler reached similar accords. This rewrote the rules for the auto industry overnight. GM emerged, at long last, from its six-decade-long experiment in providing health care as a diminished enterprise, its market share down to a pitiful 23.7 percent. Whether the UAW would be able to meet its new burden was far from clear. Its membership had withered, as had the overall population in Detroit, where some once-busy and formerly thriving neighborhoods were sadly reverting to grass and trees.

As dismal as all that sounds, many state governments are in far worse shape. They are even further behind on their pension obligations than corporations (estimates of the total deficit range from a few hundred billion to nearly a trillion dollars.)[2] And with the stock market slumping and the long-forecast real estate crash finally having arrived, the states have no ability to make good on their obligations. Illinois borrowed $10 billion to pay down its pension debt in 2003, and yet its pension funds remain a staggering $35 billion underfunded.

And most states have not accumulated *any* savings to pay for retiree health care. New Jersey, for instance, recently (and for the first time) added up the promises it has made for its retired employees' medical bills. The total was $58 billion—for which it has virtually no reserves.[3] That is *in addition* to the amount by which its pension fund is in arrears—roughly another $25 billion. Alarmingly, New Jersey does not have the option, as San Diego does, of raising taxes to normal and thus still-tolerable levels. Taxes in New Jersey are already astronomical. Governor Jon S. Corzine has been mulling whether to sell the fabled New Jersey Turnpike (much as GM has been selling *its* assets). Once you start to parcel off the farm to support the grandparents, you are in trouble. But for New Jersey and others, the alternatives are grim: they can impose austere budget cuts, raise taxes further, or both.

SEEN IN THIS LIGHT, Peter Kalikow's stand on subway pensions was long overdue. It was as principled a response in his era as Michael Quill's agitations were in his. Quill fought for decency for the workers. Kalikow drew a line so that ordinary New Yorkers would not have to pay ever higher fares to support the lavish pensions of retirees from age fifty-five possibly into their nineties and beyond. Ultimately, the union agreed to a concession on health care rather than on pensions, but Kalikow's point was made, and the strike was halted after only three days.

Though New York City's outcome was more favorable than the slow death at General Motors or the scandal in San Diego, the MTA's response is unlikely to set a practicable example for others. Few cities or states will be eager to shut down their transportation systems to tackle pension debts—and even if they were, a strike is not a solution. A GM-style "cure" of massive layoffs would be even less attractive, and the Southern California approach of pretending that the problem does not exist is worst of all. As these episodes demonstrate, our current systems no longer work. So assuming that America does not simply abandon its retirees, what can it do?

OBLIGATIONS TO RETIREES come in two forms: pensions and health care. Though pensions have a longer history as an industrial issue, in recent years employers such as GM and the MTA have come to regard retiree health care as an analogous problem. Also, the distinction between *retiree* health care and care for working-age adults has probably outlived its usefulness. Today we have an illogical patchwork; Medicare covers basic needs for people over sixty-five, but millions of younger retirees, as well as working people, are at the mercy of employers. A system that covers one should logically cover all.

Entire books have been written on how to reform the health care system, but the way out of the current mess can be highlighted without getting mired in the small points of the many recent proposals. Indeed, a solution was first suggested sixty years ago.

Walter Reuther argued that health care was too basic a need for workers to go without, and too burdensome a cost to be foisted on employers. Thus he advocated financing by the federal government. That does not mean the government would become the universal *provider* of health care. In education, for instance, Washington provides scholarships and college loans; it does not run our universities. Similarly, in health care, the government should subsidize basic coverage, on a sliding scale according to income. In a world in which people change jobs every few years, there is no reason for health care to be tied to the workplace (any more than there is for companies to provide schooling, shelter, or other basic needs). In any case, they can't afford it. Those that try, or are forced to try, such as General Motors, are gravely disadvantaged.

When Reuther and others proposed the idea of national health care, in the 1940s and '50s, Big Business, as well as the American Medical Association, viewed it as extreme and fought it every step of the way. But the world has changed. For one thing, business is global, and U.S. companies compete against foreign-based firms whose home countries *do* pick up the tab. As GM finally discovered, it cannot compete if it has to provide benefits that Toyota does not.

Moreover, the U.S. government *already* spends an enormous amount on health care. At companies with medical plans, employees receive tax-free income in the form of health insurance. This amounts to a huge subsidy—some $125 billion a year (more costly to the government than even the home mortgage deduction).[4] But it is a subsidy that no one sees. Worse, it is unequally distributed; only employees at certain firms (those with coverage) receive it.

A more direct subsidy—a voucher that could be used to purchase insurance—would be universal and thus more fair. Structurally, it could be accomplished by extending Medicare to people younger than sixty-five, with the level of coverage varying according to one's income. People would still shop for doctors and other services in the market, and still have incentives to save (since the subsidy would be limited). A similar system is being tested in Massachusetts, which has launched universal coverage at the state level. But ultimately, if the fifty states all offered competitive plans, people would move to the states with the richest benefits, just as occurred in an earlier generation with welfare. The states would then be forced to compete for residents by upping benefits. ("Move to Georgia, land of sunshine and affordable angioplasty!") Probably, a uniform national level of coverage would be best. Congress can no longer avoid the issue, and neither can the current crop of presidential contenders. If a trigger is needed, let it be the recent strike at GM that spelled the end for the Treaty of Detroit. As a coda to the settlement, GM agreed to invest $15 million in a new National Institute for Health Care, which will be dedicated to promoting access for all Americans. The time has arrived to take Reuther's proposal for government-financed care out of the showroom—and even his fiercest corporate adversary seems to agree.

PENSIONS ARE A TOUGHER FIX. Depending on how much workers earned over their careers, people need, or expect, very different levels of income in retirement. Therefore, employees or someone on their behalf has to put money aside for them, and in varying amounts, while they are working. This means that retirement benefits will always have a connection to work (if not necessarily to the "workplace"). Pensions met this condition; that is, money was saved, and lifetime benefits were guaranteed, in amounts linked to prior incomes. From the employee's point of view, pensions were close to perfect. By the late 1960s, 60 percent of the private-sector workforce had a guaranteed pension in addition to Social Security. In the next couple of decades, benefits spread to virtually all workers in the public sector as well.

But fierce economic gale winds blew this (seemingly) happy arrangement off course. In the private sector:

a) unions pushed benefits too high;
b) business went global, meaning that U.S. firms had to compete against foreign firms that did not offer pensions;
c) as the economy became more dynamic, people switched jobs more often, undermining the appeal of pensions as a retention tool;
d) life spans increased, making pensions more costly;
e) older industrial companies became less competitive (or failed outright) and their pension plans became seriously underfunded;
f) unions peaked and then faded as an economic force;
g) more jobs were created by new, start-up companies—everything from retailers such as Wal-Mart to Internet firms like Google—that refused to offer pensions.

The list above describes most of the major labor market trends of recent decades; remarkably, every item served to weaken the case for pensions. Today, only about 18 percent of private sector workers have pensions. Plummeting coverage has seriously weakened the PBGC, the federal insurer, which is caught in a vicious circle. Strong companies such as Google do not offer pensions and thus are not part of the insurance pool; increasingly, the PBGC is an insurer of the weak. It has lost billions on failed pension plans and faces a current deficit of $19 billion (that is what taxpayers will have to fork over to pay for current and predicted future losses). If numerous sponsors that are on the edge ultimately fail, or if the stock market slump deepens, the losses will be far worse.

Congress has repeatedly considered reforming ERISA so that pension sponsors would be *required* to keep their funds solvent. Each time, under pressure from corporate lobbies, Congress has backed off or created new loopholes. This is inexcusable. To require, as ERISA does, that companies fully fund their plans and then to grant forbearance to the companies that get into trouble undermines the very purpose of the law.

Even with a tougher law, it is probably too late to preserve the traditional pension system. Virtually no new companies are creating plans; the examples of GM and its ilk have scared employers off. Even GM itself is transitioning away from traditional pensions for new hires. Healthy firms such as IBM, Hewlett-Packard, Sears, Verizon, Motorola, and others are freezing their plans (such plans will pay off their existing obligations and eventually liquidate). Indeed, of the 44 million Americans with pension coverage, fewer than half are actively accruing benefits. The rest are retired, or they have left their employer, or their plans have been frozen.[5] Thus the private pension industry is gradually dying.

Whatever relief this brings to corporate shareholders, from the employees' point of view the demise of pensions is a calamity in the making. True, firms without pension plans usually offer 401(k)s, which have the attraction of mobility (employees can take their accounts from job to job). However, 401(k)s don't offer anything like the security of a pension plan.

According to the Federal Reserve, among families with retirement accounts, the median family has only $31,000.[6] That would be okay to live on for perhaps one year; to retire on it for a lifetime would be a joke. And a third of the workforce has no retirement savings at all.[7]

Even for people with larger accounts, the structure of 401(k)s is inappropriate for retirement. Employees get a lump sum, but—unlike with pensions—no annual stipend. There is no guarantee that the money will last as long as they do (or that they won't spend it or squander it along the way).

Another serious drawback is that individual plans lack the insurance feature of pensions. If you happen to retire when the stock market is depressed and the value of your 401(k) has crashed, you are out of luck. Not so in a pension plan, which benefits from the law of averages (some people retire when the market is high, others when the market is low). The recent subprime mortgage–related turmoil in the stock market should remind us that relying on individually held stocks for retirement is a risky proposition at best.

Finally, companies can reduce (or eliminate) contributions to 401(k) plans at will. Most contribute far less than they do (or did) to pensions, and, as noted, Americans' retirement accounts are woefully deficient.

Presidential candidate Hillary Clinton has offered one solution: Washington should sponsor new, national 401(k) accounts and offer matching credits to lower- and middle-income earners. Details aside, this is a sensible approach—helping people who once depended on pensions to begin to build adequate 401(k)s.

The government can take a small positive step by requiring 401(k) sponsors to offer annuities to employees as they retire. Even better, they could make annuities (as opposed to stocks, bonds, and other investments) the default option for new retirees. Annuities provide an annualized stream of income (think of them as do-it-yourself pensions). Despite the flowering of 401(k) accounts, annuities are still surprisingly rare. This is unfortunate, because annuities, like pensions, last a lifetime; they alleviate the major worry in an aging and soon-to-be pensionless society, which is that people will outlive their savings. However, this is only a solution for people who *have* enough savings to begin with.

In general, Congress should reconsider the legislative framework of 401(k)s—or rather, it should consider creating one. In the pension arena, Congress long ago demanded social trade-offs to protect the beneficiaries in return for the tax break it extended to sponsors. The point of these rules was twofold: to promote retirement savings on behalf of ordinary workers, and to ensure that the savings were invested with care. But 401(k)s essentially developed in a social and legislative vacuum. The time is ripe to enact similar protective rules for 401(k)s as well.

PUBLIC-SECTOR WORKERS such as San Diego firemen and New York City subway drivers differ from private-sector workers in two important ways. While private corporations are loath to make future commitments, in many public-sector job categories—teachers, firemen, accountants, and so on—employers still need stability in the workplace, and the old model of retaining a worker for two or three decades remains attractive. Thus, in government, pensions still make sense. Second, as unions have discovered, government workers have an extraordinary weapon—they can vote their bosses out of office. Put differently, they can use the ballot box to reinforce their negotiating leverage. Governor Schwarzenegger discovered this when he tried, unsuccessfully, to end pensions for new state workers and got clobbered in the polls. For both of these reasons—the employees' longevity and the unions' power—it looks as though, in the public sector, pensions will be here for many years to come.

Public pensions in and of themselves are not the problem; the problem is they are so often underfunded. The same political clout that enables unions to win, and keep, pensions, also enables them to push for higher benefits. As was seen in New York, the temptation for legislators to vote for higher benefits is nearly irresistible. Even worse, they are under constant pressure to keep taxes low, which creates an incentive to cheat on contributions. The seductive premise that pensions are a free lunch—or at least, a meal that need not be paid for until dessert—was pivotal to the scandal in San Diego and to underfunding everywhere.

There is one fix that is surprisingly straightforward. As Michael Aguirre proposed, states should require (by means of laws similar to ERISA) that *every* dollar of state and local pension benefits is funded as the benefit is accrued—not when the legislature or city council happens to feel like it. Such laws would need real teeth, and the federal government should help by prodding the states to pass them. Legislative details aside, the principle is simple. Legislatures cannot vote for, say, schools without also appropriating the funds. It is only in pensions that they can vote now and fund later. This is what the Aguirre statute would prevent. Pensions would still be subject to political pressures, but stripped of the illusion that pensions are "free," lawmakers would presumably make wiser choices.

FINALLY, THE FATE of pensions in the United States has strong implications for Social Security. Pensions do not exist in a vacuum; since the 1930s, they have been only one leg in the retirement triad that is also composed of Social Security and (for the well-to-do) private savings. Reuther's hope was that Social Security would be expanded to the point where private pensions would become unnecessary, but for many decades the opposite occurred. Federal benefits remained meager and were limited to a subset of the population, and the private pension network expanded. Now, those trends have reversed. In the future, as private pensions continue to wither, Social Security will be all the more essential: the retirement plan of last (and for many people, only) resort. In effect, having experimented with private pensions for sixty years, industry is throwing the burden back into the lap of government. Ironically, Social Security is itself under attack, in particular by conservative ideologues whose champion has been President Bush. It would be a tragedy to weaken the program now; as pensions fade, Social Security should be not dismantled but strengthened.

However, the lessons of failed private plans also need to be heeded by Washington. Social Security's crisis has been exaggerated by many on the right,[8] but as America ages, it does face a significant strain. The most important lesson that Social Security should derive from the private pension horrors is that benefits must be paid for *as they are earned*, so that a future generation isn't stuck with the bill. This will require a slow and expensive transition—a catch-up period so that the government can start to salt away money now for the people who will be retiring later. Currently, Social Security is a pay-as-you-go government benefit. Present-day workers and employers pay taxes that support current retirees. When today's workers retire, their children's generation will support them. This leaves the United States vulnerable to a decline in birth rates, just as GM was vulnerable when its workforce declined. Currently, there are 3.3 workers for each recipient of Social Security; by 2032 that ratio will drop by a third to *2.1* workers for each beneficiary.[9]

The country would be better served if Social Security functioned like a well-managed pension plan, with each generation supporting itself. This would mean raising taxes and locking the savings away for retirement. In actual practice, though Social Security has been collecting more in taxes than it has been paying to beneficiaries, the surplus has not been saved. Rather, the federal government has been borrowing from Social Security to plug the hole in its budget—just as San Diego did. And by 2017—less than a decade away—demographic trends will tip Social Security into a deficit, on a cash basis. At that point, payroll taxes will *not* be sufficient to pay benefits, and the Treasury will have to start repaying its debt. This will put an increasing strain on the federal budget. In other words, the bill will come due in Washington, just as it did in San Diego. But what is bad economics for a city is no less bad for the federal government. Retirement savings should not be used to paper over the budget deficit or to fool taxpayers into thinking that the government is solvent. They should be used for retirees, period.

To assure that the country does not experience a San Diego–style debacle will require political will in Congress. The payroll tax should be increased,[10] and the federal government should legislate an end to the current practice of "lending" Social Security surpluses to itself. These steps are somewhat similar to what President Bush proposed in 2005—except that the president also proposed the more extreme steps of reducing benefits and of switching to individual accounts. His plan would have converted Social Security into a national system of 401(k)s lacking any collective guarantee. A well-financed collective system would be better. Indeed, with private corporations increasingly refusing to guarantee their employees' old-age security, the government, to repeat, is the only party that can do it.

FINANCIAL DEBACLES are as old as the sun. Virtually all involve some form of borrowing, and borrowing is essentially an arrangement between the present and the future. This is why pensions are so vulnerable. Retirement schemes necessarily involve a treaty between today and tomorrow, and on a mass scale. It is no surprise that so many have run aground, or that when they do, financial upheaval is the result.

The pension schemes—public and private, federal and local—described in this book have been all guilty of similar crimes. To paraphrase Michael Aguirre, they behaved like "credit-card junkies" who charged to the card limit and made only the minimum payments.[11] Eventually, credit card bills come due. The most effective remedy—in pensions, health care, and even in Social Security—is to banish the credit card. Benefits should not be charged to a future generation; they should be paid for now.

This would not necessarily mean that benefits would be lower, or that retirees would be worse off. It *would* force legislatures to make difficult decisions about where to allocate resources. This is what legislatures are supposed to do. On the other hand, when benefits are seen to be "free," it is too tempting to perpetually ratchet them higher.

Changing this pattern will require political courage, and also a realignment across society. Business will have to face the fact that if it is unwilling to shoulder the burden, it must allow government to do so. Unions must recognize that the Treaty of Detroit no longer protects workers as much as it prices them out of the labor market. Politicians will have to look past the next election, and truly toward the "future" of which they so often speak. Lee Iacocca, the auto executive, pointed out more than a quarter century ago that the fault for the pension and health care burdens was shared three ways. Corporations, unions, and government—"the three of us," as Iacocca put it in the Chrysler boardroom—were to blame. If further catastrophe is to be avoided, all three parties must mend their ways.

ACKNOWLEDGMENTS

My editors at the *New York Times Magazine*, particularly Vera Titunik and Gerry Marzorati, encouraged me to write about pensions and laboriously worked to get a cover-length article suitable for mass readership. Without their efforts, this book would never have begun. I am deeply grateful to Vera and Gerry and to everyone else at the *Times* who pitched in.

I owe a special thanks to all of the people who were interviewed for this book. With some sources, I went to the well for multiple drinks; I am particularly grateful, therefore, to Robert Abel, John Casesa, Gary Dellaverson, Carl DeMaio, Joshua Freeman, Steve Girsky, Jack McGrory, Steve Miller, Jonathan Schwartz, and Rebecca Wilson. And I am especially grateful to Gilad Edelman, my intrepid and skillful research assistant.

Jeffrey Tannenbaum, a dear friend, and Louis Lowenstein, my father, read every word of this manuscript and offered uniquely insightful and helpful comments. My agent, Melanie Jackson, protected my commercial interests but—as always—looked out for my personal interests even more. Ann Godoff, my editor, once again proved the difference between a good editor and a great one. (Somehow, Ann sees the whole book before a word is writ.) This entire quartet has been with me since my first book, and I am grateful for their invaluable help and, in equal measure, for their steadfast loyalty.

It fell to my incomparably talented (and beautiful) wife, Judy, not only to read but also to reread, and then to re-reread (a *mal mot* that would surely catch her eye) this book in all of its wearying stages—gestational, formative, semi-complete, "almost" done (not to mention "almost-almost"), and so forth. She parsed the deepest nuances, she plumbed the technical details, she bridled at my shortcuts and evasions, she absolutely refused to let me submit a work that was less than I could make it. Hon, I am eternally grateful.

NOTES

INTRODUCTION

1. Social Security Administration; U.S. Census Bureau.
2. Pension Benefit Guaranty Corporation 2005 Fact Book, 2, 10. The latest figure is 18 percent. The agency insures pensions of 44 million people in the private sector, in addition to the 18 million covered public-sector workers and retirees. Among those in private sector plans, however, only half are currently working and accruing benefits. The rest have retired, changed to jobs without pensions, or work at firms whose plans were frozen.
3. Social Security Administration.
4. PBGC, 2006 Annual Report, 17.
5. Ibid., 2, 15. The deficit includes losses from probable future terminations. The PBGC estimates that possible future pension failures could swell the deficit by $73 billion more (p. 4).
6. See the author's "The End of Pensions," *New York Times Magazine*, Oct. 30, 2005.
7. Citizens Budget Commission.

1 • Walter Reuther and the Treaty of Detroit

The epigraph to this chapter is drawn from General Motors, *2005 Annual Report.*

1. David Halberstam, *The Reckoning* (New York: William Morrow, 1986), 327 (emphasis added).
2. 1953. The occasion was Wilson's nomination as secretary of defense.
3. Steven A. Sass, *The Promise of Private Pensions: The First Hundred Years* (Cambridge, Ma: Harvard University Press, 1997), 23.
4. Ibid., 34–35.
5. Nelson Lichtenstein, *The Most Dangerous Man in Detroit: Walter Reuther and the Fate of American Labor* (New York: Basic Books, 1995), is my primary source for the sketch of Reuther.
6. Irving Howe and B. J. Widdick, *The UAW and Walter Reuther* (New York: Random House, 1949), 29–30.
7. Lichtenstein, *Most Dangerous Man*, 33.
8. Ibid., 40.
9. Howe and Widdick, *Walter Reuther*, 193.
10. Lichtenstein, *Most Dangerous Man*, 54–55.
11. David Farber, *Sloan Rules: Alfred P. Sloan and the Triumph of General Motors* (Chicago: University of Chicago Press, 2002), 183–85.
12. Ibid., 155.
13. The Townsend episode is adapted from the author's "A Question of Numbers," *New York Times Magazine*, Jan. 16, 2005.
14. Ibid.
15. Sass, *Promise of Private Pensions*, 66.
16. Ibid., 34, 91–94.
17. Howe and Widdick, *Walter Reuther*, 4.
18. Alfred P. Sloan Jr., *My Years with General Motors* (1st ed. 1963; New York: Doubleday, 1990), 398.
19. Lowenstein, "A Question of Numbers."
20. Sass, *Promise of Private Pensions*, 118.
21. Ibid., 107.

22. Martin Halpern, *UAW Politics in the Cold War Era* (Albany: State University of New York Press, 1988), 193.
23. Benjamin M. Selekman, Sylvia Kopald Selekman, and Stephen H. Fuller, *Problems in Labor Relations* (New York: McGraw-Hill, 1958), 402–5.
24. A. H. Raskin, "UAW Seeks Pension of $100 a Month," *New York Times*, Jan. 21, 1949.
25. Walter P. Reuther, *Selected Papers*, ed. Henry M. Christman (New York: Macmillan, 1961), 39.
26. Sass, *Promise of Private Pensions*, 129–35.
27. "Labor: Turning Point," *Fortune*, April 1949.
28. Reuther was testifying to the Senate Finance Committee in its 1950 hearings on Social Security revision; quoted in Charles L. Dearing, *Industrial Pensions* (Washington, DC: Brookings, 1954), 47.
29. "A Plan for Pensions," *New Republic*, Dec. 19, 1949.
30. The author's source was the manuscript version of Jennifer Klein, "Welfare and Security in the Aftermath of World War II: How Europe Influenced America's Divided Welfare State," 20–21, 23 (subsequently published in Maurizio Vaudagna, ed., *The Place of Europe in American History: Twentieth Century Perspectives*, American Studies Series "Nova Americana," Torino, Italy: Otto Publisher, 2006).
31. Dearing, *Industrial Pensions*, 47.
32. Klein, "Welfare and Security," 26–30.
33. "Chrysler's Hundred Days," *Fortune*, June 1950.
34. Douglas Fraser, author interview.
35. "UAW–CIO Workers Security Program for Workers of the General Motors Corporation," April 10, 1950 (copy provided by UAW).
36. "The Treaty of Detroit," *Fortune*, July 1950; Sloan, *My Years with General Motors*, 395.
37. "Pensions Reconsidered," *Nation*, Nov. 19, 1949.
38. Peter F. Drucker, "The Mirage of Pensions," *Harper's Monthly*, February 1950.
39. Selekman, Selekman, and Fuller, *Problems in Labor Relations*, 426.

40. Ibid., 426.
41. Vartanig G. Vartan, "2.25-a-Share Yearend Breaks All Records for Total Payment," *New York Times*, Nov. 2, 1965.
42. "Collective Bargaining Gains by Date of Settlement, UAW–General Motors, 1937–1999," UAW Research Dept. (copy provided by UAW), 21–23. The calculation of $175 per month is as follows: Social Security was raised to a maximum of $98 a month for a single worker. GM pensions in 1955 were $2.25 per month per year of service, or $67.50 for a worker after thirty years, and $78.75 after thirty-five years.
43. Sloan, *My Years with General Motors*, 403.
44. Sass, *The Promise of Private Pensions*, 139.
45. Melvin A. Glasser, memo to Walter Reuther, Aug. 19, 1964, citing a report of the Social Security Administration, and "Corporate Retirement Policy and Practices Studies in Personnel Policy, No. 190," Conference Board, both in box 129, folder 5, Walter Reuther Collection, Walter Reuther Library, Wayne State University.
46. Glasser memo, Feb. 23, 1973, box 53, folder 10, Leonard Woodcock Collection, Walter Reuther Library. Sass said 40 percent was a typical level of underfunding for collectively bargained plans, *The Promise of Private Pensions*, 186.
47. James A. Wooten, *The Employee Retirement Income Security Act of 1974: A Political History* (hereafter *ERISA*) (Berkeley and Los Angeles: University of California Press, 2004), 68. The account here of Studebaker leans heavily on Wooten, 57–77.
48. Sass, *Promise of Private Pensions*, 186. Sass was quoting from House hearings on the Studebaker collapse.
49. Wooten, *ERISA*, 60, 74–76.
50. Ibid., 73.
51. Walter P. Reuther, "Labor's Pension Goals," typed submission to the *Journal of Commerce*, June 1, 1954, Reuther Collection.
52. Interoffice communication, Nat Weinberg to Walter Reuther, Jan. 8, 1963, box 165, folder 1, Reuther Collection.
53. Sloan, *My Years with General Motors*, 406.

54. Damon Stetson, "Union-G.M. Drama Nearing a Climax," *New York Times*, Sept. 2, 1961.
55. UAW, "Collective Bargaining Gains," 27–29.
56. "Statement from UAW to General Motors Corp.: SUB [Supplemental Unemployment Benefit]," 1, July 8, 1964, Reuther Collection.
57. John Casesa.
58. General Motors, *2005 Annual Report*, 5 ("just 31,000"). "Employee welfare or pension benefit plan for year ending Dec. 31, 1963," General Motors annual report submitted to Dept. of Labor, box 131, folder 13, Reuther Collection.
59. UAW, "Collective Bargaining Gains," 32, and Leonard Woodcock, "Summary of changes in 1964 insurance program," box 131, folder 13, Reuther Collection.
60. "Statement of Walter P. Reuther on Federal Reinsurance of Private Pension Plans," Aug. 15, 1966, 1–8, and draft of letter from Reuther to Hon. Wilbur Mills, Chairman, House Ways and Means Comm., Apr. 4, 1967, 1–4, both in Reuther Collection.
61. Senate testimony of Reuther on "Organization, costs and quality of medical care in the United States," Apr. 24, 1968, box 164, folder 5, Reuther Collection.
62. "Salient Facts Relative to Health Care in the U.S.," Reuther Collection, box 164, folder 1.
63. Elizabeth M. Fowler, "Some Analysts of G.M. Say 'I Told You So,' as Stock Drops," *New York Times*, Nov. 27, 1966.
64. The senator was Oregon's Wayne Morse. Jerry M. Flint, "New Look at G.M.: Troika at the Top," *New York Times*, Nov. 5, 1967.
65. UAW, "Collective Bargaining Gains," 36.
66. Information sheet prepared on twentieth anniversary of Ford pension, attached to memo from Irving Bluestone to Walter Reuther, Sept. 30, 1969, box 164, folder 1, Reuther Collection.
67. Robert C. Kryvicky, "The Funding of Negotiated Pension Plans," *Transactions*, Society of Actuaries, vol. XXXIII (1981): 413.
68. Lichtenstein, *Most Dangerous Man*, 436–38.
69. Jerry M. Flint, "General Motors and Union Reach Terms for Pact," *New York Times*, Nov. 12, 1970.
70. UAW, "Collective Bargaining Gains," 40.

2 • The Anti-Reuther

1. UAW, "Collective Bargaining Gains," 46–47.
2. Glasser, memo to Leonard Woodcock, Aug. 16, 1976, box 60, folder 12, Woodcock Collection.
3. Sass, *Promise of Private Pensions*, 213, and Wooten, *ERISA*, 113–14.
4. Sass, *Promise of Private Pensions*, 209.
5. Ibid., 200–01.
6. Ibid., 208, 230.
7. Ibid., 201.
8. Woodcock, letter to President Nixon, July 2, 1970, Woodcock Collection.
9. Woodcock said ERISA was a victory for the 30 million Americans with private pensions, box 39, folder 5, Woodcock Collection. Sass (217) said 45 percent of the private labor force, then about 64 million, had pensions, which yields a figure of 28.8 million covered employees. The figures do not include those with public-sector pensions.
10. Statement of Rep. Elwood H. Hillis, May 8, 1972, box 39, folder 3, Woodcock Collection.
11. See, for example, Agis Salpukas, "U.A.W. to Review Free-Trade Stand," *New York Times*, Aug. 20, 1971, and Salpukas, "U.A.W. on Eve of Meeting, Narrowing Its Social Role," *New York Times*, Nov. 13, 1971; "U.A.W. Unit Defies Chiefs, Backs Wallace in Michigan," *New York Times*, May 9, 1972; Jerry M. Flint, "Auto Makers Face Blue-Collar Blues," *New York Times*, Jan. 7, 1973; and Theodore J. Jacobs, "The Company and the Union," *New York Times*, Mar. 18, 1973; and also John Lippert, "The Fall of Detroit," *Bloomberg*, Sept. 25, 2007.
12. Agis Salpukas, "G.M. to Lay Off 30,000; Ford Cuts Pinto Price $66," *New York Times*, Nov. 22, 1974.
13. Glasser, memo to Woodcock, Aug. 7, 1972, box 9, folder 5, Woodcock Collection.
14. For instance, early retirees received $700 a month in 1978 and $915 in the first year of the new contract. UAW, "Collective Bargaining Gains," 47, 59.
15. Reginald Stuart, "New Hires Face a Loss in Auto Pact," *New York Times*, Sept. 18, 1979.

16. Douglas Fraser, author interview; also UAW, "Collective Bargaining Gains," 51, 57.
17. Jose A. Gomez-Ibanez and David Harrison Jr., "Imports and the Future of the U.S. Automobile Industry," *American Economic Review* 72, no. 2, Papers and Proceedings of the Ninety-fourth Annual Meeting of the American Economic Association (May 1982): 319–23.
18. Halberstam, *The Reckoning*, 609. The economist was William A. Niskanen Jr. During the Reagan administration he was acting chairman of the Council of Economic Advisers.
19. Sean McAlinden, author interview (the proportions apply to Americans of driving age).
20. Dan Luria, author interview.
21. Kryvicky, "The Funding of Negotiated Pension Plans," 405–35.
22. GM spokesperson, author interview.
23. Luria, author interview.
24. Robert S. Miller [hereafter Steve Miller], author interview.
25. Gerald Greenwald, author interview.
26. Ibid.
27. Greenwald and Fraser, author interviews.
28. Steve Miller, author interview.
29. Greenwald, author interview.
30. John Holusha, "G.M. Chairman Says Japanese Might Welcome Car Restraint," *New York Times*, Mar. 18, 1981.
31. John Holusha, "Driving a Hard Bargain in Detroit," *New York Times Magazine*, Aug. 26, 1984, and "Document by G.M. Shows Labor Plan," *New York Times*, Feb. 19, 1984.
32. Owen Bieber, author interview.
33. Luria, author interview.
34. Paul Ingrassia and Joseph B. White, *Comeback: The Fall and Rise of the American Automobile Industry* (New York: Simon & Schuster, 1994), 97–98, 111–14.
35. Luria, author interview.
36. James Barron, "General Motors Proposes Changes in Its Employee Health Program," *New York Times*, Aug. 16, 1984.

37. Bieber, author interview.
38. Ingrassia and White, *Comeback*, 93–94.
39. Ibid., 154.
40. Ibid., 144–46.
41. Federal Reserve Board, "Recent Changes in U.S. Family Finances: Evidence from the 2001 and 2004 Survey of Consumer Finances," A12.
42. Sass, *Promise of Private Pensions*, 229. Union representation fell from 24 percent of the private sector workforce in 1979 to 11 percent fifteen years later.
43. UAW, "Collective Bargaining Gains," 83–90; Michael H. Cimini, "Auto negotiations (General Motors Corp.–United Automobile Workers contract) (Developments in industrial relations)," *Monthly Labor Review* 113 (November 1990).
44. Ingrassia and White, *Comeback*, 430–32.
45. Ibid., 169.
46. Ibid., 307.
47. Margaret Price and Curtis Vosti, "Nicholas' Time pension low: GM director cut Smith's by 14.6%," *Pensions & Investments*, March 2, 1992.
48. Robert Stowe England, "A Question of Priorities," *Financial World*, April 25, 1995.
49. Robert Moroni, author interview.
50. Jonathan Chait, *The Big Con: The True Story of How Washington Got Hoodwinked and Hijacked by Crackpot Economics* (New York: Houghton Mifflin, 2007), 54–55.
51. Ron French, "GM's bitter pill: Automaker spends billions on drugs for aging workers, retirees," *Detroit News*, Sept. 27, 2006.
52. GM executive (name withheld), author interview.
53. "Rich Wagoner," Business Biographies, Answers.com.
54. Richard Shoemaker, author interview.
55. Gary Lapidus, "Automobiles/United States: Employee benefits stake increasing claim on Big Three value," Goldman Sachs global equity research report, May 31, 2001.
56. Steve Miller, author interview.
57. Ibid.

58. Remarks by Robert S. Miller to newspaper reporters, Washington, D.C., Oct. 28, 2005.
59. Lowenstein, "The End of Pensions," *New York Times Magazine*, Oct. 30, 2005.
60. See "The End of Pensions."
61. PBGC 2005 Fact Book, 3.
62. Gerald Meyers, author interview.
63. David Welch, with Nanette Byrnes, "GM Is Losing Traction," *Business Week*, Feb. 7, 2005.
64. Steve Girsky, author interview.
65. The pension was raised in steps over the contract life and reached $3,020 in 2006.
66. GM corporate communications.
67. *In re Delphi Corp., et al.,* Chapter 11 Case no. 05-44481, Declaration of Keith Williams, court docket #3045, 4 (available at DelphiDocket.com).
68. *In re Delphi*, Declaration and expert report of Michael L. Wachter, docket #3046, 20.
69. Monica Langley and Jeffrey McCracken, "Collision Course: Showdown on Auto-Labor Costs Looms as Delphi Goes to Court," *Wall Street Journal*, Mar. 31, 2006.
70. *In re Delphi*, Affidavit of Robert S. Miller, Jr., docket #0007, 26, 49.
71. *In re Delphi*, Declaration and expert report of Wachter, 20.
72. The workers would get a so-called cash balance plan, a newer form of pension also referred to as a hybrid because it combines aspects of defined benefit plans with those of defined contribution plans.
73. "Why GM's Plan Won't Work," *Business Week*, May 9, 2005.
74. General Motors, *2005 Annual Report*, 126. The precise figure for 2005 was $6.7 billion in benefits to U.S. pensioners, and $900 million to pensioners in overseas units.
75. General Motors, *2005 Annual Report*, 5.
76. Ron French, "Stranglehold: How General Motors and the nation are losing an epic battle to tame the health care beast," *Detroit News*, Sept. 28, 2006.
77. General Motors, *2005 Annual Report*, 5.

78. Carol Loomis, "The Tragedy of General Motors," *Fortune*, Feb. 6, 2006.
79. John Casesa, author interview.
80. David Cole, author interview.
81. Harvey Miller (no relation to Steve Miller), author interview.
82. Ibid.
83. *In re Delphi*, Declaration of Steven Gebbia, docket #3042, esp. 16–18; Tom Walsh and Jason Robertson, "Unions Irate Over Delphi's New Offer," *Detroit Free Press*, Oct. 22, 2005.
84. Steve Miller, author interview.
85. Langley and McCracken, "Delphi Goes to Court."
86. See Miller's speech to Kellogg School of Management, Nov. 7, 2005. Miller said he took the Delphi job without asking about his compensation, "and now that my salary has been cut to just one dollar a year, I guess I should have paid more attention."
87. Steve Miller, Harvey Miller, author interviews.
88. Lowenstein, "The End of Pensions."
89. *In re Delphi*, Transcript of Hearing Held on May 9, 2006, docket #3984, also Transcript of Hearing Held on May 24, 2006, docket #4136, esp. p. 145; Affidavit of Miller, 12.
90. *In re Delphi*, May 9 hearing transcript, 95–97.
91. *In re Delphi*, Declaration of Roger Struckman, docket #3779 (italics added).
92. Jeffrey McCracken, "Shifting Down: A Middle Class Made by Detroit Is Now Threatened by Its Slump," *Wall Street Journal*, Nov. 14, 2005.
93. Provided by Miller; employee's name withheld by author.
94. General Motors, *2005 Annual Report*, 130.
95. At year end 2005, GM had the following retiree obligations: U.S. pension benefits, $89.1 billion; non-U.S. pension benefits, $20.6 billion; other (primarily health) U.S. retiree benefits, $81.2 billion; non-U.S. benefits, $3.8 billion. General Motors, *2005 Annual Report*, 126.
96. Jim Millstein, author interview.
97. Ibid.
98. Millstein, Girsky, author interviews.
99. General Motors, *2005 Annual Report*, 50.

100. GM Form 10-Q, filed with U.S. SEC May 10, 2006 (period: Mar. 31, 2006); see exhibit 10.1, Memorandum of Understanding, Oct. 29, 2005, and especially Attachment E: Health Care Reform Letter.
101. Steve Miller, author interview.
102. Steve Miller, author interview, and Langley and McCracken, "Collision Course."
103. Casesa, author interview.
104. GM corporate communications.
105. Christopher Cooper and John McKinnon, "Bush Plays Down Bailout Prospects for GM and Ford," *Wall Street Journal*, Jan. 26, 2006.
106. Jerry York, author interview.
107. General Motors, *2005 Annual Report*, 3, 5.

3 • An Entitled Class

1. "New York City Retirement Systems," tables prepared by New York City Office of the Actuary.
2. Martin McLaughlin, author interview.
3. The average income for workers ages sixteen to sixty-four in the New York metro area in 2005 was $46,000; the median was $30,000 (George Borjas). Transit figures: MTA New York City Transit "Labor Negotiations Briefing Book," December 2005, Appendix N. Among the individual job categories, in 2004, bus operators earned an average of $62,551; bus maintainers, $68,152; train operators, $62,438. Other categories, such as conductors and cleaners, earned less.
4. Peter Kalikow, author interview.
5. *Report of the Police Pension Fund of the City of New York 1913*, 21–26. The history of the police fund is also summarized in Robert Tilove, *Public Employee Pension Funds* (New York: Columbia University Press, 1976), 262.
6. *Report of Police Pension Fund*, 16, 26.
7. Ibid., 17. The police contribution in 2005 was just over $1 billion.
8. Ibid., 21.
9. See the account of the strike in Robert Sobel, *Coolidge: An American Enigma*

(Washington, DC: Regnery Publishing, 1998), as well as in Donald R. McCoy, *Calvin Coolidge: The Quiet President* (New York: Macmillan, 1967).

10. Joshua B. Freeman, *In Transit: The Transport Workers Union in New York City, 1933–1966* (New York: Oxford University Press, 1989), 5. Mark H. Maier, *City Unions: Managing Discontent in New York City* (New Brunswick, NJ: Rutgers University Press, 1987), 12–13.
11. James J. McGinley, S.J., *Labor Relations in the New York Rapid Transit Systems 1904–1944* (New York: King's Crown Press, 1949), 202.
12. Freeman, *In Transit*, 13.
13. McGinley, *Labor Relations in Rapid Transit*, 213. *American Brake Shoe and Foundry Co. v. Interborough Rapid Rapid Transit Co.*, On petition for withdrawal and rescission of pension plan, June 25, 1936, Mack, Circuit Judge, In Equity, 70–364, U.S. District Court, southern district [the judge's decision contains numerous details of the 1916 IRT pension plan], 1–15.
14. L. H. Whittemore, *The Story of Mike Quill: The Man Who Ran the Subways* (New York: Holt, Rinehart and Winston, 1968), 25; McGinley, *Labor Relations in Rapid Transit*, 200; Freeman, *In Transit*, 15.
15. McGinley, *Labor Relations in Rapid Transit*, 171, 213–14, 485; *American Brake Shoe v. IRT*, Mack's decision, 2–3.
16. Whittemore, *Mike Quill*, 16, 19; Freeman, *In Transit*, 45–46, 50–51, 55. I am indebted to these two works for the early history of the TWU, as well as for the profile of Quill.
17. McGinley, *Labor Relations in Rapid Transit*, 214–15, 484.
18. Freeman, *In Transit*, 77.
19. *American Brake Shoe v. IRT*, Mack's decision, 8; McGinley, *Labor Relations in Rapid Transit*, 215.
20. Whittemore, *Mike Quill*, 3–9, 27, 37–38; Freeman, *In Transit*, 55–56.
21. Whittemore, *Mike Quill*, 86.
22. Quoted in Whittemore, *Mike Quill*, 21.
23. Freeman, *In Transit*, 70–71, 132–37, 354.
24. Ibid., 151–54, 196, 276.
25. Whittemore, *Mike Quill*, 47–49; Freeman, *In Transit*, 90, 95–97.
26. Whittemore, *Mike Quill*, 51.

27. Interborough Pension Board, "Amount of Monthly Payroll Payments and Contributions," July 13, 1953, Transport Workers Union of America Collection, Robert F. Wagner Labor Archives, Tamiment Library, New York University (hereafter TWU Collection), box 1, folder 13.
28. Whittemore, *Mike Quill*, 56; Freeman, *In Transit*, 113–14, 121–22; McGinley, *Labor Relations in Rapid Transit*, 216.
29. Maier, *City Unions*, 11; Freeman, *In Transit*, 217.
30. Whittemore, *Mike Quill*, 104–5; Maier, *City Unions*, 19.
31. Freeman, *In Transit*, 197–98.
32. Ibid., 218, 221.
33. Jonathan Schwartz, author interview.
34. McGinley, *Labor Relations in Rapid Transit*, 219.
35. Minutes of TWU board, June 27, 1941, box 1, folder 11, TWU Collection.
36. Dearing, *Industrial Pensions*, 27–28.
37. Whittemore, *Mike Quill*, 136, 143, 161; Freeman, *In Transit*, 291, 301–2, 303.
38. Maier, *City Unions*, 34.
39. Whittemore, *Mike Quill*, 126.
40. Maier, *City Unions*, 32.
41. Raymond D. Horton, *Municipal Labor Relations in New York City: Lessons of the Lindsay-Wagner Years* (New York: Praeger, 1973), 21–23.
42. Maier, *City Unions*, 34.
43. Tilove, *Public Employee Pension Funds*, 281.
44. Whittemore, *Mike Quill*, 229.
45. Charles R. Morris, *The Cost of Good Intentions* (New York: W.W. Norton, 1980), 89.
46. Maier, *City Unions*, 48.
47. Freeman, *In Transit*, 326.
48. Richard B. Freeman, "Unionism Comes to the Public Sector," *Journal of Economic Literature* 24, no. 1 (Mar. 1986): 41, 47.
49. Horton, *Municipal Labor Relations*, 49.
50. Testimony of Hillis, May 8, 1972, box 39, folder 1, Woodcock Collection, Reuther Library.
51. Robert A. Caro, *The Power Broker* (New York: Alfred A. Knopf, 1974), 735.

52. There is a good history of pension changes in New York City during the '60s in Morris, *Cost of Good Intentions*, see esp. 99–101.
53. "Summary—Pension Changes in New York City," typed report, TWU Collection.
54. Tilove, *Public Employee Pension Funds*, 283.
55. Richard Freeman, "Unionism Comes to the Public Sector," 43; Horton, *Municipal Labor Relations*, 51.
56. Joshua Freeman, *In Transit* (1st ed. 1989; Philadelphia: Temple University Press, 2001), 338.
57. Freeman, *In Transit* (1st. ed.), 333.
58. Whittemore, *Mike Quill*, 248.
59. Maier, *City Unions*, 40.
60. Letter of Oct. 31, 1963, box 25, folder 10, TWU Collection.
61. Horton, *Municipal Labor Relations*, 68.
62. Thomas R. Brooks, "Lindsay, Quill & the Transit Strike," *Commentary*, March 1966.
63. Horton, *Municipal Labor Relations*, 72.
64. Ken Auletta, *The Streets Were Paved with Gold* (1st ed. 1975; New York: Vintage, 1980), 59.
65. Theodore Kheel, author interview, and Brooks, "Lindsay, Quill."
66. Kheel, author interview.
67. Ibid.
68. Whittemore, *Mike Quill*, 284.
69. Murray Schumach, "Union Chief Irate," *New York Times*, Jan. 5, 1966.
70. Vincent J. Cannato, *The Ungovernable City: John Lindsay and His Struggle to Save New York* (New York: Perseus, 2001), 87.
71. Kheel, author interview.
72. Horton, *Municipal Labor Relations*, 81.
73. Freeman, *In Transit* (1st ed.), 335.
74. Morris, *Cost of Good Intentions*, 103.
75. Auletta, *Streets Were Paved with Gold*, 47, 150, 155.
76. Ibid., 50.
77. Schwartz, author interview.

78. Ibid.
79. "T.W.U.'s 20-Year, Half-Pay Transit Authority Pension Plan," TWU Collection.
80. Transcript of WNBC-TV's *Searchlight,* Jan. 11, 1970, panel interview with John J. Gilhooley, TWU Collection.
81. Schwartz, author interview.
82. Ibid.
83. Ibid.
84. Ibid. The only dollop of sanity in the variable supplement was that the stock market had to recoup any prior losses before pensioners were eligible for a bonus. In other words, if the market index fell from 1,000 to 900, supplements would not kick in until it again rose above 1,000.
85. Auletta, *Streets Were Paved with Gold,* see esp. 32, 289.
86. Horton, *Municipal Labor Relations,* 76.
87. Freeman, *In Transit* (2001 ed.), 338.
88. Tilove, *Public Employee Pension Funds,* 272. The figures assume the workers were married. Social Security payments were less for single workers, but even in those cases total retirement income was greater than 100 percent of final pay.
89. Ibid., 285–86.
90. David K. Shipler, "City Pension Costs Snowballing," *New York Times.* Mar. 15, 1971.
91. Schwartz, author interview. A total of sixty-one motormen retired that year on a "final salary" of at least $25,000. Shipler, "City Pension Costs Snowballing."
92. Tilove, *Public Employee Pension Funds,* 285.
93. Freeman, *In Transit* (2001 ed.), 339.
94. Ibid., 339; Auletta, *Streets Were Paved with Gold,* 146. The drop in ridership occurred roughly from 1969 to 1977.
95. Shipler, "City Pension Costs Snowballing"; Alfonzo A. Narvaez, "City Unsure of Savings in Pension Bill," *New York Times,* July 29, 1973.
96. Maier, *City Unions,* 87.
97. Barry Feinstein, author interview.
98. Ibid.
99. Quoted in Tilove, *Public Employee Pension Funds,* 280.

100. Feinstein, author interview; Tilove, *Public Employee Pension Funds*, 280; Maier, *City Unions*, 88.
101. Feinstein, author interview; Schwartz, author interview.
102. M. A. Farber, "Uniform State Pension Plan Proposed," *New York Times*, Jan. 31, 1973.
103. Ibid.
104. Farber, "Uniform State Pension Plan Proposed."
105. "Doing and Undoing," *New York Times* (unsigned editorial), Apr. 24, 1973.
106. TWU notices, Feb. 9, 1973, TWU Collection; M. A. Farber, "Coalition of 15 Public-Employe Unions Decries Rockefeller's Bill on Pensions," *New York Times*, May 16, 1973; William E. Farrell, "State Pact with Employees Called Blow to Proposal for Uniform Pension Plan," *New York Times*, Apr. 14, 1973.
107. Farrell, "State Pact with Employees Called Blow"; Francis X. Clines, "Panel Chides Governor on Pension Reform," *New York Times*, May 9, 1973; Farrell, "Albany Sets Back Pension Reforms for This Session," *New York Times*, May 23, 1973.
108. Schwartz, author interview.
109. In addition to the change cited in the text, the service requirement was raised from twenty years to twenty-five years. Schwartz, author interview; Alfonso A. Narvaez, "Kinzel Assails Panel's Pension Plan As an Endorsement of the Status Quo; Change in Age," *New York Times*, July 20, 1973.
110. Louis M. Kohlmeier, "Pension Fund Risks for Public Employees," *New York Times*, Mar. 28, 1976.
111. Edward Ranzal, "City Needs $100 Million for Tomorrow's Debts," *New York Times*, Sept. 4, 1975, and John Darnton, "Trustees of City Pensions Wary of More City Bonds," *New York Times*, Oct. 2, 1975.
112. Richard Ravitch, author interview; Schwartz, author interview; Linda Greenhouse, "A Night of Anxiety on Brink of Default," and Steven R. Weisman, "$150-Million Pact," both in *New York Times*, Oct. 18. 1975; "Saved Again from the Jaws of Default," *Time*, Oct. 27, 1975.
113. Kohlmeier, "Pension Fund Risks for Public Employees." The funds agreed to invest an additional $2.5 billion in bonds in the future, representing a total commitment of close to half their assets.

114. Auletta, *Streets Were Paved with Gold*, 206.
115. Ibid., 50.

4 • On Strike!

1. Ed Koch, author interview. See also Josh Barbanel, "Bill to Increase State Pensions Nearing a Vote," *New York Times*, June 13, 1983, and Michael Oreskes, "Mayor Attacks Bill to Improve State Pensions," *New York Times*, June 15, 1983.
2. Koch, author interview; Feinstein, author interview.
3. Ravitch, author interview.
4. Freeman, *In Transit* (2001 ed.), 339, 341, 343; Ravitch, author interview.
5. Ravitch, author interview; James Lardner, "A Reporter at Large: Painting the Elephant," *New Yorker*, June 25, 1984; and Freeman, *In Transit* (2001 ed.), 341.
6. Ravitch, author interview. See also Lardner, "A Reporter at Large"; Richard J. Meislin, "Koch Is Angered By Carey's Move to Support Pact," *New York Times*, Apr. 2, 1980; Damon Stetson, "Talks are Curtailed," *New York Times*, Apr. 4, 1980.
7. Freeman, *In Transit* (2001 ed.), 342.
8. Lardner, "A Reporter at Large."
9. Freeman, *In Transit* (2001 ed.), 340.
10. Ravitch, author interview. For a fuller and excellent account of Ravitch's effort to rebuild the subways, see Lardner, "A Reporter at Large."
11. Neysa Pranger, author interview.
12. Michael Oreskes, "A Transit Strike? Union Chief Says 'No Way,' " and "Tentative Accord Reached with City Transit Workers," *New York Times*, Mar. 18, 1985, and June 28, 1985.
13. E. J. McMahon and Fred Siegel, "Gotham's Fiscal Crisis: Lessons Unlearned," *Public Interest* no. 158 (Winter 2005), 96–110.
14. Freeman, *In Transit* (2001 ed.), 343.
15. Alan Finder, "Transit Union Head to Seek Strike Approval," *New York Times*, Apr. 15, 1992.

16. Schwartz, author interview.
17. Ibid.
18. Steven Greenhouse, "Transit Workers' Chief Quits After Protest," *New York Times*, Jan. 20, 1996; Freeman, *In Transit* (2001 ed.), 343–44.
19. Gene Russianoff, author interview.
20. Lowenstein, "The End of Pensions."
21. "Why New York's Going Broke," *New York Daily News*, Sept. 7, 2004.
22. Eric Lipton, "Mayor Eases Reins on City's Spending as Economy Booms," *New York Times*, July 13, 2000.
23. Robert C. North Jr., Adam Barsky, and Ed Watt, author interviews.
24. Pension contribution figures from the tables in "New York City Retirement Systems," prepared by the New York City Actuary (hereafter NYC Actuary) City of New York, Independent Budget Office. The $16 million represents the Transit Authority's contribution on behalf of all transit workers *except* those employed by the Manhattan and Bronx Surface Transit Operating Authority (MaBSTOA), a subsidiary of the TA that operates formerly private bus lines. MaBSTOA workers belong to a separate pension plan, also funded by the TA. Assuming their pension expense amounted to an equivalent proportion of payroll, the total transit pension payment was roughly $20 million.
25. "Why New York's Going Broke."
26. Michael Cooper, "City Foots Bill as State Upgrades Pensions," *New York Times*, Aug. 22, 2006.
27. Ibid.
28. Ibid.; New York State Board of Elections.
29. Barsky, author interview.
30. E. J. McMahon, author interview.
31. Ibid.
32. Gary Dellaverson, author interview.
33. "Why New York's Going Broke II," *New York Daily News*, Sept. 8, 2004; Bill Farrell, "Pensions Get Overdue Lift," *New York Daily News*, June 21, 2000.
34. Eric Lipton, "Giuliani Plan Would Curtail City Tax Cuts," *New York Times*, July 20, 2000.
35. Freeman, *In Transit* (2001 ed.), 346.

36. Philip Kasinitz, author interview.
37. Tom Robbins, "Underground Rumblings: A Modern Militant Vies to Revive the Transit Union," *Village Voice*, Nov. 22–28, 2000; Pete Donohue, "What Make[s] Toussaint Tick," *New York Daily News*, Dec. 12, 2005.
38. Arthur Schwartz, author interview; *Roger Toussaint, Julio Rivera, Leroy Jardim, John Samuelsen and Jose Iglesias v. New York City Transit Authority, Local 100, Transit Workers Union, et al.*, 99 Civ. 2266, U.S. District Court, Eastern District of New York, Declaration of Roger Toussaint; see also Robbins, "Underground Rumblings."
39. Nicholc M. Christian, "Chief of Transport Workers Loses to Upstart in Landslide," *New York Times*, Dec. 14, 2000.
40. The sketch of Kalikow draws on two main sources: the author's interview with Kalikow, and Craig Horowitz, "Underground Man," *New York Magazine*, Apr. 5, 2004.
41. See, for instance, Richard D. Hylton, "Sometimes Those Bare Necessities Include Yacht Docking," *New York Times*, Aug. 25, 1991.
42. Horowitz, "Underground Man."
43. Ibid.
44. MTA. The figure is as of 2004.
45. Schaller Consulting, "Mode Shift in the 1990s: How Subway and Bus Ridership Outpaced the Auto in Market Share Gains in New York City," Aug. 8, 2001, 20.
46. MTA 2006 Annual Report, "Capital Program Progress Table"; Russianoff, author interview; also Randy Kennedy, "M.T.A. Head Expected to Announce Resignation," *New York Times*, Jan. 24, 2001.
47. Russianoff, author interview; see also Robert Fitch, "New York's Real Transit Crisis," *Nation*, Dec. 30, 2005 (Web only).
48. Kevin Flynn and Charles V. Bagli, "2 M.T.A. Officials Fired in December in Bribery Inquiry," *New York Times*, Apr. 17, 2003.
49. Eric Lipton, "Big Donors' Dealings with State Give Pataki Big Advantage," *New York Times*, Oct. 11, 2002.
50. See, for instance, Sewell Chan, "Transit Chief Shows Signs of Political Independence," *New York Times*, Feb. 26, 2005. Chan said Kalikow "once . . . was

better known as a Republican donor and heir to a real estate fortune" but had developed into "a forceful advocate" for mass transit.

51. Kalikow, author interview.
52. Ibid.
53. "Why New York's Going Broke II."
54. From 2001 to 2007 the payroll rose at a rate of 2.5 percent a year, just covering the rise in the cost of living. "Financial Plan Summary, Fiscal Years 2006–2010," Mayor Bloomberg, Jan. 31, 2006, 10.
55. McMahon, author interview. The tax hike became effective in 2003.
56. North, author interview.
57. Steven Greenhouse, "The Transit Settlement: The Deal," and "The Transit Settlement: The Talks," *New York Times*, Dec. 17 and 18, 2002.
58. "Review of the Proposed Financial Plan and Capital Program for the Metropolitan Transportation Authority," Report 7-2005, Oct. 2004, New York State Comptroller, Alan G. Hevesi, 1.
59. Richard Perez-Pena, "M.T.A.'s Fiscal Predicament Is a Crisis That Many Saw Coming," *New York Times*, Oct. 25, 2004.
60. "Financial Outlook for the Metropolitan Transportation Authority," Hevesi, NYS Comptroller, Report I-2006, May 2005, and also Hevesi's Report 7-2005, 12, 30. The increase in the MTA's reliance on bond sales for capital programs is striking; during the late 1980s, 2.5 percent of the MTA capital budget was financed with debt, in the '90s, 40 percent, and from 2000 to 2004, 60 percent.
61. MTA 2006 Annual Report. MTA federal grants equaled, on an average annual basis, $630 million from 1992 to 1999 and $1.1 billion from 2000 to 2005. Inflation somewhat eroded the value of later grants.
62. Joyce Purnick, "Metro Matters; Transit Chief Has the Style of His Boss," *New York Times*, Apr. 24, 2003.
63. Sewell Chan, "Transit Chief Shows Signs of Political Independence," *New York Times*, Feb. 26, 2005.
64. MTA, NYC Transit Briefing Book; Dellaverson, author interview.
65. George Borjas; Nicole Gelinas, "Off the Rails" (op-ed), *New York Times*, Dec. 13, 2005.

66. NYC Actuary; MTA, NYC Transit Briefing Book; Steven Greenhouse and Sewell Chan, "In Talks over Transit Pact, Different Chips, Same Poker," *New York Times*, Dec. 11, 2005; and Dellaverson, author interview. The pension figures for transit include the entire workforce, including MaBSTOA.
67. Feinstein and Kalikow, author interviews.
68. NYC Actuary.
69. NYC Actuary. The actuary forecast a total pension bill for 2009 of $6.65 billion.
70. NYCERS. General employees contributed $632 million to NYCERS in 2000 and only $310 million in 2005.
71. Independent Budget Office; NYC "January 2006 Financial Plan," 61.
72. McMahon, author interview.
73. "The Case for Redesigning Retirement Benefits for New York's Public Employees," Citizens Budget Commission, Apr. 29, 2005.
74. NYCERS, Annual Financial Report, June 30, 2005, author's analysis of "Service Retirement Experience/Table of Average Retirement Allowance by Age and Years of Service," 194. Autoworkers' thirty-and-out pensions were $2,875 a month, or $34,500 annually, as of Oct. 2004.
75. Lowenstein, "The End of Pensions."
76. Bloomberg's budget message in January 2006 would state, "Pension reform is necessary in order for New York City to gain control over escalating costs." January 2006 Financial Plan, Fiscal Years 2006–2010, Michael Bloomberg, Mayor, Jan. 31, 2006, 37.
77. Pocket Veto Message—No. 188 (veto of S3325A, introduced in Senate 2003); Veto Message—No. 256 (veto of S7531, introduced in Senate 2004).
78. Dellaverson, author interview.
79. Greenhouse and Chan, "In Talks over Transit Pact, Different Chips, Same Poker."
80. Dellaverson, author interview.
81. Greenhouse and Chan, "Different Chips, Same Poker."
82. Donohue, "What Make[s] Toussaint Tick," *New York Daily News*, Dec. 12, 2005.
83. Steven Greenhouse, "City Seeks Stiff Fines for Workers and Transit Union If

They Strike," *New York Times*, Dec. 14, 2005. The Quill quote is from Robbins, "Underground Rumblings," *Village Voice,* Nov. 22–28, 2000.

84. "Subway Grinches" (editorial), *Wall Street Journal,* Dec. 15, 2005.
85. Dan Zukowski, "NY Transit Workers Ready to End Strike," Mass Transit, http://www.danzukowski.com/transit/2005/12/index.html, Dec. 22, 2005; TWU bulletin.
86. Pete Donohue, "Wheels Turn as Deadline Passes," *New York Daily News*, Dec. 19, 2005.
87. The account of the bargaining draws on interviews with Kalikow, Dellaverson, Basil Paterson, and others, as well as on the extensive coverage that appeared in the New York press.
88. "Last Stand at the MTA-TWU Corral . . . Maybe," Gothamist.com, Dec. 16, 2005; Steven Greenhouse and Sewell Chan, "Transit Talks Pass Deadline For a Strike," *New York Times*, Dec. 16, 2005.
89. Kalikow, author interview.
90. Ibid.
91. Newspaper coverage of the talks was extensive. One of the best pieces was Pete Donohue and Paul H. B. Shin, "Hopes Rose & Sank as the Clock Ticked," *New York Daily News*, Dec. 17, 2005.
92. Pete Donohue and David Saltonstall, "MTA & Union Not Talking," *New York Daily News*, Dec. 17, 2005.
93. Sewell Chan and Steven Greenhouse, "N.Y. Transit Union Rejects Offer and Calls a Limited Strike," *New York Times*, Dec. 16, 2005; Greenhouse, "Workers and the M.T.A. Stick to Lines in the Sand, *New York Times*, Dec. 17, 2005.
94. Donohue, "Wheels Turn."
95. Naomi Allen, "The 2005 New York City Transit Strike Report on the First Day, and Other Thoughts," Labor Standard, http://www.laborstandard.org/NYTransit/First__Day.htm; The Internationalist, http://www.internationalist.org./nyctransitstrike051219.html, December 2005.
96. Paterson, author interview.
97. Harry Harrington, " 'No Contract, No Work'—The 2005 New York City transit strike," Industrial Workers of the World, http://www.iww.org/en/node/2010, Feb. 3, 2006.

98. "The Daily News Says Throw Roger from the Train!" (editorial), *New York Daily News*, Dec. 21, 2005.

5 • Finest City

1. The peak official figure, as of June 30, 2005, was $1.4 billion (SDCERS). However, KPMG, the city's outside auditor, placed the deficit at approximately $1.7 billion (see the city attorney's sixth interim report on the pension case, 13). Rick Roeder, the retirement system actuary, publicly endorsed this figure as accurate given certain (more conservative) actuarial assumptions. (See Philip LaVelle, "New board for pension has tough task ahead," *San Diego Union-Tribune*, Apr. 14, 2005.)
2. Jack Jacobs, author interview.
3. Murtaza H. Baxamusa, "Bottom Line: Solutions for San Diego's Budget Crisis," Center on Policy Initiatives, April 2005, 1.
4. Measured in 2000 dollars; Jennifer Sloan McCombs and Stephen J. Carroll, "Ultimate Test: Who Is Accountable for Education If Everybody Fails?" *Rand Review*, Spring 2005.
5. Edward Fike, author interview.
6. Jack McGrory, author interview.
7. Arthur Levitt Jr., Lynn E. Turner, and Troy A. Dahlberg, "Report of the Audit Committee of the City of San Diego," Aug. 8, 2006, 34–35 (hereafter Levitt).
8. Michael Aguirre, "Interim Report Number 3 Regarding Possible Abuse, Illegal Acts or Fraud by City of San Diego Officials," 18. Aguirre, the city attorney, released seven so-called interim reports during 2005 (hereafter Aguirre I, II, III, etc). "State must return pension money," *San Diego Union-Tribune*, May 29, 1997.
9. Baxamusa, "Bottom Line," 2.
10. Matt Potter, "Married Rich," SanDiegoReader.com, May 31, 2001; John Patrick Ford, "Scandal du Jour," *Daily Transcript* (San Diego), Oct. 20, 2005.
11. John Kaheny, author interview; Philip J. LaVelle, "Rates rise, but was work done? Sanders wants look at water, sewer books," *San Diego Union-Tribune*, Jan. 22, 2006.

12. Gerry Braun, "The smooth operator," *San Diego Union-Tribune*, Dec. 18, 2005.
13. The figures were variously collected from 1997 to 2003. Baxamusa, "Bottom Line," 6, 9, 12–15.
14. Baxamusa, "Bottom Line," 23–30.
15. McGrory, author interview.
16. Philip J. LaVelle, "Mayor's retirement fund plan is opposed; City would suspend contributions," *San Diego Union-Tribune*, Apr. 16, 1994.
17. Kaheny, author interview.
18. McGrory, Gary Kaku, author interviews; Levitt, 35–36; Philip J. LaVelle, "City gets retirement pool break, $9.3 million 'loan' will avert cuts in police, fire departments," *San Diego Union-Tribune*, Mar. 25, 1995.
19. Braun, "The smooth operator."
20. Susan Golding, "A City of Neighborhoods," State of the City Address, Jan. 10, 1996.
21. John Thomson, author interview.
22. McGrory, author interview.
23. Aguirre VI, 24, 26–30.
24. Aguirre III, 9; Conny Jamison, author interview.
25. Aguirre VI, 16.
26. Aguirre VI, 38; Philip J. LaVelle, "City has a deal, but will pension trustees buy it?" *San Diego Union-Tribune*, June 21, 1996.
27. There was much debate about the size of the balloon payment that would have been required. Many said it would have been $75 million.
28. Jamison, author interview.
29. Scott Peters, author interview.
30. Aguirre VI, 46.
31. *Board of Administration v. Wilson*, 52 Cal. App. 4th 1109, 1117–1122, 1131, 1135 (1997), cited in Aguirre III, 17–18.
32. Aguirre III, 8, 18–19.
33. Ernie Anderson, author interview.
34. Ronald W. Powell, "Stadium Site Search," *San Diego Union-Tribune*, Mar. 12, 2007.

35. See the author's *Origins of the Crash: The Great Bubble and Its Undoing* (New York: Penguin, 2004), 125.
36. "Murphy for mayor," *San Diego Union-Tribune*, Oct. 15, 2000.
37. Fike, author interview.
38. "Murphy for mayor."
39. Philip J. LaVelle, "Stallings resigns," *San Diego Union-Tribune*, Jan. 30, 2001.

6 • Pension Plot

1. Aguirre II, 25–26.
2. SDCERS; Levitt, 67–68; Andrew Donohue, "Six SD Officials Charged in Pension Scandal," *Voice of San Diego* (online, nonprofit newspaper; voiceofsandiego.org), May 17, 2005; Indictment, *United States of America v. Ronald Saathoff, Cathy Lexin, Teresa Webster, Lawrence Grissom, Loraine Chapin*, U.S. District Court, Southern District of California, January 2004 Grand Jury, Criminal Case NO. 06CR0043BEN, filed Jan. 6, 2006, 14. See also E. Scott Reckard, Catherine Saillant, and Kathy M. Kristof, "San Diego Playing a Blame Game," *Los Angeles Times*, May 1, 2005.
3. Indictment, *U.S. v. Saathoff et al.*, 14–15.
4. Aguirre II, 26, 3–4, 10.
5. Ibid., 10.
6. Kroll interview of Dennis Gibson, 5–6, attached to Levitt.
7. Aguirre II, 26–27. See also Matthew T. Hall, "Ballpark built despite city's fiscal ills. Report delayed to protect bond sale, consultants find," *San Diego Union-Tribune*, Aug. 14, 2006.
8. Aguirre II, 27.
9. Levitt, B-10; Aguirre II, 11–12; also Aguirre VII, 3.
10. Carl DeMaio, author interview.
11. Aguirre II, 30.
12. Ray Huard, "City finances called sound, but new revenue is needed. Panel avoids saying how to raise the money," *San Diego Union-Tribune*, Feb. 28, 2002.
13. Aguirre II, 11, 26–29. The report said the latest (i.e., the June 30, 2001, fund-

ing ratio) was "not available." However, it had been both available and known for fifteen days.

14. Transcript of Rules Committee meeting, Feb. 27, 2002.
15. Lamont Ewell, author interview.
16. Aguirre II, 13–14.
17. Ibid., 31, 32–33.
18. Aguirre VII, 20–21.
19. Levitt, B-11; Reginald A. Vitek, letter to Sheila Leone, Mar. 5, 2003.
20. Transcript of Rules Committee meeting, March 20, 2002.
21. Aguirre II, 15.
22. Ibid., 45.
23. Richard H. Vortmann, letter to "Fellow Blue Ribbon Committee Members," Apr. 29, 2002.
24. Kroll interview of Dennis Gibson, 7, attached to Levitt, and Richard Vortmann, author interview. See also Matt T. Hall, "S.D. panelist's memo warned of fiscal woes," *San Diego Union-Tribune*, Feb. 3, 2005.
25. "Pension Violations" (editorial), *San Diego Union-Tribune*, Jan. 13, 2005.
26. Aguirre III, 16.
27. Aguirre II, 21 (emphasis added).
28. Ibid., 40.
29. Letter of Diann Shipione, May 23, 2002; Douglas McCalla, author interview.
30. Over the five years to June 30, 2002, SDCERS's investment performance was 7 percent a year. The California Public Employees' Retirement System (CalPERS), the country's biggest retirement system, said in its 2002 annual report that the average system earned 5.1 percent a year over that span, and that CalPERS earned 5.3 percent. Over the ten years ending June 2002, SDCERS's return was 10.1 percent a year, compared to 9.3 percent for CalPERS.
31. Pat Shea, author interview; Matthew T. Hall, "Lawyer's cure is bitter pill," *San Diego Union-Tribune*, June 30, 2005.
32. Vitek, letter to Leone.

33. Aguirre II, 71–76.
34. Ann M. Smith, "Heroes or Villains? It Depends on Politics, Not Facts" (guest column), *Voice of San Diego*, June 21, 2005.
35. Michael Aguirre, author interview.
36. See the author's "The Next Wall Street Scandal," *American Prospect*, Jan. 16, 2006.
37. Herring's response was by letter, as cited in Vitek, letter to Leone, and Andrew Donohue, "Concerns raised over city's ability to finance employee retirement fund," *Daily Transcript*, Dec. 6, 2002.
38. Aguirre II, 78.
39. *Record* 28, no. 2, Society of Actuaries, 1–12.
40. Indictment, *U.S. v. Saathoff et al.*, 8.
41. Indictment, *U.S. v. Saathoff et al.*, 8–9, 17. The quote is from Lexin.
42. Levitt, 74.
43. Indictment, *U.S. v. Saathoff et al.*, 18.
44. Aguirre VII, 16; Andrew Donohue, "Internal E-mail: Pension Official Pressured Attorney to Change Opinion on Deal," *Voice of San Diego*, Oct. 7, 2005.
45. Aguirre VII, 10.
46. James Gleason, author interview.
47. Kelling, Northcross & Nobriga, "City of San Diego, Facilities Financing Study," Aug. 28, 2002, see esp. 19, 54.
48. Aguirre VII, 12.
49. Ibid.
50. Ibid.
51. Ibid., 13.
52. Vitek, letter to Leone; Levitt, 75–76.
53. Robert Blum, letter to Frederick W. Pierce IV (board president, SDCERS), Nov. 18, 2002.
54. Levitt, B-17.
55. Ibid.
56. Diann Shipione, letter to the Honorable Dick Murphy and Members of the City Council, Nov. 18, 2002.

57. Diann Shipione, April Boling, author interviews.
58. Donna Frye, author interview; Donohue, "Concerns raised over city's ability to finance employee retirement fund."
59. Levitt, B-17; Aguirre VII, 13.
60. Ray Huard, "Council OKs library financing proposal. $312 million to cover new main facility, upgradings," *San Diego Union-Tribune*, Nov. 19, 2002.
61. Indictment, *U.S. v. Saathoff et al.*, 19; Philip J. LaVelle, "City Pension Plan, Part Two of Two," *San Diego Union-Tribune*, June 21, 2004.
62. P. Lamont Ewell, letter to Honorable Mayor and City Council, Dec. 6, 2002.
63. Aguirre I, 15.
64. Michael Conger, Gleason, author interviews.

7 • The Bill Comes Due

1. Conger, author interview.
2. Conger, Michael Leone, author interviews.
3. Michael Leone, Reginald A. Vitek, author interviews, and Vitek, letter to Leone.
4. Aguirre VII, 18–20.
5. Andrew Donohue, "City officials hear hard numbers on retirement fund," *Daily Transcript*, Feb. 12, 2003.
6. Aguirre VII, 14, 16.
7. *San Diego Union-Tribune*, May 21, 2003.
8. Fike, author interview.
9. Eugene Mitchell, April Boling, and Carl Luna, author interviews.
10. Conger, author interview.
11. Ibid.
12. Shipione, author interview; Paul S. Maco and Richard C. Sauer, "Report on Investigation, The City of San Diego City Employees Retirement System and Related Disclosure Practices, 1996–2004," [hereafer Vinson & Elkins], 112–114; *City of San Diego v. Orrick, Herrington & Sutcliffe*, California Superior

Court, Case No. GIC 857632, "Orrick's Notice of Filing Corrected Special Motion to Strike Complaint" (hereafter "Orrick's Notice of Filing"), 5.

13. Vinson & Elkins, 113.
14. Shipione, author interview; "Orrick's Notice of Filing," 5.
15. Vitek, author interview; see also "Defendant SDCERS' Memorandum of Points and Authorities in Opposition to Plaintiffs' Motion for Attorneys Fees and Costs," *Gleason & Wood v. SDCERS et al.* (hereafter,"SDCERS' Memorandum"), 12–13, 14, 34, 46.
16. Vitek, author interview.
17. Vitek, author interview. "SDCERS' Memorandum," 16, also refers to Herring's "profanity-laced tirade."
18. "SDCERS' Memorandum," 16.
19. Michael Leone, author interview.
20. Don Bauder, "City Lights: $20 Million In Unanswered Questions," SanDiegoReader.com, June 16, 2005; Conger, author interview.
21. Conger, author interview.
22. Vitek, author interview; SDCERS.
23. SDCERS.
24. Ibid., 4.
25. Andrew Donohue, "The History of V&E: A Special Report," *Voice of San Diego*, Sept. 9, 2005.
26. Scott Lewis, "Extra goodies for retirees added even more to pension deficit, report finds," *Daily Transcript*, May 5, 2004.
27. Scott Lewis, "Mayor puts weight behind specific pension reforms," *Daily Transcript*, July 7, 2004.
28. Scott Lewis, "Pension reform proposals met with opposition; council delays decision," *Daily Transcript*, June 30, 2002.
29. Dolores Huerta, author interview.
30. Phillip J. LaVelle, "City Hall pension politics heat up. Plan to scrap board may prove tricky for Murphy," *San Diego Union-Tribune*, July 4, 2004; Scott Lewis, "Roberts, Murphy, county, city sling pension mud," *Daily Transcript*, June 9, 2004.

31. Scott Lewis, "Retirement board overhaul will be on ballot, but with poison pill?" *San Diego Transcript*, July 21, 2004.
32. Aguirre VI, 2.
33. Matthew T. Hall, "Shea says bankruptcy is city's best route to financial recovery," *San Diego Union-Tribune*, June 30, 2005.
34. John M. Broder, "Sunny San Diego Finds Itself Being Viewed as a Kind of Enron-by-the-Sea," *New York Times*, Sept. 7, 2004.
35. Vinson & Elkins, 8; see also Aguirre I, 1–6; Aguirre IV, 1–5.
36. Aguirre I, 4.
37. Matthew T. Hall and Jonathan Heller, "Independent cash at record flow in S.D. mayor's race," *San Diego Union-Tribune*, Oct. 27, 2004. See also the press release of the Performance Institute dated Oct. 13, 2004, "Proposition J Proponents Mislead Voters to Push 'Blank Check' Tax Increase."
38. DeMaio, author interview. See also Performance Institute, "TOT Tax Increase Proposal is Flawed and Misguided," news release, July 26, 2004, and "No on Prop J. Absent Reform, hotel tax hike is waste of money" (editorial), *San Diego Union-Tribune*, Sept. 30, 2004.
39. Hall & Heller, "Independent cash at record flow."
40. John Kern, author interview.
41. Frye, author interview; see also Karen Kucher, "No Hesitations. Donna Frye's life of activism has included women's issues, the environment and politics," *San Diego Union-Tribune*, Dec. 26, 2004.
42. *San Diego Union-Tribune*, Dec. 16, 2004.
43. Aguirre II, 1.
44. Peters, author interview.
45. Phillip J. LaVelle, "Aguirre asserts control of pension legal affairs," *San Diego Union-Tribune*, Dec. 17, 2004.
46. Peters, author interview.
47. Aguirre, author interview.
48. Robert Abel, author interview.
49. Abel and Aguirre, author interviews.
50. Aguirre I, 16.

51. Abel and Aguirre, author interviews.
52. "Pension board. Will the mischief never end?" (editorial), *San Diego Union-Tribune*, Jan. 29, 2005.
53. Aguirre II, 9, 95–98 (esp. 97), 106-7. Aguirre specifically exempted members who were not on the council at the time of the alleged securities violations.
54. Philip J. LaVelle, "S.D. officials are angry over Aguirre report," *San Diego Union-Tribune*, Feb. 11, 2005.
55. Matthew T. Hall, "City pension board refuses to cooperate in deficit inquiry," *San Diego Union-Tribune*, Feb. 19, 2005, and "San Diego chaos. City is sinking dangerously in legal quagmire" (editorial), *San Diego Union-Tribune*, March 11, 2005.
56. Aguirre III, see esp. 7, 22.
57. Fike, author interview.
58. Performance Institute, "Poll Shows Skyrocketing Public Approval for City Attorney Performance and Investigations," news release, Feb. 22, 2005.
59. Aguirre VI, 2.
60. Greg Moran and Kelley Thornton, "Councilmen Guilty. Convictions," *San Diego Union-Tribune*, July 19, 2005.
61. The study was published by the Center on Policy Initiatives.
62. Tony Perry, "San Diego Mayoral Hopefuls: Read Our Lips," *Los Angeles Times*, June 20, 2005.
63. "Heck no. Frye pension plan heavy on taxes, short on solutions" (editorial), *San Diego Union-Tribune*, Oct. 27, 2005.
64. Andrew Donohue, "Figures Detail Controversial Pension Benefit Purchased by Murphy, Several Council Members," *Voice of San Diego*, Apr. 22, 2005. A year later, in June 2006, SDCERS's deficit had shrunk to a still-serious total of $1 billion, representing a funded ratio of just under 80 percent.
65. "City of San Diego Pension Comparison," Office of Labor Relations, as of Mar. 30, 2005.
66. Evan McLaughlin, "How Officials' Pensions Change If Benefits Judged Illegal," *Voice of San Diego*, Aug. 27, 2005; Caitlin Rother and Ray Huard, "City manager to step down," *San Diego Union-Tribune*, Mar. 17, 2004.

67. Braun, "The smooth operator."
68. Evan McLaughlin, "Official Embroiled in Pension Crisis Retires," *Voice of San Diego*, Aug. 5, 2005.
69. Conger, author interview.
70. Andrew Donohue, "Pension Officials Fire Back at Aguirre; Pension Whistleblower Squelches Attempts to Reinstate Her on Board," *Voice of San Diego*, July 14, 2005.
71. Aguirre VI, 1.

Conclusion: The Way Out

1. PBGC 2005 Fact Book, 3.
2. Wilshire Associates gives figures near the low end of the range; Barclays Global Investors puts the maximum total deficit at $900 billion.
3. Mary Williams Walsh, "$58 Billion Shortfall for New Jersey Retiree Care," *New York Times*, July 25, 2007.
4. President's Advisory Panel on Tax Reform, Final Report, 79; see also the author's "Who Needs the Mortgage-Interest Deduction," *New York Times Magazine*, March 5, 2006.
5. PBGC 2005 Fact Book, 9.
6. Federal Reserve Board, "Recent Changes in U.S. Family Finances: Evidence from the 2001 and 2004 Survey of Consumer Finances," A12.
7. Social Security Administration.
8. See the author's "A Question of Numbers."
9. Social Security Administration.
10. The transition costs of such a plan would be large, because the payroll taxes of present workers aren't being "saved"; they are used for benefits of current retirees. If payroll taxes *were* saved, Social Security would need other revenues to pay current benefits. This is why the transition cost would be so big.
11. Aguirre III, 7.

Index

Abel, Robert, 211
Agnelli, Gianni, 50
Aguirre, Michael
  and United Farm Workers, 205
  early case, voting rights lawsuit, 160–61
  pension funding proposal, 229
  pension racketeering, efforts against, 204–5
  SDCERS pension reform activities, 160–61, 186–87, 210–14, 219
Airline industry, bankruptcies, 65, 72
American Express, pension fund (1875), 11
American Federation of Labor (AFL), 89
American Liberty League, 15
American Motors, 29
Anderson, Warren, 118, 122
Annuities, 228
Automobile industry
  automation advances, 51
  decline of, 35, 37, 46, 51, 221
  early labor unions opposed by, 14–15
  layoffs, 51
  as oligopoly, 28, 31
  organized labor. *See* United Automobile Workers (UAW)
  pension funding deficits, mechanism of, 46–48
  pension funding reforms (2007), 222
  recession, impact on, 48
  See also General Motors (GM)

Becker, Harry, 22
Benevolent associations, 88
Bethlehem Steel, decline/bankruptcy, 63–64
Bieber, Owen, 51–52
Bloomberg, Michael
  tax increases under, 136
  transit strike, 146-152
  TWU pension/wage deal, 142–52
Blum, Robert, 185, 187–88, 190–92, 204
Briggs, Lisa, 205
Brooklyn Rapid Transit (BRT)/Brooklyn-Manhattan Transit (BMT), 89, 92, 95
Brotherhood of the IRT, 90
Brown, Chris, 73
Bruno, Joseph, 129
Bugas, John, 19, 27
Bush, George W., 230–31

Califano, Joseph A. Jr., 49
California
  budget surplus (1998), 172

Proposition 13, 159
referendum system, 159
See also San Diego
California Public Employees' Retirement System, 162
Callan Associates, 184
Carey, Hugh, 115, 119–22
Cerberus Capital Management, 221
Chrysler
financial crises, 49–50
health care cost burden, 49–50
purchase of, 221
strike against (1950), 24
Citizens Budget Commission (NYC), 141
Civil Service Employees' Association, 130
Clinton, Hillary
health care reform, 35, 58
pension fund proposal, 227–28
Communist Party
and Quill, 91–93, 95–98
and Reuther, 13–15, 21–22
organizing of transit workers, 91-93, 95-97
Conger, Michael, 194–201, 218
Conway, E. Virgil, 125, 133, 135
Coolidge, Calvin, 89
Corzine, Jon S., 222
Coughlin, Charles, 93
Cuomo, Mario, 124, 134

D'Amato, Alfonse, 134–35
Daschel, Tom, 66
Davis, Gray, 172
District Council 37, 111
Debs, Eugene, 12
Defined benefit plans, 23, 128
Dellaverson, Gary, 137–38, 143–51
Delphi, 67–78
bankruptcy, 72
costs/pricing increases, 67–68
establishment of, 61–62
financial downslide, 65–66, 68, 70, 72–73
forced retirement plan, 67–68
health benefits reduction plan, 77
health care cost burden, 68
Miller as CEO, 70–73, 77
pension fund deficits, 65–66, 72–73
pension fund obligations, 62
retiree health benefits, 72, 74
UAW agreement to, 61–62
Delta Air Lines, 72
DeMaio, Carl, 178, 203–4, 207
Detroit, Treaty of, 25, 28, 36, 97, 225, 231
DeVetter, Steven, 207
Dies, Martin, 93
Dinkins, David, 123
Dole, Bob, 171
Drucker, Peter, on pension catch-up obligation, 25, 29
Dunne, Henry J., 94

Employee Retirement Income Security Act (ERISA), 45, 213, 226
Enhanced pensions, 41–42
Enron, 181
Ewell, Lamont, 193–94

Feinstein, Barry
drawbridge protest (1971), 111–12
pension negotiation, 117–19
Fike, Edward, 198
Final salary, 107, 109, 129
Financial Accounting Standards Board (FASB)
FAS 87, 56–57
FAS 106, 58
Fink, Stanley, 118
Fire fighters' union (New York)
heart bill, 108
variable pension supplement, 108, 128
Fire fighters' union (San Diego)
endorsement of Murphy, 206
pension gains, 172–73, 176
political influence of, 167, 184, 190, 205–6
public exposure, activities of, 167
Fisher, George, 78
Ford, Henry, 15–16
Ford, Henry II, 19, 42
Ford Motor Co.
first pension plan, 19, 21
pension fund deficits, 25, 47
Reuther at, 13
Strike against (1941), 15
401(k)s
negative aspects of, 55, 227–28
operation of, 54–55
states' adoption of, 141
Fraser, Doug, 24, 26
Freeman, Joshua, 91
Freezing benefits
GM pension freeze, 78
mechanism of, 85, 227
Frye, Donna, 174, 193, 203, 208–9, 216–17

Garry, Shirley, 103
Gaurisco, Annette, 66

General Motors (GM)
auto parts subsidiary. *See* Delphi
bonds sale (2003), 66, 69
buyout package offer (2006), 221–22
enhanced pension, 41–42
health care benefit cuts and plan to reduce benefits, 67, 74-77
health care cost burden, 52, 66–67, 69
health care counseling effort, 59
idle workers, spending on, 55–56
and import quotas, 50–51
jobs bank program, 52–53, 55
layoffs, 51, 77
oil prices, impact of, 68, 74, 77
pension costs, rise in, 42, 45, 48
pension fund deficit, scope of, 58
pension payments by 2000s, 10, 69
pension plan freeze, 78
pension underfunding solution, 59–60
Plan B approach to health care burden, 75, 222
profit gains and losses, 9–10, 27, 31, 33, 35, 52–54, 56, 60, 65–69, 74, 77–78
resale value of autos, 53
retiree health benefits, 2–3, 46, 59, 223
Smith (Roger) as CEO, 50–58
Smith (Jack) as CEO, 59–61
strikes against, 4, 15, 32, 37, 60, 222
surplus vehicles, 53
thirty-and-out retirement plans, 40–42, 55
UAW benefits/pension deals, progression of, 24–25, 32, 35, 37, 45–47, 52–53, 67, 222
Wagoner as CEO, 62–63, 66–70, 74–79
Gerard, Leo, 64
Gettelfinger, Richard, 68–71, 76–77, 222
Gibson, Dennis, 182
Gilhooley, John J., 107
Girsky, Steve, 74–75, 78
Giuliani, Rudolph, 127, 129
Gleason, James, 189, 194
Gleason case, 194–202
Goldberg, Arthur, 108
Golding, Susan, 162–66, 171, 202
Gompers, Samuel, 89
Google, 226
Gotbaum, Victor, 107, 111–12
Great Depression, 13, 90–91
Greenwald, Gerald, 48–50
Grissom, Larry, 176–77, 180–82, 188–89, 199

Hall, Sonny, 123–24
Hamilton, Dwight, 169
Harrington, Harry, 152
Health care benefits
Chrysler, burden on, 49–50
employer costs, rising, 39–40
FAS 106 rule, 58
GM benefits, 59, 66–67, 74–77
GM cost burden, 52, 66–67, 69
reform efforts, 35, 58, 224–25
for retirees. *See* Retiree health benefits
Reuther/UAW advocacy of, 17, 24–25, 28, 32–35
for San Diego workers, 160, 169, 196
and state deficits, 222
TWU benefits, 94, 98–99
Heap, Elmer, 192
Heart bill (NYS), 108, 129
Hell on Wheels, 123, 125
Herring, Bruce, 180, 187, 201, 218
Hillis, Elwood H., 44
HIV bill (NYS), 129
Hoffa, Jimmy, 111, 205
Honda, American plant, 51, 52
Howe, Irving, 14
Hudson, 29
Hybrid vehicles, 60

Iacocca, Lee, 48, 50
Idle workers, 55–56
Import quotas
rationale for, 51
UAW support of, 44
Inflation, impact on pension funds, 36
Interborough Rapid Transit (IRT) Co., 89–95
pension system of, 90

Jackson, Jesse, 144, 146
James, Willie, 125, 130–31
Jamison, Conny, 170
Japan
auto industry competition, 34, 46
auto industry development spending, 69
auto profit margins, 67
and U.S. import quotas, 50–51
Jarvis, Howard, 159
Jobs bank (GM), 52–53
Johnson, Lyndon B., 42

Kagan, Marc, 142
Kalikow, Peter S.
biographical information, 84, 133–36
as car buff, 84
and D'Amato, 134
as MTA chairman, 135–50, 223

as observer of GM, 84
and Pataki, 83, 133–36, 138–39
pension cut, demand for, 86
pension obligation concerns, 83–84
as public advocate, 85–86
and Toussaint, 86–87, 133, 137–38, 142–52
transit service cuts, 86
TWU benefits negotiation, 133–50
Kelling, Northcross & Nobriga, 189–90
Kennedy, John F., 30, 100
Kennedy, Robert F., 205
Kerkorian, Kirk, 69, 74
Kern, John, 198, 206, 208
Kinzel, Otto, 112–14
Klein, Herbert, 158
Klein, Jennifer, 23
Koch, Ed, 117–23
KPMG, 203, 207, 210, 213, 219
Kravis, Henry, 122
Kroll Inc., 213
Kryvicky, Robert C., 47, 60, 62

Labor unions
auto industry opposition to, 14–15
NLRA provisions, 18
pension deals, basic elements, 4–5
pension insurance, opposition to, 43
See also Private unions; Public unions
LaGuardia, Fiorello, 94–95
Lam, Carol, 202
Landon, Alf, 16
Lapidus, Gary, 62
Lawe, John, 119–20
Leone, Michael, 196, 201
Levitt, Arthur, 156, 213, 219
Lewis, John L., 20, 94
Lexin, Cathy
dislike of Shipione, 199
indictment of, 214
and MP-2, 181, 183–86, 193–94
pension deficit concerns, 176
Lichtenstein, Nelson, 13
Lindsay, John V., 103–9
Little Wagner Act (1958), 100
Lundgren, Terry, 145
Luria, Dan, 47, 49

McCall, H. Carl, 127–31
McGhee, Mike, 184
McGrory, Jack, 163–71, 218
Madaffer, Jim, 182
Manager's Proposal 2 (MP-2), 183–89, 196
Manchester, Doug, 207
Metropolitan Transportation Authority (MTA)
borrowing/debt repayment, 125
city transit inclusion in, 110
and cronyism, 135–36
Kalikow as chairman, 83–87, 135–50, 223
pension costs, rise in, 83–84
subway revitalization (1980s), 122
transit system cutbacks, 86
Microsoft, pension-free structure, 62
Miller, Robert S. ("Steve")
and Chrysler bail-out, 48–50
as Delphi CEO, 70–73, 77
Bethlehem Steel reorganization, 63–64
biographical information, 40, 63–64
plan to downsize Delphi, 72–73
Millstein, Jim, 75
Mooney, John, 147
Moores, John, 174
Moral hazard, 85, 155
Moroni, Rob, 58–59
Morris, Charles, 106
Municipal Assistance Corporation (Big Mac)/ MAC Securities, 114–15
Murphy, Richard
biographical information, 173–74
Blue Ribbon Committee, 177–80
as indecisive, 173–74, 181–82, 197–98
pension deficit, neglect of, 181–82, 197–98
and pension investigation, 202–16
resignation of, 213–17
San Diego management award, 178

Nader, Ralph
auto industry expose, 34
pension fund plan, 44
Nash, 29
National Institute for Health Care, 225
National Labor Relations Act (1935), 18, 92, 99
National Labor Relations Board, 20
New Deal, 15, 18, 21, 92
New Directions (of TWU Local 100), 125, 130, 132–33
New York City, fiscal crisis (1975), 114–16
New York City Employees' Retirement System, 96
pension deficit, 109
New York City transit system
and BMT, 92, 95
as part of state agency. *See* Metropolitan Transportation Authority (MTA)
city pension plan, 96
decline in services (1970s), 110, 119, 121–22

establishment of, 95
fare hikes, 86, 97–98, 122
historical view, 89–90
and IRT, 89–95
size of, 86–87, 95
strikes against, 4, 87, 90, 98, 104–5, 120–21, 146, 151–52
subway revitalization (1980s), 122
transit system cutbacks, 86
union. *See* Transport Workers Union (TWU)

New York City unions
Christmas bonus, 108, 128
drawbridge protest (1971), 111–12
final salary, 107, 109, 129
heart bill, 108, 128–29
HIV bill, 129
legislative power of, 100–101
official recognition of, 99–100
pension fund financing, 85–86, 136
pension fund gains, 106–9, 112
pension fund payouts, 110, 116, 127
pension funds, historical view, 87–101
pension guarantee provision, 85
pension reorganization, 111–16
political influence of, 84–85, 100–101, 129–30
power re-asserted (1980s), 117–19, 124
See also DC 37; Teamsters Union; Transport Workers Union (TWU); United Federation of Teachers (UFT)

Nixon, Richard, 45
North, Robert Jr., 127, 130–31
Northwest Airlines, 72

O'Brien, Michael, 151
O'Brien, Thomas, 94
O'Dwyer, William, 97–98
O'Grady, Joseph, 104
Oil embargo, 44
Oil prices, impact on GM, 68, 74, 77
Organized labor. *See* Labor unions; Private unions; Public unions
Orrick, Herrington & Sutcliffe, 199, 219
O'Shea, Thomas, 91

Packard, 29
Partnership for New York City, 145
Pataki, George
and Kalikow, 83, 133–36, 138–39
MTA borrowing under, 125, 135–36
pension legislation under, 129–31, 142
and TWU strike, 147
Paterson, Basil, 144–45, 150–51

Patrolmen's Benevolent Association (PBA)
heart bill, 108
pension fund bargaining, 100–101
pension fund gains, 106

Pension Benefit Guaranty Corporation (PBGC)
deficits, 2, 65, 226
establishment of, 45
future view of, 226
operation of, 45
pension bailouts, 64–65
union exploitation of, 65

Pension fund(s)
and FASB accounting rules, 56–58
as compared with 401(k)s, 54–55, 227–28
defined benefit plans, 23, 128
and early retirement, 27–30, 41–42, 109
enhanced pension plans, 41–42
freezes, 78, 84, 227
inflation, impact on, 36
new-age companies, lack of, 62–63, 226
private, historical view, 11–12
public, historical view, 87–101
Reuther/UAW advocacy. *See* General Motors; Reuther, Walter
smoothing principle, 126–27
stock market, impact on, 64–65, 125–26, 131–32, 136, 171–73
tax benefits of, 26
thirty-and-out plans, 40–41, 55
variable pension supplement, 108, 128

Pension fund deficits
and employee overpromises, 3
at GM. *See* General Motors (GM)
mechanism of, 46–48
post-9/11 losses as cause of, 65–66
San Diego. *See* San Diego City Employees' Retirement System (SDCERS)
statistics on, 2
unfunded plans, collapse of, 28–31

Pension insurance
necessity of, 29–30, 44
opposition to, 42–43
PBGC, establishment of, 45
Reuther/UAW support, 34, 43

Perkins, Frances, 15–16, 95
Peters, Scott, 210
Police Life and Health Insurance Fund (NYC), 87–88
Politics
moral hazard, as element in, 85
public union influence, 84–85, 100–101, 129–30, 161, 166–67, 228–29

public unions established, 95, 97
and Reuther, 30–31
universal health care, Republican opposition to, 58
See also Republican Party
Population aging
early versus late retirement, 27–30, 41–42
statistics on, 1, 17
Presidential Leave benefit (San Diego), 183, 188–90
Price, Robert, 105
Private unions
pension fund problems, causes of, 226
pension funds, historical view, 11–12
See also United Automobile Workers (UAW)
Proposition 13 (California), 159
Public unions
New York City. *See* New York City unions
pension fund problems, causes of, 83–84, 225–26, 228–29
political influence of, 84–85, 100–101, 129–30, 161, 228–29
San Diego. *See* San Diego City Employees' Retirement System (SDCERS)
strikes as illegal, 87, 102
See also specific unions

Quill, Mike
biographical information, 91–92, 103
Communist Party, alliance with, 91–93, 95
Communist Party, break with, 97–98
leads 1966 strike, 103–6
and Lindsay, 103–5
pension issue as focus, 91–92, 94
as TWU founder/president, 91–99, 102–5

Railroad(s)
pension funds, 11–12
pension funds failure, 17
Ravitch, Richard, 115, 119–22
Reagan, Ronald, 51
Recessionary economy, impact on auto industry, 48, 65
Referendum system of California, 159
Republican Party
and San Diego politics, 156–57, 166, 170–71, 185
Social Security, attacks on, 4, 230
universal health care, opposition to, 58
Retiree health benefits
Delphi, 72, 74
GM, 2–3, 46, 59, 223
NJ state deficiencies, 222
NY City workers, 104, 110, 124, 223
San Diego city workers, 160, 169, 197
steelworkers, 62
Retirement funds
annuities, 228
Clinton proposal for, 227–28
funded plans. *See* Pension fund(s)
historical view, 11
median family account balance, 227
Reuther, Valentine, 12
Reuther, Victor, 13
Reuther, Walter, 14–37
biographical information, 12–15
health care advocacy, 17, 24–25, 28, 32–35, 224
pension fund advocacy, 15–25, 27–30, 33
on pension insurance, 34
political influence of, 30–31
and socialism, 13–15, 21–22
Rifkind, Simon, 115
Roberts, Ron, 202–4, 207–9
Roche, James, 35
Rockefeller, David, 122
Rockefeller, Nelson A., 111–13
Roeder, Rick, 170, 185, 188, 190–91, 194
Rohatyn, Felix, 114
Roosevelt, Franklin D., 15–16, 95
Ryan, Ed, 165, 179, 202

Saathoff, Ronald
biographical information, 167
indictment of, 214
and MP-2, 183–84, 206
Murphy, endorsement of, 206
negotiations with city, 172–73, 176, 181, 205–6
political influence of, 166–67, 176, 190, 205
Presidential Leave benefit, 183, 188–89
See also Fire fighters' union (San Diego)
Sanders, Jerry, 216–17
San Diego, 155–219
bond market lockout, 200, 203, 206–7
Chargers' ticket guarantee, 164–66, 171, 173
corruption, history of, 157–58
fiscal crisis (2005), 206–7, 215–17
Golding as mayor, 162–66, 171
governmental system, 158
KPMG audit of, 207, 210, 213
McGrory's management of, 163–71
Murphy as mayor, 173–74, 178, 181–82, 193, 197–98, 202–16
Padres' stadium corruption, 173
pension system. *See* San Diego City Employees' Retirement System (SDCERS)
political culture of, 156–57

public unions, influence of, 161
removal from Social Security system, 160
Republican convention (1996), 166, 170–71
retiree health benefits, 160, 169, 197
Sanders as mayor, 216–17
SEC investigation of, 202–3, 207, 213–15
stadium revitalization, 166, 171
stripper-gate scandal, 197–98, 215
undertaxation, impact of, 157, 163–64, 166, 179, 190, 217
voting rights lawsuit, impact of, 160–61
Wilson as mayor, 157, 159–62, 171
Zucchet scandal, 190, 197–98, 206, 215
San Diego City Employees' Retirement System (SDCERS)
accounting system manipulation of (1991), 161
Aguirre probe of, 210–14, 219
blue-ribbon report (2002) on, 177–80
board, conflicts of interest, 165, 176, 187–88, 196, 203, 214
deficit, causes of, 157–58, 160–62, 165, 168–70, 172–73, 177, 183–84
deficit, scope of, 155, 177–79, 181, 188, 194, 217
Gleason lawsuit, 194–202
Golding's underfunding of, 164–70, 202
grand jury indictments, 214
Manager's Proposal 2 (MP-2), 183–89, 196
Murphy administration, 177–82
pension credits, sale of, 177
pension increases (1996), 168–70, 177, 185
pension increases (2000), 172–73
pension increases (2002), 181–83
Pension Reform Committee and, 196, 204–5
Shipione challenges to, 184–86, 189, 192–94, 197, 199–200, 209, 211, 218
Surplus (13th check), distribution of, 159–60
trigger plan of, 170, 180–81, 184, 188, 191
Wilson's exploitation of, 160–62, 171
San Diego Union-Tribune, 158, 163, 173, 174, 180, 189, 193, 217
Sanitation workers (New York)
heart bill, 129
pension fund gains, 106
Santo, John, 91–92, 96–97
Sass, Steven, 18
Schwartz, Jonathan, 124, 129
Schwarzenegger, Arnold, 141, 204, 229
Seabrook, Norman, 128–29
Sept 11 attacks, stock market decline caused by, 64–65, 136, 175–76
Shanker, Albert, 113, 115
Sharpton, Al, 146
Shea, Pat, 185, 186, 206, 215
Shipione, Diann
MP-2, fight against, 189, 192–94, 218
attacks on, 197, 199, 209, 213, 218
biographical information, 185
political contacts of, 185–86
SDCERS challenged by, 184–86, 199–200
SDCERS files, access to, 211
testifies in pension case, 218
Shoemaker, Richard, 61–62, 68–70, 74–75
Silberman, Richard, 162
Simon, Bruce, 72–73
Sloan, Alfred
GM growth under, 15, 53
organized labor, opposition to, 15, 17
Treaty of Detroit, 25
and UAW strike (1937), 15
Smith, Ann, 168
Smith, C. Arnholt, 157
Smith, Jack, as GM CEO, 59–61
Smith, Roger, as GM CEO, 50–58
Smoothing principle, 126–27
Socialism, and Reuther, 13–15, 21–22
Social Security
and enhanced pensions, 41–42
future importance of, 229–30
origins of, 16
reform proposal, 230–31
Republican attacks on, 4, 230
San Diego, removal from system, 160
solvency, Reuther's concerns, 34
working income, portion replaced by, 43
Spanos, Alex, 164, 166
Spitzer, Eliot, 146
Stallings, Valerie, 174
State pension funds, deficits, 2, 222
Steel industry
decline/bankruptcies, 63–64
pension funds, 20
Stein, Herbert, 56
Stock market
climb (1990s), 125–26
impact on pension funds, 64–65, 125–26, 131–32, 136, 171–73
plunge (2000), 131–32
post-9/11 decline, 64–65, 136, 175–76
Strikes
federal intervention in, 18, 20
public, as illegal, 87, 102
Taylor Law, 105
See also individual unions

Struckman, Roger, 73
Studebaker, 29–30, 42, 45

Taft, Robert A., 21
Taxation
  401(k)s and, 54–55
  pension fund benefits and, 26
Taylor Law, 105
Teachers' union. *See* United Federation of Teachers (UFT)
Teamsters Union
  drawbridge protest (1971), 111–12
  Feinstein negotiation, 117–19
  Local 237, 111–12
13th check (San Diego), 160
Thirty-and-out plans, 40–42, 55
Thomas, Norman, 13
Toussaint, Roger
  alienation from supporters, 142–44
  biographical information, 132–33
  and Kalikow, 86–87, 133, 137–38, 142–52
  leads transit strike, 146–52
  and New Directions, 125, 130, 132–33
  TWU president, 132–33, 137
Townsend, Dr. Francis, 16
Toyota, 67
Transport Workers Union (TWU)
  Bloomberg era pension/wage deal, 142–46
  2005 transit strike, 146–52
  early communist affiliation, 91–93, 95–97
  establishment of, 90–93
  final salary defined in contract of, 107, 109
  first contract, 99
  health care benefits, 94, 98–99
  James as president, 125, 130–31
  Local 100, power of, 86–87, 123
  minority dissent, 102, 120, 123
  New Directions faction, 125, 130, 132–33
  pension fund gains (1930-1950s), 91–92, 94, 98–99
  pension fund gains (1960s), 105, 107
  pension hike milestone (2000), 131
  Quill as president, 93–99, 102–5
  strikes, 4, 98, 104–5, 120–21, 146, 151–52
  Toussaint as president, 132–33, 137
  20/50 pension, 106, 123–24, 142
Treaty of Detroit. *See* Detroit, Treaty of
Truman, Harry, 18, 21, 97
20/50 pension, 106, 123–24, 142

Uberuaga, Michael, 180, 202, 203, 218
United Airlines, 65
United Automobile Workers (UAW)
  Bieber as president, 51–52
  Fraser as president, 45–50, 48
  Gettelfinger as president, 68–71, 76–77
  import quotas, support of, 44
  origin of, 14–15
  pension/benefit gains. *See* General Motors (GM); Reuther, Walter
  pension insurance, support of, 43
  strikes, 222
United Federation of Teachers (UFT)
  and New York City bailout, 115–16
  pension fund gains, 107, 109
  pension plunder protest, 113
United Steelworkers, 64
Unsafe at Any Speed (Nader), 34

Van Riper, Ellis, 106
Variable pension supplement (NYC), 108, 128
Vinson & Elkins, 203, 207, 211, 213, 219
Vitek, Reginald, 196, 201
Vortmann, Richard, 175, 177–79, 182, 187, 192

Wagner, Robert F. Jr., 99–100, 103, 119
Wagner Act (1935), 18, 92, 99
Wagoner, Rick
  appointed GM CEO, 62–63
  benefit reduction efforts, 66–70, 74–79
  biographical information, 40
  and GM auto parts subsidiary. *See* Delphi
  international positions, 54
  UAW health care trust established, 222
Wallace, George, 44
Wallace, Henry, 97
Wal-Mart, pension-free structure, 62
Wear, Byron, 179
Webster, Terry, 176, 178, 182, 183, 184, 214
Weingarten, Randi, 150
Welfare states, European, 22
Whitman, Christine, 126, 142
Whittemore, L. H., 99
Wilson, Charlie, 9–10, 20, 22, 23
Wilson, Malcolm, 112–13
Wilson, Pete
  employee rights, violation by, 171
  as San Diego mayor, 157, 159–62
  SDCERS fund, exploitation of, 160–62
Woodcock, Leonard, 42
Wooten, James, 29
World War II, 95–96

Zucchet, Michael, 190, 197–98, 206, 215

FOR MORE FROM ROGER LOWENSTEIN, LOOK FOR THE 

The definitive account of the dot-com boom and bust—from "one of the best financial journalists there is" (*The New York Times Book Review*).

Origins of the Crash
The Great Bubble and Its Undoing
The 1990s were a feverish time of extraordinary excess when values seemed momentarily unimportant—why be honest when you could be rich? Even government gatekeepers—the SEC, Congress—lapsed under the all-powerful sway of "shareholder value." And then, the bubble burst on boom time. As corporate scandals at Enron, WorldCom, and too many other respected, publicly traded companies were brought to light, it became clear the giddy '90s had been made possible by wide-scale corruption in accounting practices, compensation schemes, and business ethics in even the most esteemed and established boardrooms. Just like that, it was over. America's great boom ended quickly and so badly.

Lowenstein's riveting *Origins of the Crash* is the definitive examination of the rise and fall of the 1990s bubble. With his singular gift for rendering complex financial events eminently comprehensible, he lays bare all the most labyrinthine events at Enron and elsewhere. He presents all the dizzy mania of the 1990s economy, revealing jaw-dropping details of the excesses of CEOs and the appalling lack of oversight on the part of our government gatekeepers, and also delves into our past to find its origins in the reckless policies and practices of the 1970s and '80s. Lowenstein traces the causes of the bubble and draws a clear line straight through to our current financial morass—a cautionary tale we would all do well to heed.

ISBN 978-0-14-303467-4